Before The Escape

Maria & Ric Repasy

With the exception of Maria's specific memories, this is a work of fiction. Names, characters, places, and incidents are products of the author's imagination or are used fictitiously and are not to be construed as real. Any resemblance to actual events, locales, organizations, or persons, living or dead, is entirely coincidental. In this story, Hitler is the Devil, certain politicians are his satanic disciples, and Hungary is an invented hell on earth.

For my Grandchildren. May they all persevere and find love, inspiration, and purpose. – Nagymama

"Those who cannot remember the past are condemned to repeat it." – George Santayana

"History, despite its wrenching pain, cannot be unlived, but if faced with courage, need not be lived again." - Maya Angelou

"Our lives are so important to us that we tend to think the story of them begins with our birth. First there was nothing, then I was born... Yet that is not so. Human lives are not pieces of string that can be separated out from a knot of others and laid out straight. Families are webs. Impossible to touch one part of it without setting the rest vibrating. Impossible to understand one part without having a sense of the whole." – Diane Setterfield

Table of Contents

Forward

Our first few interviews were frustrating and disappointing. My impatient persistence only hardened Mom's resolve.

"You are giving me illogically sequenced and incomplete fragments of events," I complained.

"What do you expect? You are asking me about something that occurred seventy-eight years ago."

"There is no story here."

"I really don't remember anything," she softly murmured.

After an unpleasant silence on the phone, I tried a different tactic. "Do you remember how you felt?"

"Our brains naturally repress unpleasant memories. They are best left buried."

I finally realized that our problem lied with the interviewer. I was unprepared to ask the right questions. Like an attorney preparing for a deposition, I needed to do my own research first, to learn the chronology of events during those first twenty-three years of Mom's life in Hungary. She was born at the peak of the Great Depression, lived her adolescence during the Nazi rise, bunkered down through the Second World War and the Siege of Budapest, and spent her teen years during the rise of a tyrannical Soviet Republic.

But even that was not enough. I needed to go further back in time to understand Hungary's tragic history. Five hundred years of foreign rule. Eerily similar failed revolutions occurring centuries apart. The rise of the great Austro-Hungarian Empire and Budapest, the Paris of the East, at the turn of the century. The railroads that transformed the economy and enriched our family. The Treaty of Versailles that took away two-thirds of the kingdom. The radical political swings. Hatred and blame counterbalanced by the great sacrifices of tragic heroes.

I am eternally grateful for the plethora of uncited research and online references from which I assembled that chronology. Because I was too lazy to properly cite those sources, we declare this book to be a memoir. Better yet, a work of fiction. We also translated László Szesztay's (Mom's grandfather) memoir and Mom and Dad's diary written during their escape and first years in America.

As we worked together through that timeline, we experienced the miracle of how a human brain can unlock and retrieve long-lost snippets of memories. We were able to unscramble and anchor those random montages into the context of history. But that wasn't all. Mom's mind miraculously opened up to new memories that emerged like fading fragments of dreams. Writing this book became a joyous adventure. A shared hobby during the COVID lockdown. A cherished bonding. I knew we were on the right path because the process, not the end state, became our passion. I was in no hurry for it to end, despite the fact that Mom was approaching her 90th year on Earth.

This is a story about the formative first 23 years of Mom's life anchored in the greater history of Hungary. We often spoke about her grandchildren as our target reading audience. Our hope that they would discover their beautiful, yet tragic, ancestral country. Learn a history barely even mentioned in American schools. Build an understanding and pride for their heritage. An appreciation of what their grandparents went through to start a new life in America, and how different life was in a world not very far away and not very long ago.

Mom is not the type of person who lives in conflict with her world. She creates no drama. Of the two of them, Dad was the ponderer, the one tormented by circumstances. He was the planner. Mom was a doer who made no claims to accomplishments that uniquely defined her. She observed and simply made the best of whatever life put in front of her. She remains content and looks back with few regrets. But one epiphany we made while writing this book was that all the challenges she overcame were vastly offset by the selfless kindness of others along the way. That good fortune was truly a blessed gift born of the goodness that exists alongside the evil in this world. The Devil took center stage, but God quietly and subtly prevails.

Ric Repasy, January 2023

1

The Escape, December 1956

With unmistakable strain on his face, Ricsi emerged from the late-into-the-evening closed-door meeting with the other doctors at Zalaegerszeg Hospital. He held his index finger to his lips to indicate silence as he quickly ushered me back into the clinic room that served as our makeshift apartment.

"It's much worse than I imagined," he said with a wince. "Dr. Imrédy overheard at today's Party meeting that the ÁVH will come for us tomorrow. Me and Dr. Husvét."

"Did he say why?" I reached out and grabbed his hand.

"For interrogation regarding my involvement in revolutionary activities."

For over a decade, the *Államvédelmi Hatóság* (ÁVH) terrorized and violated civil liberties of the populace. When this rabble of thugs wearing their blue uniforms with green epaulettes fired into an unarmed crowd in front of Radio Budapest, they lit the spark that turned a peaceful protest into a raging revolution. When the rebels gained the upper hand during the uprising, they turned their violent rage against these secret police officers. However, after the revolution was brutally crushed, the ÁVH circled back to take revenge on anyone even remotely connected to the revolution. In the first two months after the revolution, eighty-thousand Hungarians fled the country to avoid prosecution. Ricsi was just another loose end.

Hungary had devolved into a society in which distrust reigned. We never knew who was deceiving us in attempts to garner incriminating evidence for the ÁVH. We imagined spies lurking in every dark corner, probing our statements and thoughts for signs of opposition to the Party. We dreaded the sound of our doorbell ringing in the middle of the night signaling that the ÁVH had come to drag us into dungeon prisons, to torture us until we confessed to crimes we hadn't committed. We even suspected that close relatives were potential agents.

However, within this haunted environment, a strong circle of trust evolved among our small cadre of doctors at the Zalaegerszeg Hospital. While Ricsi lacked the temperament to swallow his dislike for the Party, his friend, Dr. Imrédy, had the farsightedness to keep his enemies close. In public, Dr. Imrédy was an ardent, active Communist Party member. In private, Ricsi implicitly trusted Dr. Imredy's intel.

"This so-called interrogation will not turn out well. He says I'll probably end up in prison. And all for what?"

Ricsi took a deep breath and then answered his own question, "He says when the ÁVH have you in their sights, the significance of your crimes is irrelevant."

He grabbed my outstretched hand and stared into my face. "I was stupid. There is no reason that you should be dragged into this situation. The problem is mine."

"What do you mean by that?" I pleaded.

He stared at me. His rapid breaths broke the silence. "Dr. Husvét and I are leaving at dawn. But you? You could still take Andris back to Father in Tata."

His suggestion that we separate clearly weighed heavily on him. But I understood his logic. He was thinking of our safety. We still had no word on how many of those eighty-thousand refugees had actually made it across the border. We might be killed or captured en route. He might lose his family either way. He wanted to give me a choice. To know that I could easily opt out of his dilemma.

We had never discussed or even considered joining the masses fleeing across the border. Our life here was undoubtably difficult. We lived out of a single pediatric clinic room surrounded by sick patients who perpetually infected our baby Andris. But I only thought about persevering. I prayed for a better future. I simply endured.

Squeezing his hand I replied, "It would never be my choice to have you go alone."

In the pre-dawn on a wintery Thursday, December 20, Ricsi, Andris, Dr. Husvét, his wife, their three-year-old daughter Kuki, and I walked from Zalaegerszeg hospital to the town center railway station. Ricsi had been "on call" and hadn't slept for the last 24 hours. He was determined to keep his routine as normal as possible to avoid any indication of our intention to flee. I had also stayed up all night worrying and trying to decide what to bring along. I settled for one briefcase, a baby bag, and a blanket tied up into a sling to carry Andris.

In the excitement of the moment, I completely forgot about my exhaustion as we purchased our train tickets to Zalalövő. I was more than a little unsettled as the train conductor winked at me knowingly. Even though we were wearing double layers of clothing, we had tried so hard to dress and appear like two families on an innocent little outing. But who did we think we were fooling? Even I could see the unconcealed panic in the eyes of the other adults. Disembarking at Zalalövő, we paid a truck driver to take us five miles into the forested hills that extended to the border. From that point, the rest of the journey would be on foot.

The previous night, we had cut out a 3.5" x 3.5" section of a map to guide us to our destination. We were aiming for a tiny village called Szentgotthárd. However, as we tried to navigate through the hills and little villages, our map turned out to be useless. We were completely lost and growing desperate. We finally encountered a nervous young man who agreed to lead us to his house in Farkasfa.

Our cadre of escapees grew to nine when three young men joined our little group. "Thank God you found us," the largest teen confided. "We have wandered lost for three days on our own."

The hike was much more rigorous than anticipated. Despite the winter weather, we sweated through our multiple layers of clothing. Other than the brioche and black coffee we consumed before leaving the hospital, we had not eaten all day. In my previous night's overwhelmed frenzy, I completely forgot about packing snacks or water. I pushed fatigue, hunger, and thirst out of my mind and forged ahead. Our child's fate was in our hands.

We quickly realized that carrying a child was much more challenging than anticipated. Andris felt much heavier than his 33 pounds weight. The method that I had worked out back at the hospital of carrying him in the blanket slung over my neck did not work out as planned. But we struggled on without adjusting the sling. We traded off carrying him in three mile intervals. Just when we were about to beg our guide for a break, a second villager joined our group and carried Andris on his bicycle, giving us a blessed mile of reprieve.

Our guide avoided roads. The three times we stepped on an actual road were only to hurry across back into the safety of the forest before being spotted by Russian patrols.

As we crossed fallow agricultural fields, the uneven frozen plowed earth threatened to twist an ankle. At low points, our feet broke through thin ice and our city shoes soaked through with ice cold water.

In the afternoon, cramped and cold, Andris got crabby and started to act up. We gave him his first dose of "Sevenal" (a sleep-inducing phenobarbital). We had dressed him in so many layers that it was difficult to expose a section of skin to administer the injection with the partially frozen syringe. We were not sure how much medication he actually received. It did not knock him out as expected. But he quieted.

By eight that evening, we were still several miles away from our guide's house in Farkasfa. It was dark and the temperature had dropped considerably. I could no longer ignore my fatigue, hunger, and dehydration. Despite the cold, Ricsi was sweating. I didn't want him carrying Andris in his state. But I was so exhausted that I could not take on that burden. Normally, I was the type who would have been concerned about dirtying my clothes in the mud. But that evening, I repeatedly collapsed and sat wherever I fell. Taking deep breaths through swollen, cracked lips, I tried to regain my fortitude.

We finally arrived at our guide's house in Farkasfa. The first thing I asked for was a chamber pot for Andris. I had packed four diapers, but of all days, on this first day of our escape, our 18-month-old child decided to be toilet trained. Then, I collapsed at the table and slept.

We remained in our guide's farmhouse until sundown the next day, resting, eating, and speculating about the rest of our journey. Ricsi helped rig up a better way to carry Andris. Using a wooden board as a seat, he tied the blanket into a makeshift backpack. At 5:00 p.m., a different guide led us to two more houses where we rounded up more escapees. In the last house, a larger crowd was already gathered. Our numbers had grown from nine to twenty, including a four-year-old boy.

Listening to the crowd, I realized that most were not fleeing because of imminent threat of government retaliation. Those types of refugees had fled long ago, immediately after the revolution. The majority of this crowd was leaving Hungary for the promise of a more prosperous future in the West. Some even saw this escape as a swashbuckling adventure. Three secondary-school-aged girls particularly annoyed me by their lack of seriousness about the situation. One of them blurted out "I wouldn't even mind if we encounter a little shooting."

Our third and final guide had escorted another group across the border the night before and was still sleeping. His wife told us not to expect to leave until 3 a.m. But when this guide awoke at eleven and saw the group he was to escort, he decided to leave immediately. He was concerned that the three small children among us would slow our progress. Within the first few steps from the house, our new guide demonstrated heroic selflessness. He put the four-year-old boy on his back and walked on at a deliberate pace. We followed like a line of ducklings.

Because our group was so large, he decided to reroute us though deeper forests to avoid being seen. We faced another ten mile walk in the bitterly cold night air. Ricsi appeared revived after our day of rest, but I still felt exhausted and dreaded the pending trek. The first few miles were a pleasant walk through gorgeous pine forests. The pine needle laden path gave the frozen ground some give. I held the briefcase and baby bag. Carrying Andris, Ricsi's initial exuberance lasted until we reached the first hill.

Ascending a steep 700-foot rise, the bag and briefcase suddenly felt twice as heavy. I quickly became winded. I kept losing my footing. Ricsi forged ahead without complaint, but he was clearly struggling. I tried to push him uphill from the back, but he begged me to stop because it only caused him to lose his balance.

At the summit, as we took a moment to catch our breath, our guide gave each of us a few squares of chocolate and a sip of *Pálinka* brandy as he calculatingly assessed our condition. He had the stamina of a wild buck that constantly roamed these forested hills. In contrast, we town folk were in terrible physical shape. I sighed deeply when he informed us that we still were only halfway to our destination. The guide grabbed Andris from Ricsi, slung our son onto his back, and led us on once again. Our pace quickened for the next hour, until we reached an inundated meadow. The chilly water rose up over our indoor dress shoes to our ankles. But the numbing cold almost felt good.

As we began to climb again, I was thankful that our route was sheltered and concealed by the surrounding pine forest. I imagined that the trees were our guardians. Their snow-laden pine boughs quenched my thirst. They reached out to me at the right time to provide handholds to help me keep my balance while maneuvering the steep descents. But then, I slipped while still holding a branch and painfully sliced open my palm.

At the bottom of a steep slope, we traversed an obstacle course of 12" deep trenches of eroded and then frozen mud. In the pitch black of night, we could barely see the terrain. One false step and someone could easily twist or break an ankle. By the grace of God, we all made it across this precarious frozen section.

We took our final rest stop in a dense patch of forest two miles from the border. Ricsi gave Andris the last portion of the sedative. He related how miserable it felt to give that injection to the little exposed patch of Andris's skin by the light of one burning matchstick. He could not tell how much of a dosage he was actually injecting. We heard tragic tales of other families overdosing their children in this same situation. However, it was a necessary precaution. The cries of one child could endanger the lives of the other 19 escapees in our group.

At the final road crossing, our guide crept off to study the timing of the border guards' movements. He made us wait for 30 minutes to ensure nobody was within eyesight. Running across this road, we reentered the forest thicket. Then we suddenly came to a forty-foot wide clear swath cut through the deep forest. This was the border. Several months back, this had been an impassable section until the first groups of fleeing Hungarians had cleared the six foot-wide roll of barbed wire placed there by the Russians in 1948–the physical manifestation of Churchill's literary "Iron Curtain." The bright beams of a late rising moon glistened on our guide as he carried Andris on his back across the clearing.

Watching the others cross the border, I was struck by the bittersweet realization that the little boy on that guide's back may not have any memories of the world we left behind. That he would not understand the reasons nor the choices we made. Through the folly of humankind, this crossing was such an arbitrary division of two worlds. Simple lines on a map that divided tyranny from freedom, tragedy from hope, our homeland from a new life abroad. Our son needed to know the history of this beautiful yet troubled land that was once our home. The story of the life we had left behind.

2

László Comes to Budapest, 1863-1910.

My maternal great-grandfather, Károly Szesztay, watched in stunned silence as the Nagykálló town hall buzzed on the night that the railroad developers presented their proposal to locate a train station in the town center. He had a gut-feeling that this railroad would cause problems for the town. However, not in the way that these townsfolk were envisioning.

The year of that 1863 town hall meeting, railroad lines drew only a meager skeletal cross on the map of Hungary. An east-west line ran from Debrecen to Vienna, and the north-south line ran down the middle from Pest down to Timosvár. The developers tried to explain how the proposed rail line would connect Debrecen in the south to Ungvár (now Uzhgorod, Ukraine) in the north. That this transportation link would ensure the town's future political and commercial growth.

However, the townsfolk inimically shouted over them in protest. Nagykálló citizenry remained united in opposition to the new railway proposal. A train passing through town would destroy their town's quaint rural character. One man described how these wood-powered steam locomotives spewed out pungent black clouds of smoke that left a trackside swath of dirty soot. A line passing through town center would blacken their elegant square, church, and town hall. No, this new technology was not to be so eagerly embraced. The developers, dumbfounded by this opposition, agreed to reroute the track through the next biggest town of Nyíregyháza, located ten miles to the northwest.

Though he couldn't articulate his unease about the town's decision that evening, Károly felt sure that it was wrong. The world was changing. Clinging to old ways of thinking would only leave you in its wake.

Nagykálló[1] originated as a fish pond, thrived as a market since the 14th century, and served as county seat for the last 120 years. It was one of the many small towns and villages dotted throughout the verdant floodplains of the great Tisza River in eastern Hungary. Second in grandeur only to the Danube River, the Tisza fed a flourishing civilization as far back as historians are able to trace. Fecund sedimentary soils yielded agricultural bounties that gave birth to an enriched land-owning noble class who cleverly and brutally consolidated wealth on the backs of generations of serfs.

But Károly was neither an aristocrat nor a farming peasant. Like his father, Károly was a lawyer. A year before this town hall meeting, Károly completed his law studies at his father's alma mater, the regionally renowned Protestant University in

---

[1] The name of the town Nagykálló means "large gathering area" because of its market.

Sarospatak.[2] He moved from his boyhood village of Fényeslitke and opened a law practice. However, after that town hall meeting, Károly's suspicions bore out. The railroad killed this once prosperous town.

The timing could not have been worse. He had just met and had fallen in love with a dark-haired, devout Catholic girl named Anna Maria Koranyi. Anna had not always been a devout Catholic and "Maria Koranyi" had not always been her name. At her birth in 1841, she was Kornelia Kornfeld, daughter of medical doctor, Sebald Kornfeld. They were German speaking Ashkenazi Jews whose descendants had migrated to Eastern Hungary in the 18th century to escape persecution up north. Both intolerance and a refusal to assimilate led to Christian and Jewish culture clashes. But Dr. Kornfeld assimilated. He changed the family name to Koranyi and joined the Catholic Church.

When Károly and Anna married in 1865, her Jewish past was not an issue. Károly's problem was that her zealous Catholicism conflicted with his Lutheran upbringing. They struck a compromise. Their three daughters would be raised Catholic like their mother, and their four sons would be raised Lutheran. My grandfather, László Szesztay (whom I called "Nagypapa"), born in 1870, was the eldest of those seven children.

The new railroad segment bypassing Nagykálló had been fully operational for several years by Nagypapa's second birthday. However, the short-sighted victory of the citizens of Nagykálló over the rail line developers had already taken its toll. Unconnected from the new economic life-force the railway provided, Nagykálló lost its commercial vitality and withered on the vine. Its population and economy waned. Nyíregyháza, on the other hand,

---

[2] which translates as "muddy stream"

16

became the region's new thriving metropolis. Its population grew to 70,000. It became the new county seat. Károly Szesztay closed his fledgling law practice and moved the family from Nagykálló to Nyíregyháza.

But this is not the story of a dying town. It is the story of an expanding railroad network and of the influence that it had on the course of Nagypapa's life. The era of the railroad had just begun. A complex network would soon cover the map of Hungary. The railroad introduced an invigorating new circulatory system that transformed the country's underdeveloped economy. Towns connected to the network thrived.

Three towns of Pest, Buda, and Óbuda officially merged to become one city: Budapest. It sat like a spider in the centroid of Hungary's web-like rail network. The closer you got to Budapest, the denser became the network. Additional short rail segments between markets and population centers fed the spider. Urban growth was meteoric. Landed gentry left their estates to participate in city politics. Freed serfs and immigrants crowded into shared apartments. An unprecedented construction boom was underway. In the eighteen years between Nagypapa's birth and the day he would move there, the population of Budapest doubled. Nagypapa would become one of those fortunate enough to catch a ride on the wave of railroad expansion. One who saw and seized a future of opportunity and growth.

Like his forefathers, Nagypapa excelled in the formal education strictly required of all Szesztay children. At the Lutheran

Secondary School, he received high marks in religion, grammar, poetry, German, Greek, and Latin. He could recite from memory the great Magyar poets Petőfi, Arany, Vörösmarty, and Tompa. But Nagypapa found his calling in the technical sciences. He even volunteered after school to help professor Ferenc Mészáros prepare chemistry and physics experiments for the next day's class. By the time of his 1888 secondary school graduation, he already knew that he wanted to design railroads.

That summer, Nagypapa got his first job associated with the railroad industry. Working long days, he led Design Engineer József Scheiber's four-person survey team that took measurements for the Nyíregyháza/Mátészalka railway line. Mr. Scheiber rewarded Nagypapa with much more than spending money for his pending move to Budapest. He also taught him about the many opportunistic private start-up railway developers who quickly lost their fortunes. They built short segments with hopes of being bought out by the new Hungarian State Railway (MÁV), but were unsuccessful because their tracks, stations, or sheds failed to meet MÁV standards. The lesson learned was that the industry was badly in need of technical experts. Nagypapa set off for Budapest to become such an expert.

Being the first Szesztay to leave Eastern Hungary to study, Nagypapa's first trip across the city engraved a lasting memory. The evening train from Nyíregyháza arrived early the following morning at *Keleti Pályaudvar*, Budapest's eastern train station. As the train slowly pulled into the five-year-old station, Nagypapa and his three school companions gawked at the biggest and most impressive building they had ever seen. They loaded their luggage onto a *konflis* (a horse-drawn carriage taxi) and crossed the bustling, overwhelming city in jaw-dropped silence. Rákoczi út (road) was walled-in by three and four stories of apartments above ground-floor shops, bakeries, bars, bookshops, confectionaries, and produce markets. Despite the brisk fall morning air, curtains billowed in open windows underlined with flashy bright geraniums. Turning onto the narrower and even more dense Dohány *utca* (street), they entered a Jewish district crowded with black-robed orthodox Jews sporting long beards and curly locks of hair emerging from under black hats. They inhaled the rich odoriferous scents of leather and wine, fishmongers, ripe horse manure, freshly baked bread, pungent sauerkraut, and the sweet whiff of women's perfume. Turning right at Károly *Körút* (circle), the konflis passed through the elegant "Elizabeth" district lined with opulent multistoried mansions belonging to Hungary's well-known aristocratic families: the Eszterházys, Károlyis, and Wenckheims. A shiny new commuter rail line, the HÉV, shared the crowded street with a horse drawn tram.

The *konflis* finally arrived at Deák Ferenc Square stopping in front of a building that even dwarfed that massive train station. The Károly Military Barracks was the largest building in Budapest. He and his three companions spent their university years adjacent to the barracks down a narrow side street, in two rooms on the second floor of Lajos-*bácsi*'s apartment.[3]

---

[3] In Hungary even unrelated elders are respectfully referred to as uncle (*bácsi*) or aunt (*néni*). Lajos Tokaji-Nagy was an attorney who used to share an office in Nagykálló with Nagypapa's father, Károly Szesztay.

The *Budapesti Műszaki és Gazdaságtudományi Egyetem* (Budapest University of Technology and Economics) located on Museum Circle was and is still the premier technical university in Hungary. It was the first institute in Europe to train engineers at the university level. But Budapest had much more to offer a young man than just engineering studies.

Nagypapa took advantage of cheap "rooster" seats, which were offered to students, to frequently attend plays and concerts. From the highest balcony of the National Theater, he watched the finest theatrical talent in Europe and became infatuated with the female stars. The Hungarian actress Mari Jászai, after whom a theater would later be named, shined as the leading role in the classic tragedies. His heart was forever touched by the beautifully sad songs of the nation's *csalogánya* (nightingale) Blaha Lujzá. He was also enamored of Ilka Pálmay, the bewitching prima donna whose unmatched artistic performances left the city buzzing for weeks.

Politics provided him another primary form of entertainment. He followed parliamentary debates like a national sport. As a student, he was granted access to the government halls located on Sándor *utca* to hear the great speakers of the day.[4] These were the glorious years of high Parliament. He heard speeches from the renowned leaders of the time: Count Albert Apponyi, Gábor Ugron, Dezső Szilágyi, Nándor Noránszky, Count István Tisza, Bartha Miklós, Count Gyula Andrássy, and Dániel Diri. Even though he often found the ideas of these parochial gentry outdated, their great oratory skills made even insignificant issues

---

[4] The beautiful landmark parliament building that you now see standing along the Danube River had not yet been built. At that time the Parliament building was on Alexander utca opposite the Museum garden.

worth listening to. The Magyar Parliament forbade the "reading" of speeches. Members delivered speeches extempore.

Hungarian historian Antal Szerb wrote that "Hungarian is a declarative language that tends to monologue rather than dialogue. It is rational rather than mystical. Lyrical rather than metaphorical." In public speaking, this directness and terseness allows for an intoxicating rhetoric. A politician's reputation was built on his speech-making abilities. Nagypapa recognized and respectfully raised his hat to these great parliamentary intellectuals whenever he passed them on the street.

Nagypapa also participated in political parades and demonstrations, adding his voice to the emerging public opinion of the nation. He was deeply offended by one bill before parliament in 1890 that proposed to allow for civil marriages. He took to the streets to protest this bill. He joined the crowd gathered in front of the opposition leader's apartment and cheered as the politician emerged on his balcony to speak a few encouraging words. He also gathered before and stoned the windows of deputy Prime Minister Abzug's apartment for having introduced the bill. Calvary policemen called to scatter the protestors were sympathetic with the youth. The crowd dispersed with courtesy and without injury. This was a golden era for Hungarian politics.

In November of 1892, now a university graduate, Nagypapa joined the Mandel-Hoffmann-Quittner entrepreneurial company as it prepared to construct the Murány Valley railway. He temporarily relocated to the small town of Pelsőcz (now Plešivec, Slovakia) in the Sajó Valley to lead on-site survey work for the design of bridges, stations, and retaining walls. The new line rose steeply into the Tatra mountains and carved ledges that traversed steep mountain walls. Surveying this route for the designers was extremely challenging and dangerous. Nagypapa climbed large trees and, after tying himself on with ropes, rappelled down with his tripod and theodolite to take these measurements.[5]

In June of 1893, Nagypapa's former Professor of Railway Engineering, Sándor Lipthay, announced that he was traveling abroad and asked Nagypapa not only to cover for him in his absence but also to become his successor at the university. They arranged a schedule which allowed Nagypapa to hold lectures and to continue his private practice. Preparing drawings and diagrams for Professor Lipthay and spending many hours conducting research in the well-stocked library of the University of Applied Sciences, Nagypapa renewed his passion for technical design. It shaped the rest of his life. He got into the right type of business at the right time. His success mirrored the rapid expansion of Hungary's railroad network. Lowered fares boosted passenger demand. Both construction and manufacturing boomed. In the decade between 1890 and 1900, Hungary's railroad network expanded by over 150% from 7,025 to 10,632 miles. The increase in the number of locomotives was even higher, rising from 1,680 to 2,917. And more and more of those locomotives were being built within country by the Hungarian State Engine Factory, MÁGEV.

Nagypapa's father once advised him that "to catch large fish, you need to fish in a big pond." Rather than returning home to Eastern

---

[5] These early surveying challenges inspired Nagypapa in later years to promote the innovative technique of photogrammetry for engineering data collection

Hungary along the Tisza River, he stayed in Budapest. And in the spring of 1894, Nagypapa caught one of those big fish.

The former revolutionary officer and politician Count Alexander Károlyi invited Nagypapa to his estate in Fót, north of Budapest, to discuss potential consulting services. Rolled out on top of Count Károlyi's large library desk, was a map of Újpest, an area directly north of the city. The Károlyi family owned most of this land. "I want you to prepare civil development drawings for this particular parcel." The Count declared as he pointed to the map.

"I must respectfully decline," Nagypapa replied. "It does not make sense to only look at one isolated parcel. Rather, an expansion plan for utility services for the entire area should be drawn up first."

"You do not want my commission?" The Count replied with surprise.

"I don't want to be part of the haphazard way in which development has been occurring so far in Újpest. In the long run," he added, "a comprehensive plan would increase the value of all of the Count's land."

The Count stared at this audacious young engineer. Then, with a flick of his finger, he dismissed Nagypapa without a word.

"That was the end of that," Nagypapa said to himself, questioning his impertinence.

But a few days later, an apology letter arrived from the Count in which the Count admitted that Nagypapa was right and that he eagerly awaited Nagypapa's cost proposal for the Újpest urban expansion plan.

Thus began his many-year creative collaboration and friendship with Count Alexander Károlyi. As this multi-decade expansion plan came to fruition, Újpest developed into an industrial and commercial center with a new port and a major rail hub. The population of this area doubled. The Count made a fortune and Nagypapa received generous royalties.

He and the Count shared a passion for Hungary's expanding railroad. In 1863, Count Károlyi had developed one of Hungary's earliest railway segments between Pest and Újpest. The socially-minded Count saw the railroad as a means for Hungarian farmers to compete in the European markets. The Count also introduced Nagypapa to a widowed countess who had him design an entire new village called Leányfalu[6]–a place where girls could go to deal with unplanned pregnancies or to avoid prostitution.[7]

Nagypapa's relentless pursuit of knowledge continued to reward him. His professional renown led to requests for private tutoring and nationwide lecture engagements on railway design. His reputation also opened doors to a higher social class. He became a member of the National Casino and Hunnia Boating Association whose membership included the most notable personalities of Budapest. It also had one of the finest casinos in Budapest. An exclusive, class-conscious, member-only gentlemen's club. He seldom partook in smoking or drinking alcohol, however he spent many an evening at a card table. He later hosted his gentlemen friends at his apartment to play around his special green felt-covered game table with its ornate copper bowls in each corner.

As a bachelor with the wherewithal to participate in the vibrant social life of the capital, Nagypapa began to take his evening meals

---

[6] which translates as "village for girls"

[7] The village of Leányfalu thrived longer than the Countess did. Having lost her fortune when the communists took power, the townsfolk cared for her in her last years.

at the novel New York Cafe.[8] Devilish fauns adorning the building's facade gazed down at him as he entered to dine on lavishly prepared beef goulash, fishermen soup, paprikas chicken, wiener schnitzel, and grilled foie gras. After coffee, dobos, sacher and Eszterházy cakes, he settled in to peruse the cafe-supplied stacks of foreign magazines and to play cards or chess with playwrights, directors, and other bourgeois intelligentsia.

Arriving one evening at the Casino with the intent of a good card game, Nagypapa found himself in the midst of a debate with local politicians who were also Casino members. On that March 1894, evening, they resolved to defy Austro-Hungarian Emperor, Franz Josef. Even though this dual-monarchy was an era of unprecedented prosperity, a disobedient nationalism still simmered in Magyar hearts. In the eyes of most Hungarians, this king was just one more in a long line of foreign rulers. Five hundred years of Ottoman sultan and Habsburg rule.

The exiled revolutionary, Lajos Kossuth, had just died in Turin. The Emperor, fearing that a celebration romanticizing Kossuth's life might rekindle those flames of dissent against the Austro-Hungarian empire, refused to declare Kossuth's death a state-sanctioned day of remembrance. The Emperor forbade the ringing of church bells. The national theaters and Opera were

---

[8] Alajos Hauszmann, the famous architect who designed the eclectic Italian Renaissance-style building that housed this cafe would later become László's by-marriage-relation.

directed to continue with performances. Schools were to remain in session. These directives were too much of an insult for the Hungarians to swallow.

Nagypapa felt a special kinship with this tragic hero, Lajos Kossuth. Kossuth was also born and raised along the Tisza river in a village a stone's throw from Fényeslitke. Kossuth was also a Sarospatak University educated attorney. However, what Nagypapa admired most about Kossuth was his renowned oratorial ability to rouse a crowd to a jubilant frenzy. Kossuth's passionate speeches in Budapest's Pilvax Cafe ignited the 1848 revolution. Hungary's new independent government survived for more than a year until the Austrians crushed it with the assistance of 100,000 Russian troops.

Casino members vowed to bury Kossuth in grand fashion befitting a national hero. They blocked theater entrances to prevent patrons from entering. Nagypapa and other university professors cancelled their lectures. County and city delegations from all over the countryside, and thousands more, poured into Budapest to honor him. Buildings along the funeral procession route were shrouded in black mourning flags that fluttered in the spring breeze. At Kossuth's gravesite, the now-aged and renowned novelist, Jókai Mór, gave an impassioned commemorative speech for this revolutionary leader. Mór, who participated in that revolution as a young novelist, cited his novel penned during the revolution in which the protagonist said, "It is better to suffer defeat in a righteous cause than to triumph in an unrighteous one." This sentiment epitomized Hungary's affinity with its tragic heroes. He ended his speech by repeating the chants made by those rebel students in 1848 as they marched through city streets, "Equality, Liberty, and Brotherhood." These 1894 acts of defiance had no lasting impact on the political state of the Empire, however the

Emperor had been wise to be wary. A sublime rebelliousness still smoldered in Hungarian hearts.⁹

It was a sunny day in June of 1896. From the vantage of Count Károlyi's downtown apartment balcony, Nagypapa watched the millennium parade passing by below. The celebration marked one thousand years since Prince Árpád led Magyar tribes from east of the Caucasian Mountains to settle in the Hungarian plains.

The city had prepared for the millennium as if it were simultaneously hosting the Olympics and the World's Fair. Budapest opened the world's first underground electric subway line, the *Ferenc József Földalatti Villamos Vasút,* under Andrássy Avenue between Gerbeaud's confectionary shop on Vörösmarty Square out to Városliget Park. Its comfortable yellow coaches smelled of freshly varnished wood and ozone emitted by the electrical current. The city completed construction of the boulevards that form the Pest rings. Both the Gallery of Fine Arts and the palatial High Court of Justice opened that year. The city

---

⁹ In addition, Nagypapa's new friend, Count Alexander Károlyi de Nagykároly, was also one of the few noblemen who had supported the 1848 revolution. While most nobility believed that the revolution threatened to upend their advantageous privileges, the idealistic seventeen-year-old Count saw it as an opportunity to reverse social injustices. He served as an army lieutenant and later fled to Paris to avoid capture. During his exile he was inspired by progressive thinkers to resolve social tensions by improving workplace welfare. He returned to Hungary and became a liberal member of the House of Lords of Parliament and of the Academy of Sciences.

also renovated Városliget Park, adding the lake and its adjacent late medieval Transylvanian Vajdahunyad Castle.[10] Large colorful hot air balloons hovered over the city park. Cannons thundered. Green-trousered heralds blew silver trumpets. Endless music rose from the cavalry bands that accompanied regiments from all over the Hungarian countryside, all dressed in centuries' old military finery. This was more than a celebration of the millennial. It was a celebration of Budapest at its peak of culture, progress, and economic growth. The city proudly promoted its adopted nickname, the "Paris of the East!"

As the parade passed below them, the Count pointed out notable dignitaries participating in the procession. The city's mounted delegation included two recently ennobled Jewish magnates who made their fortunes milling wheat. Alongside rode Mr. Haggenmacher, the Swiss-born owner of the largest brewery in Budapest. The royal couple, Franz Josef and Empress Queen Elizabeth rode in a restored, crystal-paned 100-year-old baroque carriage originally built for Queen Maria Theresa. The Emperor wore a Hungarian Hussar military uniform. Melancholy Elizabeth wore a frozen smile through the endless parade. Their daughter, Archduchess Stephanie, snapped photographs using the first Kodak box camera that Nagypapa had ever seen.

The Count pointed out two of his nephews who were not brothers, but cousins raised in the same aristocratic household located in what is now called Baktalórántháza. Both had traveled abroad to study and both would soon play critical roles in Hungarian politics. However, they were of much different political temperaments. Representing Arad County, where he would soon

---

[10] In front of this castle there now stands a statute of Nagypapa's friend and client Count Alexander Károlyi.

28

be appointed *Ispán* (Count), Gyula Károlyi de Nagykároly was extremely conservative. He favored Hungary remaining a kingdom, the status quo, and the political structure of counties led by the aristocracy.

Leading the regiment from the County of Heves, wearing a doublet of armor, was the young Mihály Ádám György Miklós Károlyi de Nagykároly. Unlike his cousin Gyula, Mihály was a westward leaning liberal who favored France and Britain. Twenty years after this parade, when the Great War was ending, Mihály Károlyi ended centuries of continuous Habsburg rule and established the Democratic Hungarian Republic. But that was still years away. At this point in time, he was a rambunctious, spoiled young man. Caught up in a decadent lifestyle permitted by his social standing, he wilded away in the vibrant Budapest clubs and French spa towns. He hunted, attended international horse and automobile races, and amassed large gambling debts. The Károlyi family eventually reined him in and leveraged their connections to secure him a government job.

This Millennium ceremony was the last time the royal couple would visit Budapest. On September 10, 1898, an Italian anarchist in Geneva fatally stabbed Queen Elizabeth. The following January, the king's son, Rudolf, died under mysterious circumstances. Then tragedy would strike for the third time on July 28, 1914, when the heir to the Austrian Habsburg throne, Francis Ferdinand, would be assassinated.

Legend has it that in 1849, in the town of Arad, as the thirteen martyred generals of the Hungarian Revolutionary Army gasped their last breaths as they hung in their nooses, Austrian general Julius Jacob von Haynau and his fellow Austrians clinked their beer glasses in toast.[11] When repeated tragedy struck Emperor Franz Josef, the Hungarian public called it "the hand of God." Retribution for Austria's crimes against the Hungarian people and those thirteen generals. These Habsburg tragedies signaled the beginning of the fall of the Austro-Hungarian Empire.

When Nagypapa married Margit Seidl in 1901, he "married up." Not because she was two inches taller than he, but because he was marrying into a well-respected Buda family. The bride's father, Ambrus Dezső Seidl, was founder of the first credit union in Hungary, a member of the House of Magnates, and an active leader in the Catholic church. The Seidls were descendants of Germanic families who had settled in Buda after the Habsburg Monarchy defeated the Ottoman Turks. Margit was one of ten children growing up in a stylish villa nestled in the Buda hills. German was her native tongue, as it was for nearly three-quarters of the Buda population.

Nagypapa met comely Margit through one of her older brothers when she was only fifteen. But he would not ask for her hand in marriage for nine more years. He was determined to first establish himself professionally and financially. To provide his "princess" a lifestyle that compared with her upbringing. This commitment reflected his temperament and his determination.

---

[11] Based on that legend, Hungarians still consider it bad manners to clink glasses of beer.

By the time they married, he ran a successful engineering consulting and investment company. He was also a tenured professor at Budapest's top technical university. He fluently spoke Hungarian, German, French, and English. He'd traveled throughout Europe to visit universities and the most innovative transportation facility construction of the era: massive bridges, long tunnels, viaducts, and modern ports. He was admired for the profundity of his academic and technical knowledge. He commanded respect and an unquestioned patriarchal authority. He proved unquestionably capable of maintaining the quality of life to which his prized bride was accustomed.

For the first decade of their marriage, Nagypapa and Margit rented an apartment in the heart of urban Pest. It fronted the congested József Circle, a major thoroughfare that formed the second concentric semi-circular ring boulevards encircling the city center. In those years before the Great War, the city was vibrant, prosperous, and exciting. Though Vienna reigned as the capital of the Austro-Hungarian empire, Budapest was its cosmopolitan centroid. The city was a magnet for every countryside fortune seeker. Its blossoming factories competed in European markets. A Hungarian had invented the first telephone exchange and Budapest was an early adopter. Budapest bustled with the exuberance and progressiveness of the newly rich. Supporting a nationalist "Buy Hungarian" campaign, Hungarians pinned red cloth tulips to their jacket lapels.[12] By 1905, Nagypapa's business financier, Commercial Bank President Leó Lánczy, was driving one of the world's first electric cars. The city was growing so rapidly

---

[12] That ended when one newspaper revealed that these cloth tulips were made in Bohemia, an Austrian province.

that newly-built apartments surrounded and crowded out factories that were originally located on the outskirts of the city.

In their new apartment, Margit gave birth to the first four of their five daughters. As they grew, these Szesztay daughters toiled endlessly to achieve their parents' ambitious educational objectives. The girls would never have to work, but much was expected of them. Foreign nannies contributed to the children's fluency in French and German. Tutors and dance instructors filtered through the apartment. These girls were being groomed to retain their standing in Budapest society.

When the girls became "apartment crazy," the family strolled over to the large open Tisza Kálman Square[13] where the girls ran and played with other neighborhood children among the carriages, horses, umbrella-covered vegetable stands and canvas-tented stalls. However, both of the two eldest daughters, Margit and Ilonka (my mother), started showing asthmatic symptoms and had trouble breathing. It was then that Nagypapa observed that other children at this square were suffering from eye and lung ailments. Something was amiss. Though he could not prove it, Nagypapa suspected that these symptoms were somehow connected to the nearby gas production facility. The couple decided to get their children out of Pest.

---

[13] Now called II János Pál Pápa Tér

3

The Kelenhegyi House

After moving from Pest, Nagypapa and Margit rented an apartment located directly across the Franz Joseph Bridge[14] behind a grand villa that fronted on Béla Bartok Boulevard not far from where the Gellért Hotel would later be built. This apartment became the epicenter of daily family adventures into the Buda hills in search of the perfect home. One can travel only so far on foot, especially along steep hillsides with young asthmatic girls in tow. Fortunately, the girls recovered rapidly in the fresh air of the forested hills under a sky that lacked the obscuring smoky haze that covered Pest.

The Szesztay family fell in love with the area, but they found nothing for sale. This was when Nagypapa realized the invaluable benefit of having married into a well-connected family from Buda.

---

[14] On August 20, 1946, this bridge was renamed the Szabadság "Liberty" Bridge.

Through his banker father-in-law, Nagypapa learned of plans to construct a new street directly behind the apartment they rented. Manyoki *utca* would traverse the hillside and provide access to formerly inaccessible parcels. Nagypapa also learned that Baron Béla Gerster, in urgent need to liquefy assets, had sold half of his villa property to the Henry Freund and Son Entrepreneurial Company.

Nagypapa rushed over to the Company's Pest Hold street office and made an immediate offer on the property. They asked for 80,000 Koronas. He offered 75,000. They sent him away promising to consider the offer. Their stiff demeanor left him unsettled. Riding the *villamos* (trolley) back over the bridge, he contemplated that this was a seller's market. He might have been wiser to meet their asking price or even to exceed it. He needed to immediately secure this contract. There was no other site as suitable as this.

"What an ass I am," he thought. He spent a sleepless night regretting the loss of the most perfect site over only 5,000 Koronas. He still wasn't used to the fact that he was now extremely wealthy. His increasing fortunes had grown in alignment with Hungary's rapidly expanding rail network. Hungary now had the 6th most dense railway network in the world, ahead of Germany and France. It was time to leverage his wealth to establish his family estate.

The next morning, already dressed in his crisply pressed suit and sipping his espresso, he prepared to return to the Freund and Son office to make a preemptive second offer when the telephone rang. The company had accepted his offer.

In 1911, Nagypapa hired architect and renowned urbanist, Antal Palóczi, to draw up blueprints for the Kelenhegyi house. Following architectural trends of the time, functionality trumped ornate beauty. The structure could support additional floors or be expanded horizontally. This multi-directional expansion potential required solid foundations and load bearing shear walls. An unanticipated benefit of this design feature was that it made the house a somewhat better bomb shelter than the houses nearby.

The orientation of the Kelenhegyi property was one of its best attributes. This south eastern facing hillside welcomed a delightful morning sun, was shaded from the mid-day sun by centuries-old trees, and it remained cool in the afternoon as the hot sun tucked behind the hill's ridge. This hillside was also sheltered from winter's chilly north winds. At that time, Kelenhegyi *utca* was just an unpaved walking path with conveniently placed benches offering rest to pedestrians undertaking the strenuous ascent.

Though it was highly unlikely that the Kelenhegyi house was designed to withstand an attack, such considerations would not have been completely far-fetched. This Gellért hillside upon which the new house stood had actually been subjected to six sieges during the past millennium since the Magyars first arrived in Hungary. The ruins of an ancient fortress still blankets its peak. With its commanding view over the city and the natural defense offered by the river, this hill provided the ideal defensive terrain. It was the spot from which several desperate last stands were made against overwhelming odds.

The Islamic Ottoman Turks conquered Gellért Hill in 1541 and held it for 145 years. In that period, they planted the majestic hazelnut trees that surround our property. Notably accepting of other religions, these Turks peacefully coexisted with a large Jewish population numbering approximately 1,000. In the subsequent siege of Buda, the "Holy League" of united Hungarian and European soldiers encircled the hill and conquered the Turks. These soldiers then massacred 3,000 "heathen" Turk civilians, including women and children. They also massacred half of the Jewish population for having stood alongside the Turks to defend their homes. However, these bloody episodes were ancient history. It was preposterous to even suggest that such brutal warfare could ever happen again in these modern times.

On gridded paper, Nagypapa sketched out concepts for the surrounding gardens anchored around the two large Turkish hazelnut trees. He would construct large retaining walls above Kelenhegyi *utca* to level the lot. The sunniest northeast corner would be the winter garden. He added palms, ficus, flowering annuals, rose bushes, apple trees, a vine-covered seating area, and a children's play area with swings and a sandpile.

During construction, with the same meticulous exactitude that defined his success, Nagypapa kept ledgers of every minute expense associated with the project. Tightly penned numbers and itemized expenses filled pages of a compact book that survived longer than he. He kept this book in the pocket of his crisply pressed three-piece suit, his attire even on Sundays.

The Szesztay family moved into the Kelenhegyi house in May of 1914. Nagypapa contentedly noted in his little book that credit payments on the new house were comparable to the rent they had been paying for their Buda apartment – an outrageous three times the rent they had paid back on József Circle.

On moving day, three generations of Szesztay women piled into a taxi with armfuls of bouquets, which they intended to use as decorations for a rooftop housewarming celebration. But the motorized taxi could not make it up the hill. The women had no choice but to haul the armloads of flowers up by foot.

One month after the Szesztays moved into the Kelenhegyi house, the Great War started. Hungary reluctantly joined the Austrian Emperor in declaring war on Serbia. Though the Great War inflicted immense death and economic loss, life at the Kelenhegyi house progressed with minimal disruption. Nagypapa was at the zenith of his successful career. The Kelenhegyi house maintained its reputation for fine hospitality. Live-in maids prepared delicious feasts and weekday afternoon coffees. Gardeners maintained the exquisite gardens. The sunny main living and dining area of the first floor (above the ground floor) was large enough to accommodate a massive table. Wide doors opened to expand the room for use as a conservatory for concerts, dancing, or other social events. Nannies and tutors educated the girls in dance, music, languages, exercise, and preparations for Catholic high school. Margit, an accomplished pianist in her own right, accompanied the dance performances.

For Hungary, the years immediately following the Great War were even more turbulent and difficult. However, inside the protected, idyllic compound of the Kelenhegyi house, life blissfully carried on. Nagypapa's five daughters blossomed into beautiful young ladies, well-groomed to become happy perfect brides.

4

Béla Comes to Budapest
1918-1933

Some say that a mutt is a better animal than a pure breed. Genetic intermixing results in improvement of the offspring. Though clearly not born into a noble heritage, my father, Béla Jaszai, epitomized the benefits of being a mutt. In his veins flowed the blood of half of Europe's population. Untethered to inherited landholdings, his family roamed western Transdanubia and intermingled with other nationalities. His genealogy is much more complicated and less documented, a consequence of formally undereducated generations.

His maternal Hungarian grandfather married a half-French girl whose surname had changed from Badieu to the more Magyar sounding Badog. During Napoleon's 1812 invasion of Russia, French infantryman Badieu lost a leg and hobbled back from

Moscow to the Hungarian town of Győr where a companionable Hungarian peasant girl nursed him back to health and later became his bride.

Father's paternal grandparents were Czech and German. They changed their name from Jelenek to the more Magyar sounding Jaszai.

Father never saw his mother, my paternal grandmother (née Maria Angyal), wake up or go to bed. Ever present, she kept vigilance over her playful husband and rollicking children as she perpetually cleaned house, mended clothes, raised pigs and chickens, tended the garden, skinned rabbits, and quartered venison. With only brief intervals between births, she was either nursing one child or pregnant with the next. Father remembered her as positive, happy, and strong. Sweat dripping down from her smiling face as her thick strong arms kneaded the daily bread.

Father's father, my paternal grandfather (also named Béla Jaszai), was vigorous from a life lived in forests. He was fun-loving, good-hearted, and boyishly simple in his ambitions. However, his passion for wine and cards became a problem for the welfare of the family. He never gave up the wine, but he stopped playing cards–though not completely at first. One day, word reached back to Grandmother that Grandfather was once again holding the "Bible of the Devil" (playing cards) in his hands. Grabbing a wooden cane, she raced out of the house in search of her delinquent husband. He was winning at that instant she struck him on the side of his head. The blow knocked him out of his chair. He fell to the ground. Without even bothering to tend to the blood spurting from his forehead, she marched back home. Grandfather was left with a permanent white scar on his forehead. He never gambled in cards another day of his life. In fact, he refused to even touch playing cards, even when his children begged him to play.

Because Grandfather migrated around western Hungary in search of employment, the births of his five sons and four daughters were registered in different towns. Two of those nine children died before their first birthdays. Father, born in 1898, was their fifth child. For most of Father's childhood, the family resided in the village of Balatonendréd where Grandfather worked as a *Jager* (Forest Guard) tasked with protecting the vast Benedictine church land holdings from wildlife poachers and illegal timber harvesting. Though the Forest *Jager* position paid a meager salary, it entitled the family to use a forest manager's residence. The isolated house was adjacent to a stream that flowed north through the town of Zamárdi and then emptied into Lake Balaton. When it rained, this stream overflowed and turned their lot so muddy that Father had to carry their dog out to do its business.

Grandfather knew how to reap the bounties of the forest. In a household daily ritual, his children would help him unpack his backpack to reveal that day's treasure: wild pears, berries, mushrooms, baby birds, and even bunnies.

Though all seven surviving children attended elementary school, Father was the only child to achieve a higher than secondary school level of education. As a teen, he was tall, strong, handsome, intelligent and charming when he needed to be. Father earned the right to attend university by joining the Army at the age of seventeen. In 1915, the Great War had already started, but word of the tragic mounting death toll had not yet trickled back to the masses. Being such a strong outdoorsman, he anticipated easily managing the discomforts of army life. The upside, the opportunity to expand his horizons and better his life, was too tempting to resist. That summer, Father marched with the

Austro-Hungarian Army to the Italian Front to fight in the Battles of Isonzo. He soon found that the Army took much more than it gave.

❖

Béla and brother Géza, 1916

With promises of territorial gain, including most of Slovenia and Croatia, the Western Allies lured the previously neutral Italy into the Great War. Italian leaders pinned their hopes on promises from Italian Field Marshal Luigi Cadorna that he would easily break through the Slovenian plateau, take Ljubljana, and then push through to Vienna. Because the majority of Italians were still firmly opposed to entering this war, these leaders secretly signed the Treaty of London, hoping that this promised glorious victory would win over the Italian population after the event. But there was no glory and no victory. The Italians found themselves mired in a bloody series of twelve battles which cost them 300,000 lives. Half of their entire Great War death total occurred along the Isonzo River. The Hungarians lost 200,000 soldiers, more than in all other battles of the Great War.

The twelve battles of Isonzo, which took place between June 1915 and October 1917, were unquestionably the worst conflict experienced by any Hungarian soldier. Father's unit was stationed high in the Slovenian Alps where the Isonzo River[15] carved steep canyons before it emptied into the northernmost reaches of the Adriatic Sea. As summer turned to winter, bitter cold and disease claimed as many deaths as war wounds.

That first Christmas Eve, there was a pause in the fighting. On one side of the Isonzo, the Hungarians sang a Christmas song. When they finished, the Italians sang a Christmas song. Thus the two sides continued throughout the night, singing for each other as if they were old friends rather than enemies. At sunrise, the fighting resumed as if the surreal previous evening had never occurred.

Captured the following spring, Father spent the last two years of the war in a prisoner of war camp near Naples, Italy. In camp, he built a lasting friendship with fellow soldier Jenő Prettenhoffer. Jenő would later become my godfather. Years later, their bond of friendship would be severely tested.

The physicians were still deployed to the battlefront caring for the troops, when the Spanish flu surreptitiously boarded Europe's efficient railroad network and detrained in every city, town and village. While in camp, Father was nearly felled by the Spanish flu. Emaciated and gasping for breath, he would have died had Jenő

---

[15] Called the Sôca River in Slovenia

After the Great War, Jenő and Béla (seated)

not carried him like a child in his arms to a medical clinic to save his life.

Many interesting comparisons can be made between how society dealt with this 1918 influenza and the 2019 COVID-19 virus: the wearing of face masks; the government's initial whitewashing of the seriousness of the situation; the government's initial reluctance to mandate restrictions; the introduction of "guidelines" for operation of cinemas, theaters, and streetcars (such as keeping tram windows open); the press blaming the authorities for being unprepared and indecisive; the government belatedly acknowledging the flu's deathly reality and imposing restrictions that came too late to have an impact; establishment of separate hospital wards for Spanish flu patients; and the closing of churches, schools and other gathering areas.

The Spanish flu ended up killing more Hungarians than both the Great War and the subsequent political shenanigans that followed. As the year 1918 came to an end, Father slowly recovered in Naples while, back in Hungary, the ailing Austro-Hungarian Empire collapsed.

On the morning of October 31, 1918, Count Mihály Károlyi[16] and his Social Democratic Hungarian National Council (HNC) followers emerged from the dark paneled rooms of the Hotel Astoria into the blinding morning brightness. Affixed to their hats they wore their signature aster flowers. In an all-night strategy meeting, they had finalized plans for a coup d'état.

They broke into Prime Minister Count István Tisza's villa, murdered him, seized public buildings, and declared Count Mihály Károlyi President of the First Hungarian People's Republic. Believing that the Triple Entente (Western allies) would recognize

---

[16] Count Alexander Károlyi's carefree Western-leaning liberal nephew

Hungary's opposition to the war and would want to establish diplomatic relations directly with him, Count Károlyi naively dissolved Hungary's army. But the Entente had no interest in engaging with Hungary. It had already brokered deals with Romania, Yugoslavia, and Czechoslovakia, whose troops now roamed unopposed throughout the Hungarian countryside reclaiming large portions of Hungarian territory. The HNC floundered politically and economically. Social unrest festered. In less than six months, the stage was set for a second *coup d'état*.

On March 21, 1919, the political pendulum swung even further to the left when communist leader Béla Kun led a Soviet takeover of the republic. Just as Mihály Károlyi had banked on support from the Entente, Kun pinned his hopes on receiving support from Russian revolutionary leader Vladimir Lenin, now in power after Czar Nicholas II abdicated his throne. But Lenin was preoccupied with ongoing internal struggles pitting the Bolshevik "Reds" against the conservative "Whites" and the "Kulak" peasants. Russian Bolshevik support never materialized.

The Hungarian Soviet regime was as ill-prepared to lead the country as the HNC had been. It passed senseless regulations that were broadly ignored. It established a worthless currency. By the summer of 1919, residents of Budapest were beginning to starve and become restless. The Soviet regime retained control by suppressing internal discontent and terrorizing dissent in what became know as the "Red Terror." But this heavy-handed approach backfired on them with bloody consequences. The only notable consequence of their 132-day long experiment was that it spurred Hungary's far-right faction to take action.

Count Gyula Károlyi[17] had been imprisoned and his vast estates in Arad seized by Romanian troops. After his release in May 1919, he fled to the southern town of Szeged, where he and a Transylvanian Count named István Bethlen united to form a counterrevolutionary movement. Their right-leaning vision emphasized continuity of rule by the landed class and traditional Hungarian values.

This counterrevolutionary group formed a militia, called the National Army. Radical-right soldiers volunteered en masse. Vice-Admiral Miklós Horthy became its Minister of War. He had recently been forcibly retired from his admiralship after Hungary ceded to Yugoslavia its only access to the sea. Horthy had the popular appeal of Ronald Reagan. He had the war-hero military bearing, physical stature, and voice needed to fill the leadership void. Hungarians rallied behind him.

As expected, the Soviet Republic self- imploded when Romanian forces entered Budapest on August 6, 1919. The communist leaders fled. The Rumanians lingered only long enough to loot the city. The dust had settled by the crisp clear morning of November 16th, when Admiral Horthy mounted a large white horse and marched into Budapest. Horthy paraded his small National Army through the city streets to its newly established military headquarters at the Gellért Hotel. Amid great pomp, the retired Admiral spoke from the grand hotel staircase to the gathered crowd. He accused Budapest of betraying the nation, of abandoning its one-thousand-year history.

---

[17] Count Alexander Károlyi's other nephew

"Budapest trampled the crown and our beloved red, green, and white colors in favor of red communist rags," he shouted as he contrasted the idyllic, racially pure countryside with the corrupt, anti-national liberal, communist, decadent, urban culture that imposed this Bolshevik revolution on the rest of the country.

A conservative coalition that favored restoring the Kingdom of Hungary swept the January 1920 countrywide elections. In March, the National Assembly elected Horthy to serve as regent of the restored "kingdom without a king." A month later, on June 4, 1920, Hungarian emissaries went to France to reluctantly sign a treaty which they weren't even given a chance to discuss beforehand. The Versailles Treaty formalized the dismemberment of Hungary.

In the stroke of a pen, Hungary lost 71.4 percent of its territory that existed during the dual monarchy-era Kingdom of Hungary. In one day, Hungary's population dropped from twenty million to only seven million people. Two-thirds of the country was divided up and turned over to the neighboring Kingdom of Romania, the newly-founded states of Czechoslovakia, the Kingdom of Serbs, Croats and Slovenes (the future Yugoslavia), and Austria.

It was as if you awoke after an accident and found three of your four limbs amputated. The population was disorientated, humiliated, and afraid. Even those involved in drafting the Treaty of Versailles expressed concerns about its global consequences. It was too harsh. But because citizens of France and England passionately hated Hungary and Germany, no Western politician dared speak in opposition to the treaty. Weakened Eastern European countries were unable to defend against the growing Bolshevik threat rising in the East. Italy turned to National Fascism. In Germany, the Nazi Party emerged.

Hungary's political pendulum swung firmly to the right. Politicians blamed the communists and liberal urban capitalists–the "foreign element"–for corrupting Hungarian society. These foreign culprits also happened to be Jews.

It didn't matter that most successful Jewish business leaders were conservative anti-bolsheviks. It didn't matter that 90% of the Hungarian Jewish population opposed the revolution. These statistics were tossed aside for the simple reason that Béla Kun, the leader of Hungary's bolshevik revolution, and many of his most notable followers, were Jews. Also, the majority of the liberal urban capitalists and intellectuals in Budapest were Jews.

One quarter of Budapest's population were Jews. They significantly influenced the city's business, industry, and cultural life. Almost all of the Hungarian mines, heavy industrial enterprises, banking, wholesale and retail trade were owned by Jews. They owned nearly all of the Budapest newspapers. They comprised 70% of the journalists, and 50% of the city's lawyers and doctors. Despite this influence, it wasn't until 1895 that the Jewish religion was officially recognized and given the same rights as Protestant and Catholic religions. But now that social progress would be nullified. The pendulum of Jewish tolerance would swing violently back in the opposite direction.

In September, Prime Minister Pál Teleki pushed a law known as the *Numerus Clausus* (Closed Number) through the National Assembly, which law stipulated that the number of students from various "races" and nationalities admitted to universities in Hungary could not exceed the proportion of the given race or nationality within the country's total population. Though this law did not cite any specific race or nationality, it was manifestly intended to reduce the number of Jewish students studying at universities from over 25 percent of all students before the First

World War down to six percent to match the proportion of Jews within the total population of Hungary.

Concurrently, a faction of the counter-revolutionary National Army began roaming the country and brutally punishing revolutionary sympathizers. In counterpoint to the Soviet Republic's "Red Terror," this new movement was dubbed the "White Terror." The militias ruthlessly assaulted anyone associated with the communists. Soon, they arbitrarily attacked anyone who was Jewish.

Horthy initially gave tacit approval to the White Terror simply by ignoring the militia's shockingly violent activities. But he soon found that he could no longer politically condone their capricious and unaccountable attacks. He and the prime minister disbanded the wayward detachments. By the time that they were able to dissolve the White Terror units, there had been over five thousand killings and thousands of arrests.

While imprisoned during and after the war, Father learned to speak Italian. Upon his release, he loitered around the shipyards of Naples, Italy, in search of work and passage to America. Though he had the good fortune to have avoided the chaos and bloodshed of the short-lived Hungarian coups, he had no luck in making a living in Italy or obtaining passage to America. He returned to Hungary to leverage his military scholarship to attend the University of Sopron, located near Hungary's western border with Austria. Hoping to have successfully avoided the post-war political upheaval, he found himself smack in the middle of another political intrigue.

The same time Father arrived in Sopron, a group of wayward, prosecution-fleeing, White Terror officers also showed up. What better way to distract attention from their crimes than to foment more social unrest? They called themselves the Ragged Guard and their stated mission was to reestablish the monarchy. Secretly, the current prime minister, Pál Teleki, and other members of the Christian National Union Party backed this wayward militia. The Ragged Guard declared Burgenland, the region surrounding Sopron, a new independent country called Leitha Banat (*Lajtabánság*). All they needed was a king.

The last Emperor of Austria, Charles I[18] had been a disappointment and an embarrassment to the great Austro-Hungarian Empire. When Emperor Franz Josef died in 1916, the throne passed to Charles only because the heir presumptive, Archduke Franz Ferdinand, had been assassinated in Sarajevo in 1914 (leading to the start of the Great War). Charles was considered a buffoon even by his closest advisors who complained that "he can't even write properly," and that "he is 30-years-old, looks 20, and thinks like a 10-year-old." At war's end, he fled to Switzerland, but refused to formally abdicate. This out-of-his-depth dilettante left the collapsing empire mired in confusion and chaos.

Hungary's rightwing "Legitimists" reached out to this exiled politically naive, self-absorbed monarch and convinced him that Hungary's adoring population would embrace his return to power. They led him to believe that Regent Horthy would eagerly and

---

[18] Charles was also the last King of Hungary (IV Károly), last King of Croatia, last King of Bohemia (Karel III), and the last monarch of the House of Habsburg-Lorraine.

voluntarily cede power back to him. Charles shaved off his signature mustache and traveled incognito on a forged Spanish passport from Switzerland to Sopron. But Regent Horthy immediately dismissed Charles on the grounds that the Entente and neighboring states had vowed to invade Hungary if such a monarchal return was ever attempted.

The Ragged Guard came to Father's university to recruit students to join the rebellion. Entranced by their "make Hungary great again" glorification of the past, many students joined their ranks. However, Father declared himself a pacifist and remained unsupportive. He was an ardent nationalist, but was skeptical about the reverence given to the monarchy.

Back when Father was ten years old, Grandfather took him out to the town of Zamárdi's main avenue to witness the parade as the Austro-Hungarian king, Ferenc Jozsef, passed through. The entire town gathered streetside to catch a glimpse of this venerable man. As the king's carriage neared, Grandfather, in his booming voice, shouted out *Éljen a Király* (long live the king). Surprised by the abrupt exclamation, the king abruptly jerked his head to face the noise. His royal crown slipped off to expose his small pale bald head. Grandfather laughed aloud at the confusion he had caused. For some reason, the homely image of that king caused Father to question the omnipotence of royalty.

Father also felt that he had experienced enough warfare for one lifetime. As it turned out, he made a wise choice. The attempted succession was quickly crushed. Sopron and eight nearby villages held a plebiscite on December 16, 1921, in which they voted to remain in the Kingdom of Hungary (even though the population of this area was slightly over half German).[19]

The British Royal Navy forcibly escorted Charles and his wife Zita into permanent exile on the Portuguese island of Madeira where, several months later, the humiliated Emperor died of pneumonia. An embarrassed Pál Teleki relinquished the prime ministership to Count István Bethlen de Bethlen who, with Machiavellian discipline, built an unstoppable conservative political machine that held power for the next decade. The Hungarian Diet passed a law nullifying the "Pragmatic Sanction of 1713," dethroning Charles as king of Hungary and abolishing the House of Habsburg's rights to the throne of Hungary. Hungary was now officially a kingdom without royalty.

When Father graduated from Sopron in 1923 with a forestry/civil engineering degree, Hungary was in the midst of a post-war recession. He joined ranks with the unemployed who made their way to Budapest. One university-learned skill that he found marketable in the city was his ability to work with survey equipment to make maps. That skill led him to Nagypapa, László Szesztay. The still expanding railroad network development had an insatiable need for good surveyors. Design and construction was bottlenecked without them. Father joined Nagypapa's small

<hr/>

[19] The city of Sopron thereafter became known as Hungary's *Civitas fidelissima* (Most Faithful City).

team of civil railway designers, who worked in the Kelenhegyi house.

The years flew by. Father excelled at his craft and won Nagypapa's favor. But Father was not satisfied with being a member of someone else's team. He was eager to launch a business of his own. At that time, the Hungarian government was debating a potential law that would take agricultural land from the largest land-holding nobility and redistribute it to disenfranchised farmers. A few extremely powerful noble families and the church owned nearly all the prime land in Hungary. One percent of the population owned over fifty percent of the country's land! This underlying power structure had evolved over the centuries, regardless of who controlled the country. In order to implement such a radical redistribution proposal, the country needed accurate records of land ownership. For that, they needed surveyed plots. Though a land reform bill would not pass until after WWII, Father pounced on this speculative business opportunity and started his own surveying business.

Even with Father's optimism and drive, this was an extremely difficult time in Hungary to start a new business. Post-war inflation was still rampant. In January of 1927, a new currency called the Pengő replaced the Hungarian Korona. Prime Minister Bethlen pinned Hungary's post-war recovery strategy on wheat, the most widely produced and consumed cereal grain in the world. Even after losing two-thirds of its agricultural land, Hungary was still among the top six wheat exporters in Europe.[20] Throughout the 1920s, Russia's continuing Bolshevik civil war disrupted its wheat

---

[20] Fun Fact: The practice of wheat hybridization to create hardier strains evolved from heredity experiments performed 50 year earlier by the monk Gregor Mendel in the gardens of a Hungarian monastery in Brünn.

Happy groom to be Béla (Father), 1929

production and world-market wheat prices remained high. But Hungary was only a bit player on the worldwide wheat stage. The "big players" of wheat, Canada, Argentina, Australia and the United States, produced 90 per cent of total world wheat exports. Stronger strains of wheat, newly mechanized farming equipment, droughts, and floods led to market gluts and shortages. The extreme price fluctuations wiped out smaller farms. Then, the big

The Kelenhegyi House

players dragged the rest of the world down into the Great Depression. After the crash of "Black Thursday," October 24, 1929, world grain prices followed the stock market down. Hungary's agriculturally-based economic framework buckled.

While the world's media focused on the impact of the Great Depression in western countries, Hungary was nearly flatlining as it struggled for survival in the shadows. The country's crop prices fell by more than 50 percent. Unemployment skyrocketed to 36 percent. Foreign credit dried up and short-term loans were called in. Major banks failed, including Hungary's primary creditor, the Österreichische Creditanstalt bank in Vienna. The national bank depleted its supply of precious metals and foreign currency. Eighteen percent of Budapest lived in poverty. Peasants reverted to subsistence farming. Industrial production stalled and businesses went bankrupt. Prime Minister István Bethlen's masterful political reign came an end. In August of 1931, Bethlen's counter-revolutionary cohort, Count Gyula Károlyi de Nagykároly took the reins and tried in vain to regain control of the tailspinning economy. His emergency measures failed to improve the situation, and a defeated Károlyi resigned the prime ministership in September of 1932.

Father's surveying contracts slowed to a trickle and he struggled to pay his employees. But he never completely closed up shop. He remained hopeful. Life was looking up. He had fallen in love.

5

Love in the Kelenhegyi House, 1930-1939

I f you ever visit Budapest, you can easily find the Kelenhegyi house. Cross the Szabadság Bridge from the frenetic Pest side of the Danube River to the bucolic Buda side. You will run directly into the elegant art-nouveau Gellért Hotel nestled into the foot of the surrounding verdant Gellért Hill. With its famous hot baths, the hotel has been a major tourist landmark since it opened in 1918. Alongside this hotel, Kelenhegyi *utca* climbs the steep slope past the outdoor baths and gardens.

Beyond the hotel grounds, palatial villas line the street. Massive pillared wrought-iron fences surround and protect immaculate gardens with grand old trees that shade the homes of the upper class, rich industrialists, politicians, foreign dignitaries, and old nobility. Among these villas, after the first hairpin turn, you will reach 23a Kelehegyi *utca*. If you miss our villa and follow the

My parents Béla and Ilona in the Kelenhegyi house
garden, 1930

winding road up to the top, you will reach the ancient citadel with
its commanding views back over to the Pest side.

Our house was surrounded by others owned by the rich and
famous. The old widow of the publisher of many of Hungary's
most popular novelists owned the closest neighboring villa. She
would silently stand like a vulture at her window overlooking our

garden and watch us play. Directly uphill, along Minerva *utca*, lived Nagymama's brother, Ambrus Seidl.[21] Directly adjacent to our north was the Zwack Villa built by the family that created the famous Unicum liquor. Next to them, the Swiss Embassy occupied the yellow-walled Bayer Villa with its fairy-tale copper domed roof. Directly below us was the Finnish Embassy. And these were just the neighbors within a stone's throw of our gardens.

We may have been encircled by wealth, but we did not live a lavish lifestyle. In fact, in all the years I lived just above the hotel, I never swam in its overpriced but thoroughly enjoyable thermal baths. My father refused to throw away money while there were so many available reasonably priced swim options. The wealth that sheltered the family during the Great War, the subsequent political upheaval, and the Great Depression, belonged to Nagypapa. Fittingly, it was Nagypapa who invited all of his new sons-in-law to join his beloved daughters and live in the Kelenhegyi house.

It's possible that Father stopped working for Nagypapa to avoid the awkwardness of courting his boss's daughter and living in the same house. If not for Nagypapa, Father would never have met my mother, Ilona. Their paths in life would not likely have crossed. She, in her mid-twenties, was the epitome of urban bourgeois

---

[21] Minerva utca got its name from the large, still-standing, ancient Roman statue of the goddess Minerva, uncovered during an excavation on Castle Hill and moved to the villa garden of the renowned architect, Alajos Haussmann, who also married into our well-connected Seidl side of the family.

Béla and Ilona Wedding, June 16, 1931

elegance. Compliant to her parent's wishes, refined by years of tutelage in liberal arts and social etiquette, but innately shy. She felt less attractive than her sisters, but possessed a soft, pastel, serene beauty and a most pleasant comportment.

He endeavored to emulate the mannerisms of the urban upper class, but that was not how he saw himself. He noticed the raised eyebrows of surprise at his social naïveté. Unfamiliar references to a common past that the others shared constantly reminded him that he came from a foreign, less-sophisticated background.

She passed her time in parlor tea parties, leading a Catholic Women's Association, and organizing charity events to help the needy.

He escaped into the woods when he wasn't toiling endlessly to keep his surveying business afloat. Her interest in social causes began to wain as she became infatuated with this lanky, handsome backwoods blond. She joined him on long walks through the hills.

His strength, passion, and otherworldliness excited her. She admired that he was the only one of six siblings to attend college and start his own business. It was a testament to his diligence and work ethic.

He was drawn to her warm brown eyes and her unruly hair. He much preferred her quiet modesty over the combativeness of her competitive sisters.

She admired him for his character, not his social standing. He believed that her nonjudgmental, even temperament ideally counter-balanced his passionate zeal.

Their mutual desire was electric, but properly restrained. Before proposing, Father felt obliged to demonstrate a steady income from his struggling business. Ilona waited until after her 27th birthday for them to marry.

Father may not have been the man that Nagypapa initially envisioned for his daughter, however, he warmly welcomed his new son-in-law into the Kelenhegyi house. The newlyweds moved into one of the attractive, recently added, mansard rooftop apartments. Still committed to her Catholic charities, Mother took her extra breast milk down to a local maternity ward after my older brother Laci was born in 1932. By the time of my birth, a year later, Mother had abandoned her committees and activism and had become a devoted housewife and mother.

Throughout the years, the large Kelenhegyi house morphed and easily absorbed the growing families as husbands moved in with their wives and more grandchildren came. Within a few short years, all of the Szesztay sisters married.

The defiant eldest, Margit, married first at the age of 20. She moved far away, gave birth to two girls, divorced, returned to the house, remarried, and moved away again.

Gizela, who was beautiful despite having a very distracting lazy eye, ended a tragic love affair with a kind Jewish boy whom she was forbidden to marry. She eventually entered into an unhappy marriage with a lawyer who spent most of his time at the horse race track or with his other, illegitimate, family. She coped by focusing her neurotic attention on her only daughter Margarita. Obsessively over-protective, she kept Margarita locked up in their third floor apartment. They didn't have a piano in their apartment and came to borrow ours for daily practice. Gizela-*néni* hovered over Marga during those practice sessions. When she heard a misplayed note, she smacked her poor daughter's hands. The number of errors invariably increased and these sessions quickly went downhill. It was painful to watch.

The prettiest fourth daughter, Erzsébet, had expressed an initial interest in my father, but ended up marrying another young engineer employed by Nagypapa named Jozsef Vietorisz. Józsi-*bácsi* was quiet and not very exciting, but he was a brilliant engineer and businessman. In 1935, Józsi-*bácsi* earned a directorship position in a major metal parts production factory and moved Erzsébet-neni and their young daughters to Diósgyõr.

This same year, the youngest Szesztay daughter, Klára, married the affable László ("Laci") Majoross. They met on the tennis court when she was fourteen and he twenty-one. An athletic build, a clean-shaven movie star face, he never smoked and was uncommonly health conscious for this era. He was unburdened by the opinions of others. After earning his doctorate in law, he opted for a less lucrative government position resolving estate and inheritance legal issues. In lieu of work, he filled his hours with sport and adventure. Besides tennis, he was an avid soccer player. Though she shared the alpha personality tendencies of her older sisters, Klára obediently followed Laci's lead. She quickly embraced his free-spirited outlook on life. The couple kept a 34 foot-long two-person shell along the Danube and rowed on brisk mornings. Summers were spent on long camping trips. In winter, they hiked to the top of undisturbed snow-covered mountains with their skis on their backs.

Though she was only seven years younger than Erzsébet, Klára seemed to have come from a different generation altogether. She was progressive, stylish, and extremely liberal. She dressed in the latest fashions and even made some of her own clothes. She shared her husband's sense of invincibility and hunger for fun. I remember standing in the bathroom door watching Klára-*néni* prepare for one of her many evenings out dancing with Laci-*bácsi*. With a hairpin, she scraped out the last bits from a lipstick tube. In contrast, my mother never wore lipstick. Unlike the other aunts and Mother, Klára was more often away from the house, spending much of her time with Laci's sister and her husband. The two couples became so tight-knit that they decided to marry on the same day after Klára turned eighteen.

Me and Béla, 1936

Among all the household servants, Bálint-*néni* and her husband Bálint-*bácsi* stand out in my memory. She began as a kitchen helper at the Kelenhegyi house at age 16. By the time I was born, she was already in her fifties and serving as the Ház-Meister (house manager). Bálint-bácsi was already a skeletal, old curmudgeon. He was our handyman. They shared an apartment in the northwest corner of the ground floor behind Nagypapa's engineering office that occupied the entire eastern half of the ground floor.

Bálint-bácsi looked at me in a way that made me feel as if I were an intolerable inconvenience. I never possessed a key to the house nor the front gate. Whenever I returned to Kelenhegyi house, I had to ring the bell. He would limp out to open the gate. The older I got, the later I came home, and the more I dreaded having to wake him to let me back in.

I picture only his dour face lit by orange flames as he steadily shovels coal through the iron opening of our modern centralized steam furnace. Meanwhile, faceless deliverymen groan as they carry wheelbarrows of black coal up the twelve steps from the street to the separate utility entrance. In the adjacent room faceless maids pull wet clothes from large tubs, turn crank wringers, pin laundry up on lines, iron, and fold in the adjacent laundry room. From among all of the cogs of the household machine, only Bálint-*bácsi*'s face haunts my memories. Soon after the Russians took power, this bitter, old handyman died a silent but tortured death choking on a fish bone from his soup.

In 1938, my baby sister Ilonka and Gizela-*néni*'s daughter Margaréta joined our Kelenhegyi world, and Nagymama (Margit Anna Klára Szesztay) left us. With failing kidneys and a weak heart, she had spent much of the prior years in bed. With some regret, I admit that I remember more about the hired help, who actually watched over me, than my dear Nagymama. And, though Nagypapa had been devastated by her death, he seemed to get along well afterwards on account of the established retinue of hired help who cooked, cleaned, shopped, washed, mended, and kept us grandchildren out of his hair. The house I was born into was a well-oiled operation.

Even in retirement Nagypapa maintained a professorial daily discipline. He rose early, dressed formally, and often departed the compound. He remained aloof and uninvolved in the matters of raising the children and running the household, leaving Bálint-*néni* to manage the hired staff.

Though Nagypapa generously provided for our well-being and comfort, he was not a warm-hearted person. He was smart and socially cordial, but it took his extreme self-discipline to overcome his natural preference for solitary projects and contemplation. He expected his daughters and grandchildren to demonstrate the same militaristic self-discipline which had propelled him to his success. We grandchildren were not permitted to dine with Nagypapa until we mastered proper table etiquette and conversational skills. Since I was always more interested in playfully defying authority than joining the dinner table, I seldom ate with Nagypapa.

When he was home, Nagypapa spent most of his time in his office, a sanctuary that we children were not permitted to enter. His office door was usually closed. I felt shut out of his life. That is why I defiantly snuck into his office when unoccupied. I quietly, curiously poked through the drawers of his large desk and shelves piled high with books and drawings. A waste basket below the heavy desk contained his discarded papers, including unopened "junk mail" of that period. Rifling through that basket, I chanced upon coffee advertisements. Those advertisement contained glued-on coffee bean samples, which I removed and chewed. From his private toilet closet, I stole his finest quality toilet paper. I did not use this stolen paper for its intended purpose. Rather, I used it as tracing paper with which I copied drawings from books and magazines.

When Nagypapa came out to sun himself on one of the recliner chairs in the garden, his heart warmed and his disciplined intensity melted away. He removed his shoes and socks and placed pebbles between his toes to allow sun and air to reach every surface. In those sunny moments, he spoke to me about things that I found to be the antithesis of what I expected to hear from him. He spoke of ghosts. Of departed acquaintances who sent him messages that helped him resolve perplexing dilemmas. I didn't know what to make of these stories, but I relished those infrequent intimate moments.

In his 65th year, Nagypapa gave up his ground floor office. We remodeled it into both a comfortable apartment and an office for Father's growing surveying business. I can still walk through our ground floor apartment in my mind.

Entering the foyer fronting the eastern side of the building, you encounter three doors. The door on the right leads to our maid Roza-*néni*'s room. When my parents left us alone and escaped upstairs to socialize, they usually returned to find me in Roza-*néni*'s bed. I was also quarantined in Roza-*néni*'s room when I came down with the measles. Despite efforts to keep me away from the rest of the family, I passed the measles on to my father. His lungs never fully healed after the Spanish Flu, and the measles went deep into his lungs. He battled pneumonia until he luckily obtained imported penicillin, a drug not readily available in Hungary at that time.

The middle door enters a hallway leading to our narrow, dark kitchen, with its one small window providing limited natural light. The adjacent food pantry included an ice box, kept cold by two large blocks of ice delivered weekly by the iceman's horse-drawn wagon. The kitchen may have been dusky, but it was in constant use. I can still smell the delectable aromas that filled the entire apartment.

The door on the left leads into Father's office. Father and two draftsmen labored away at three large desks positioned in front of the bright, east-facing windows. In the evenings, this office became our family entertainment room. I was allowed to click away on his typewriter or play the upright piano. Passing through his office, you enter our parents' corner bedroom, from which another door led west to the children's bedroom. Our large bedroom had two south-facing windows that looked out into our neighbor's wooded garden. In early December, we placed our shoes on those wide windowsills in anticipation of gifts from Saint Mikulás. Laci and I shared the one large bed. Later on, two smaller beds were added for Béla and Ilonka.

A second door on the north side of our bedroom leads down a long pass-through storage corridor (called the *átjáró*) lined with built-in floor-to-ceiling cabinets accessed via a sliding ladder, and jacket hooks lining the opposite wall. The *átjáró* and the front hallway intersected at the bathroom. I bathed in its large, claw-footed iron bathtub and I gave my dolls their baths in the *bidét*. Many a wintery day, we blew off steam by running the loop through our apartment, passing through the office, bedrooms, *átjáró*, front hallway, and foyer. Then again, back through the office, bedrooms, *átjáró*, front hallway, and foyer. Again and again, until winter turned to spring and we could play in the garden once again.

68

My Jaszai grandparents' 50th wedding anniversary, me in
mother's lap, 1938

One sunny summer day, we rode the train west to Veszprém to
my paternal grandparents' fairy-tale two-story house situated on a
postage stamp size parcel that had space for only one pear tree.
The dusty and well-lived-in old house smelled of potted rosemary
and flowering geraniums. The ground level consisted of an open
living room. Upstair a small kitchen was tucked in-between two
tiny bedrooms. I imagined that if all of Father's sisters and
brothers and their children arrived simultaneously, we would be

crammed in like a can of sardines. Even our family of five seemed to max out the house's capacity. How had father's entire family once lived in this tiny house?

Our visits never lasted more than a few hours. I would not sleep overnight in that house until my university years. We sat, ate, and talked in the living room until Grandfather rose with broad grin rising under his broad white painter's mustache, "Would you children like to come see my garden?" he asked with childlike exuberance. Eager to be rescued from the monotony of more idle chatter we followed him several blocks away to his hillside garden plot. A stream flowed along the sloped garden's lower edge. He taught us how to fold paper boats and float them down a small stream. We excitedly chased our boats down and relaunched them until they began to disintegrate. He next pulled out his buck knife and cut several fresh willow branches growing near the streams. We carried them into the cave that he had carved into the hillside on the uppermost garden edge. Shaded from the sun, we huddled together on two small handmade stools watching as he pounded the willow stick bark until it slipped off the wood. Then he deftly carved the stick into pull-whistles. While we tooted like cats in heat, he reached over to a shelf carved into the cave wall for his stash of wine. He had given up playing cards, but never his wine.

Grandfather's face was weathered resulting from his many years exposed to the elements. While he had long since retired from his forest manager position, he still was strengthened by nature. Observing Grandfather, I came to understand that Father's upbringing had been quite different from Mother's sheltered life in Budapest.

This difference became even more evident on a subsequent trip where we spent an entire month away from the Kelenhegyi house. We accompanied Father on his surveying job in a village called

Bakonynana, located about 13 miles north of Veszprém. As a teenager, Mother went on trips to Vienna, Zurich, and Sweden for the purpose of improving her language and cultural skills. But those trips always included the highest levels of comfort and protective oversight. Even a casual stroll through town was chaperoned under the watchful eye of a trusted family friend. It was not until she met my father that she spent any time in the Hungarian countryside. She could never have imagined that she would spend an entire month surrounded by villagers still struggling in the post-Great Depression poverty. This village so dramatically contrasted her sheltered city upbringing. Her over-protective sisters were aghast that Father would bring his family to a place like this.

A different side of Father emerged in this village. The well-groomed educated engineer became a rougher, more masculine and exciting country boy. He easily bridged the great societal gap and spoke to the local hired laborers as if he were one of them. But he also made sure that Mother felt loved, safe, and comfortable.

There was no running water in this village. No flush toilets like those at the Kelenhegyi house. At one home I visited, there wasn't even an outhouse. The matron told me, "Just go anywhere beyond the animal pen. You dig your own hole."

I will never for get the emaciated 10-year old boy whom I met on one afternoon walk around the village. He was weeding alone in a large watermelon patch. I stopped to watch him work. When he paused to look back at me, I asked him what he would eat for lunch. He replied that he had a cracked watermelon. I watched as he hungrily scooped out the red flesh with a spoon.

Further down the road, a group of village women incessantly stirred large metal vats over open fires. "This will be plum butter," they explained. I offered to stir the pot but they kindly yet firmly declined my offer. "If we stop stirring for even a minute, the blue plums will burn and the entire batch will be ruined." However, they promised to teach me how to milk a cow and invited me to help string up the bright red peppers that would later be ground and sold as paprika.

I felt a bit like a celebrity among the Bakonynana children, who all wanted to play with me. They imagined that I, the city-girl, possessed some worldly wisdom. Perhaps I failed to admit how sheltered I really was back in my sanctuary. My world within the larger universe of the idyllic Kelenhegyi house, surrounded by beautiful gardens, enclosed within large metal fences and locked gates, situated among other magnificent villas creating their own worlds, within a highly desirable hillside neighborhood overlooking, but safely removed from, the heart of the city across the river. In blissful ignorance of the dangers lurking much closer to me than I realized.

Back row: Gizela, Ilona, Margit, Erzsébet & Klára.
Middle: Judit, Laci, Zsuzsa, Nagypapa holding Ilonka,
Kato, & Éva. Front: me, Margareta, Klára, Éva, & Béla.

Laci and me on Father's lap, surrounded by his
workmen, 1937

6

The Gestation of a War, 1938-1939

Hungary's next prime minister, Gyula Gömbös, was the first foreign head of government to visit Adolf Hitler after he became Germany's Chancellor. During this visit, Gömbös spoke of Hungary's desire to restore wrongly confiscated territories. This was the revisionist pipe-dream that alarmed Western Allies and lured Hungary into its ill-fated alliance with Germany.

Gömbös followed up his visit with a letter to Hitler in the spring of 1934, in which he argued that the restoration of historic "Greater Hungary" was not only in Hungary's interest, but also essential for German imperial policy. When he wrote of uniting with Germany to check the "unwarranted ambitions of small nations," he was referring to the burdensome "Little Entente," an agreement signed by all of Hungary's neighbors,[22] with strong backing from France, to prevent Hungary from mushrooming back to its former glory.

Radical-right Hungarian politicians were awed by Hitler's rapid consolidation of power and his audacious defiance of the prohibitions imposed by the Versailles Treaty. The Führer of Germany passed laws that nullified civil liberties and allowed the police to take people into "protective custody" at Dachau.[23] He took personal control of the military, formed the Gestapo, outlawed trade unions and all competing political parties, and purged his own Nazi party. He even had the audacity to pass a law exempting himself from paying income taxes, and then to direct the government to buy his embellished autobiographical manifesto *Mein Kampf* to be given as wedding gifts to newlywed couples.

Hitler even established the *Reich Luftwaffe* (Air Force). This revealed a plot years in the making. He had used the German airline Lufthansa as a front to offer government funded pilot training. The new pilots were actually being trained as fighter pilots for his secret state-of-the-art air force. In addition, citing the "Protocols of the Elders of Zion," a fictitious novel about a Jewish conspiracy to take over the world, he boycotted Jewish shops and businesses. The wolf was starting to show his teeth.

---

[22] Including Romania, Czechoslovakia, and the "Kingdom of Serbs, Croats, and Slovenes"

[23] Germany's first concentration camp

The Munich Agreement, signed on September 29, 1938, was the turning point at which Hungary finally crossed the proverbial Rubicon. In exchange for the opportunity to reclaim a small portion of lost territories, Hungary formalized its fateful alliance with the Devil. By this time, Hitler had already militarily occupied the Rhineland, a region which the Treaty of Versailles specifically stipulated was to remain demilitarized. Hitler had also paraded Germany's army into Vienna in a masterful publicity stunt captured on film newsreels. Happy, smiling children waved Swastika flags, and wholesome women pinned flowers onto the lapels of marching soldiers.

Hitler would repeat this pattern of highly effective Nazi propaganda campaigns with increased audacity in Czechoslovakia and Poland. Nazi propagandist Joseph Goebbels utilized every type of media made available by the latest technologies. The Nazis made movies and even dabbled in television. However, with Hitler's renowned oratory skills, the radio remained their most effective propaganda tool. By 1938, 75% of German households owned a radio. Everybody had access to radio one way or another. It surpassed the printed media as the public's primary news source. And radio waves did not stop at borders. Hitler reached out to a wide audience with intense intimacy. People were inclined to believe what they heard on the radio. And Hitler had no qualms about manipulating public sentiment by broadcasting fake news.

The Sudetenland was a predominantly German-speaking region along Czechoslovakia's northern border. To take control of this region with the least amount of worldwide outcry, Hitler staged devious political theater by spreading false reports that the Czech government was repressing the German minority. Feigning outrage over the supposed mistreatment of German people, Hitler demanded that Czechoslovakia cede the Sudetenland to Germany or be prepared to face war. British, French, German and Italian leaders rushed to Munich to diffuse this trumped-up conflict. The outcome of this meeting was the Munich Agreement.

In addition to clearing the way for Germany to annex Sudetenland, the Munich Agreement also ceded a part of Slovakia to Hungary, including the town of Levice (*Léva Vára*). Hungarians were ecstatic with this first reclamation of taken territory. In honor of this historic event, Father gave my sister, Ilonka, the middle name of Léva when she was born on November 26 of that same year. For years, we called her "Lévababa." Hitler proved that he could actually accomplish what Hungarian politicians had only promised to do for the past eighteen years.

No matter how hard some Hungarians tried to stop it, the post-Great Depression political climate in Hungary kept swinging further to the extreme right. Gyula Gömbös was brazenly anti-Semitic. But before regent Horthy allowed him to take office, he demanded that Gömbös disavow his extreme anti-Semitism and allow Jews to retain their government positions. Gömbös publicly recanted his previous antipathy toward Jews. The Jewish political leadership, in turn, supported his appointment. Gömbös kept his promise and refrained from enacting any racially motivated laws or causing economic harm to the Jews. But his successors were not bound by such promises of restraint.

In May 1938, immediately after former banker Béla Imrédy assumed prime ministership, he pushed through Hungary's first formal anti-Jewish Law. It defined Jews by religious affiliation and limited Jewish participation to 20 percent in civil service, industries, and institutes of higher learning. Ironically, Imrédy was soon forced to resign the prime ministership when it was revealed that his great-grandfather was Jewish.

Me, Nagypapa, Laci, Klára, Béla, 1938

Kelenhegyi swing set, Laci, Éva, Béla, me, Klára & Marga

On May 5, 1939, Pál Teleki, who returned for a second run as prime minister, pushed the second anti-Jewish Law through the Diet. It further restricted Jewish representation in industry and business, pushing many Jews into poverty. This time, however, the delineation of "Jewish" expanded to align with Germany's infamous Nuremberg Laws. Now, members of the "Israelite faith," or any person with two Jewish grandparents - including 100,000 Hungarian converts to Christianity and their offspring - fell victim to these laws. But Hungary's anti-Semitism paled in comparison to what was concurrently happening in Germany.

In the fall of 1938, Germany invalidated the passports of all its Jewish citizens and reissued passports with the letter "J" stamped in red. The Nazis justified these new passports as a response to requests by Sweden and Switzerland who wanted a way of easily denying Jews entry into their respective countries. A month later, in response to the murder of a German consular aide in Paris by a Polish Jew, the Nazi's launched the "Kristallnacht pogrom." Throughout Germany, thousands of Jewish shops and synagogues were looted, burned, or destroyed. The Nazis also forced Jews to turn in their radios to local authorities.

In January of 1939 Hitler gave a speech to the German parliament in which he prophesied that there might be another world war. Jewry and Bolshevism, not Germany's aggression, would cause this war. He vowed to prevent the Jewish race from ruling the earth. Hitler didn't hide his agenda of conquest and annihilation of the Jews in Europe. He explicitly laid it out in *Mein Kampf*. The world just didn't take him seriously.

Sadly for Hungary, whenever he held out the promise of recapturing taken lands, we were too eager to join his side. Hungary was merely a disposable pawn in Hitler's chess match with the world. In February 1939, he promised to restore more of

My grandfather, Béla Jaszai, in his Veszprém
garden, 1938

our former borders. Hungary signed the anti-Comintern pact with Italy, Germany, and Japan and withdrew from the League of Nations.

Hitler's top foreign policy advisor and negotiator, Ulrich Friedrich Wilhelm Joachim von Ribbentrop, was an opportunist. Hitler's reliance on Ribbentrop annoyed other Nazi Party members who thought him superficial and lacking in talent. One German diplomat later recalled, "Ribbentrop didn't understand anything about foreign policy. His sole wish was to please Hitler." He had a talent for memorizing Hitler's pet ideas and then later presenting them as his own, a practice that much impressed Hitler. His knowledge of other countries and his skill in duplicity grew out of years traveling throughout Europe as a wine salesman after marrying the daughter of a wealthy Wiesbaden vintner. In Hitler's chess game with the world, Ribbentrop was Hitler's knight, jumping from country to country implementing a foreign policy built on deceit.

When Ribbentrop advised regent Admiral Miklós Horthy to start concentrating troops on our northern border, Horthy had no idea that Ribbentrop would simultaneously warn Slovakian Prime Minister, Jozef Tiso, about the Hungarian troop mobilization. Ribbentrop then presented Tiso with two choices: either declare independence from Czechoslovakia, with the understanding that the new state would be in the German sphere of influence, or see all of Slovakia absorbed into Hungary. The Slovaks chose to declare independence.

Hitler then used the ensuing divide in Czech-Slovak relations as a pretext to take over Czechoslovakia. He summoned Czechoslovakian President Emil Hácha to the Reich Chancellery in Berlin presumedly to chastise him for his failure to keep order in his country. When President Hácha arrived on the evening of March 14, Hitler watched a film and deliberately kept Hácha waiting for hours. When they finally met at 1:30 a.m., Hitler toyed with the President before revealing that German troops were marching into Czechoslovakia at that very moment. By 4:00 a.m., Hácha had reluctantly signed a protectorate agreement.

As they had done in Austria, German troops marched into Bohemia and Moravia without facing any organized resistance. Without firing a shot Hitler had dissolved the second Czechoslovak Republic. Again, the publicity cameras rolled as Hitler led a triumphant parade up to Prague Castle and proclaimed his bloodless victory. An emboldened Hitler had conquered the Rhine, Austria, and now Czechoslovakia without facing any military resistance.

The Nazis repeated the pattern they had established in Austria. As soon as the cameras were turned off and the world's attention drifted away, the Nazis reneged on their false promises of protection. Instead, they implemented *Generalplan Ost*, designed to eradicate the Czech nationality through assimilation, deportation, and extermination. The plan assumed that only 50% of Czechs were fit for Germanization. Czech intellectuals were to be removed not only from Czech territories but from Europe completely. Two hundred thousand intellectual elites and middle class passed through concentration camps and another 250,000 died during the German occupation.

Hungary took advantage of the chaos that followed Hitler's conquest of Czechoslovakia to invade the ethnically-Ukrainian Sub-Carpathian Ruthenia region. We subsequently invaded an unmobilized and unprepared Eastern Slovakia. On April 4, 1939, Hungary and Slovakia signed the Budapest Treaty which turned over a strip of eastern Slovakia extending north to the Polish border that included the towns of Uzhhorod and Sobrance. Strategically, Hungary wanted this land to establish a buffer to protect the railway that passed through Uzhhorod along the Uzh River up to Poland. This was the same railway line that bypassed Nagykálló around the time of Nagypapa's birth.

Hitler pushed his luck too far when he decided to play a similar game with Poland. Though the United Kingdom and France had guaranteed to defend Poland if Germany invaded, Hitler doubted that Chamberlain had the stomach to go to war in their defense. But to hedge his bet, he needed to ensure that the Soviet Union would not interfere with his plans. To mitigate the Soviet risk, on August 23, Germany and the Soviet Union signed the Molotov-Ribbentrop Pact, which contained secret provisions for the joint occupation of Poland and Soviet occupation of Finland and Bessarabia.

Since the majority of the German population was opposed to invading Poland, the Nazi propaganda machine started spreading false stories about atrocities committed against German populations living within Polish borders. The Nazis accused Polish

Our family in 1939

authorities of organizing violent ethnic cleansing of ethnic Germans living within Poland. This propaganda was only the first stage of operation *Konserve* (canned good).

In the next stage, German troops, dressed in Polish uniforms, stormed various border buildings, frightened the locals with inaccurate shots and acts of vandalism. When they retreated, they left behind corpses in Polish uniforms. The corpses were actually prisoners from concentration camps killed by lethal injection before they were shot. Staged attacks took place at a railway station, a customs office, a forest service station, and a communication station. But the most notable attack took place at the German-language radio station in Gleiwitz. On the first day of September, the morning after the Gleiwitz incident, in a speech in the Reichstag, Hitler cited twenty-one border incidents as justification for Germany's "defensive" action against Poland. That same day, German and Slovakian forces invaded Poland. Though Hitler had tried to entice Admiral Horthy with the offer of additional territory, Hungary refused to participate in the invasion of Poland. World War II had begun.

Laci and me, 1939

7

Summers in Rezi, 1940

I excitedly pirouetted around the apartment when I learned that the Vietorisz family would move back from Diósgyőr to the Kelenhegyi house in early 1940. Having my cousins back meant more interesting play time. They filled in the years around me. Kato was 10; Zsuzsa and Laci 8; I was 7; Béla and Klára 5; Éva 4; and Marga and my sister Lévababa (Ilonka) both 2 years old. The family moved into the large first floor apartment, which had exclusively belonged to Nagypapa. Now a widower, he only needed his bedroom, his toilet with its fine tracing paper, and his office with its treasure filled wastepaper basket. I anticipated an entirely new level of excitement on the swing-set, at the sandpile, and in our feeble attempts to play ping-pong. But to my disappointment, play time barely improved. Not only that, their presence introduced tensions into the household for reasons I was too young to comprehend.

Józsi-*bácsi* had moved back to Budapest to start a new prestigious job. He was director at *Magyar Állami Vas Acél es Gépgyár* (the Hungarian Royal State Iron, Steel and Machinery Factory). Employing thousands of workers, MÁVAG was the largest Hungarian rail-vehicle producer and Hungary's second largest industrial enterprise behind only the Manfréd Weiss Steel and Metal Works. He became director of the machinery division. Since we were now allied with Germany, nearly all of the factory's production had been diverted to support the German war effort. He was in a favorable position with the Nazi Party. He possessed written papers signed by Hermann Göring that allowed him to travel anywhere within German controlled territories. He was often away from home, traveling through Hungary, Austria, and Germany to oversee production of items I could only imagine being very important to the war effort.

The Vietorisz family arrived at the Kelenhegyi house in a brand new Mercedes sedan driven by an ever-present chauffeur. I had never even ridden in a car. The husbands of the other families sharing the Kelenhegyi house–the Majorosses, Jezierszkys, and Jaszais– all had decent jobs. But none of them could even consider affording a car.

The chauffeur driven car was only the first of many obvious lifestyle differences we would observe. Because of the war, food and other goods were becoming scarce. However, the Vietorisz family always secured what they needed. They often held afternoon teas in their large apartment. I went for the cookies, which were elegant but absurdly tiny. I was never allowed to take my fill of these unsatisfying diminutive cookies.

"Why don't you bake more robustly-sized biscuits like those we bake?" I asked, feigning an air of superiority. In reality, cookies had become an infrequent luxury in our apartment.

And this wasn't my only snide criticism. I made a fool of myself trying to impress the adults because I coveted what Kato had. Like her, I wanted to be treated like a young lady rather than a little girl. Her three additional years seemed to entitle Kato a different status with the adults. They fawned over her for her drawing and painting artistic aptitude. She wore beautiful dresses and coats that Erzsébet-*néni*'s seamstress sewed for her and her sisters. After enduring nagging complaints born out of my envy, my poor mother contracted with a different, more affordable, seamstress to make a coat and hat for me. But these somehow just did not compare to my cousins' clothes. I tried to pretend thankfulness to my mother, but I did a terrible job of hiding my disappointment. By the look on her face I am sure Mother saw through my weak stoicism. I am still ashamed, 80 years later, for hurting Mother because of my childish envy.

I sought companionship among my cousins in the Kelenhegyi house but was frequently disappointed. I always felt like I wanted to play with them more than they wanted to play with me. Not wanting to miss a chance to interact, I would wait out on the swings. But my cousins were often content to stay inside their apartment and play among themselves. I envied that they were closer in age to each other. My sister, Ilonka, was too small to be a meaningful playmate. So I played mostly with Laci.

I had no trouble keeping up with my older brother. As the first born male grandchild, great expectations were thrust upon him. Laci didn't meet those expectations. He was young for his age, slight of build, and extremely introverted. Father would make him do exercises, but he never bulked up. However, Laci was my perfect play partner. We were inseparable. After Laci, my most frequent playmates within the Kelenhegyi house were my two-year-younger brother, Béla and our cousin Klára. While Klára-*néni* was one woman in the house that I most admired, my role model, her daughter Klára confessed to me that she simultaneously idolized me as her role model.

They said I was a tomboy who jumped from one piece of furniture to the next without touching the ground. I didn't get that from my mother. Father tried to teach mother to ride a bicycle. He bought her a helmet and padding for her knees and elbows. On a flat street along the Danube, he ran alongside, pushing the seat from behind. He tried everything but Mother never rode for more than a few yards. Father passed the bicycle down to me and Laci. It was too large for me to be able to sit on the seat, and the handle bars were up near my chin. However, I quickly learned to ride and proudly circled the lot.

On a chilly May morning, I shivered in my bathing suit poolside at the Rudas *Uszoda* (swimming pool) as my indifferent gray-haired swimming lesson instructor tied a rope to a belt and then strapped the belt around my waist. Once I was in the water, he pulled me up with that rope each time I went under but only after I took in a mouthful of water. I must admit that his draconian methods quickly taught me how to swim.

Father took us to ice-skate, to the Budapest Zoo in Városliget Park, or to swim. On one of those swims on Margit Island, my nose got so sunburnt that I still have the red patch it left. However, Father's favorite way to pass free time on a Sunday was to take us for a hike in the woods. He could name any plant we passed. Out there, he was truly in his element and the most animated. He loved the forests and I loved those outings. I would hold his large fingers as he explained everything about the woods. Different trees, how they should be taken care of, the need to remove dry branches before they started to decay. He knew every bush, bug, and bird. He would capture a field mouse or some interesting insect. Holding it gently in his hand, he taught us not to be afraid and that every creature was beautiful and perfect in its unique way.

Though the two sides of my parents' families did not mix, Father did his best to maintain contact with his brothers in Pest. The oldest brother József-*bácsi* never came to our house. He had married an even older, obese woman who ran a bar in the distant Zugló district of Budapest. Never wanting to lose their faithful patrons, they were perennially stationed at the bar. When we visited them, his wife would serve me delicious glasses of raspberry soda, which I drank sitting at the bar among inebriated adults.

We saw more of his younger brother Feri-*bácsi* who occasionally brought his two daughters to the Kelenhegyi house. And then, just before the siege, Father's youngest brother Géza and his German-born wife Trudi came to stay only a few houses down from us with her relatives.

When I got the chance to venture outside the protective bubble of our Kelenhegyi compound, I did notice more German soldiers on the streets of Budapest. They looked handsome in their crisp uniforms and, as far as I could tell, acted properly and respectfully. The older girls sang a song about trying to capture and marry one of these young eligible bachelors. Though I didn't really understand the gist of the song, I memorized the lyrics and repeated it.

The war crept up on us like an insidious fog. The shelves in the small shops slowly emptied. I don't know if it was because of the war or the food rationing, but starting in 1940, my parents sent us children every summer to my aunts in Rezi, a small village five miles north of Keszthely on Lake Balaton. All three of Father's sisters, Teri-*néni*, Mariska-*néni*, and Ánna-*néni*, lived together in a small cottage.

With no children of their own, these aunts showered us with welcoming love. Their joyous home had no electrical service nor indoor plumbing. We took our water in buckets from the well and, after we graduated from the *bili* (chamber pot), did our business in an outhouse. In the evening, we gathered intimately in the one gas-lantern lit room. My aunts sat around happily chatting as they constantly crocheted or knitted. Ornate doilies and tablecloths covered the walls, chairs, tables, and beds. I slept in a large bed quilted with feather-filled billowing white sheets. I was so worried that I might have an evening accident and pee in the bed. But I never did. I felt so comfortable sharing in their simple contented lives.

Teri-*néni* had recently stayed with us at the Kelenhegyi house for a few months on her way back from Czechoslovakia. She had been forced to give up her teaching position in a small village near Prague after Hungary's territorial takeover soured relations with that country. I will never forget the wonderful box of homemade cookies she brought with her, baked for her by the grateful families of her former students. She appeared with those cookies around the time when the only available options were those served upstairs in my cousins' apartment.

The middle sister, Mariska-*néni*, was the only one of the three to have married. A year after their wedding, her husband–the Mayor of Rezi–found it necessary to reprimand the *Falusi Bolond* (village idiot) for some minor transgression. The idiot became enraged and hit the Mayor over the head with a rock. He died instantly and left Mariska a widow.

Anna-*néni*, the youngest sister, was as kind and warm as her two sisters, but suffered from what was probably Elefantiasis. Her legs were as large as tree trunks. All three aunts were accomplished piano players, but Anna-*néni* was the best. Unable to afford lessons, she taught herself to sight-read music and played exceptionally well. I was amazed at how she could beautifully play a brand new musical score the first time it was placed in front of her. Her sisters sang harmonies as she pounded out both folk and popular currently-aired songs. Anna-*néni* would borrow and then hand-copy scores of sheet music. I still have a large album of these beautifully written out songs. Music has always lifted my spirits. But whenever I hear one of the songs I learned in that cottage, I fondly remember our summers spent in Rezi.

Their large property had plum, cherry, and apple fruit trees, a vegetable garden, and a vineyard. I scratched the backs of their friendly piglets, and played with chickens and ducklings. The *pínce* (wine cellar) rose from the ground in a concrete mound that was excellently suited for climbing, sliding down, and playing king of the hill.

They gave us minor chores. We pulled weeds in the vineyard and collected fallen walnuts. But we quickly got distracted and ran off to chase each other through the rows of grapevines, roll down the grassy *Csalit* hill, or search the woods for *Vargánya* mushrooms. We were especially drawn to the stream that flowed just below the cornfield because it was where we met and played with other children from the village. Though I don't remember it, it was here, along this stream that I caught lice at the age of three. My aunts shaved off my luxuriously curly baby hair, only to have it grow back as the stiff lumpy hair I struggled with when that started to matter to me.

One summer day, we took a trip to the hot baths of Héviz. I barely remember the baths, but will never forget the harrowing carriage ride there and back. We rode a horse-drawn wagon on a hilly, precarious dirt road. When we came to steep downhill sections, the driver placed a log through the spokes of the wheels and skidded and twisted the wagon down the steep slope. While it must have been preferable to racing down uncontrollably, the sensation made my stomach drop.

Our aunts filled us with homemade pasta and bread. They kneaded bread dough in a large wooden trough, and then divided the dough into three round woven baskets to rise while they prepared the brick oven, known as a *Kemence*. They started a raging wood fire inside, then quickly brushed out the ashes, and slid in a wooden pallet holding the risen dough. The aroma of the beautifully browned bread was intoxicating.

I had no understanding of the financial hardships most Hungarians faced at this time. But even in Rezi where residents could maintain gardens and livestock, we still felt the impact of food rationing. A large portion of the village harvest, dairy, and livestock went toward feeding the war effort. Meat, sugar, and milk were all taken away from villagers to be given to the army. One time, my aunt took us to the village dairy. A female worker ladled out a sample for me of the cream that had risen to the top of one of the large steel milk cans awaiting collection. The smooth thick liquid going down my throat was unforgettably delicious, made ever more memorable because we hardly ever consumed milk at that time.

That first August leaving Rezi, we brought an extra person back with us when we returned to Budapest. My father hired Roza-*néni* to be our live-in cook. The sixteen-year-old daughter of a Rezi neighbor, Roza-*néni* was of an age at which she longed to find a way out of the constraints of village living. She dreamed of living in Budapest. She worked out decidedly well for our family. But I always wondered whether her Budapest adventure met her expectations.

My brother Béla in Rezi, 1941

My father was a minimalist, and was completely content with austere furnishings. A bit obsessed about the cleanliness of our apartment, he refused to allow us to have curtains or rugs. He called them "dust collectors." It wasn't until Roza-*néni* came, with her extra house-cleaning assistance, that he allowed my mother to lay down some of the beautiful oriental rugs that her father had given her.

I started first grade in September 1940. As there was no pre-school or kindergarten at that time, this was my first year of formal schooling. First grade through fourth grade was called "elementary school." The next four years were "middle school." After that, we had four years of "secondary school." At the public *Horthy Miklós Altalanos* public elementary school, I was not required to wear a uniform. I wore a skirt, blouse, cardigan, knee-high socks, and leather shoes. I actually preferred it later when, in September of 1944, I started attending middle school where navy blue pleated skirt and white blouse uniforms were required. When everybody looked the same it eliminated the instinctive proclivity of young girls to try to out-dress each other.

My mother walked with me twice that first week. After that, I was on my own. The school was a short run down on Orlay *utca* to Béla Bartok Boulevard and then about 400 yards to the right. I need to emphasize the word "run." I invariably ran or skipped the entire way down steep Orlay *utca*. On those crisp fall mornings, the large horse chestnut trees lining the street dropped loads of leaves and shiny brown buckeye nuts. I rushed into the ankle deep soft mess, kicking up a cloud of leaf litter while pocketing a few chestnuts to use in self-defense of a potential ambush. I made sport of kicking them to my imaginary companions. My brother and I once carved smoking pipes out of the chestnuts and stuffed them full of dried tree leaves as the tobacco. The ghastly taste cured me of any desire to smoke for the rest of my life.

Two thirds of the way down Orlay utca, the large homes gave way to inviting little shops pushed up adjacent to the sidewalk. There was the old shoemaker, who once made me a pair of shoes styled to look like "Mary Janes." I waited in great anticipation for that dream pair of shoes, only to have outgrown the shoe size by the time they were finally delivered. There was a tiny general store crowded with aisles packed with shelves of hardware that I loved to examine. The buildings became larger as I approached the Boulevard. Nestled among the bank, bakery, and drugstore, was the one store that earned most of my childhood attention, the candy store.

At eight o'clock, we began with reading, writing, arithmetic, gym, and finally music. Academics always came easily to me and I scored near the top of the class through high school. At ten o'clock, we had a snack break called *Tízórai*. It consisted of the sandwich, fruit, or crackers that I brought from home each day. As the war rationing ramped up, parents no longer had access to snack foods. To ensure that the children ate something, the school started providing tiny bottles of white or chocolate milk and a bun.

First and second graders were released at one o'clock. That was when I gathered with my classmates in front of the candy store. We chatted as we stared at the colorful candies. We said our goodbyes before I trudged alone back up steep Orlay *utca*. Though I truly enjoyed my schoolmate friendships, we always went to our respective homes for the main meal of the day. The distances between our homes were too far to walk alone and we had no cars. The only play dates I can recall were the rare scheduled birthday party where a few hours of free play was capped by cocoa and cookies. But these events never yielded deep friendships.

The tree defined the holiday. On Christmas Eve, all of the Szesztay grandchildren eagerly waited in Nagypapa's office for the hand bell to ring signaling the moment that we could return to the dining room to witness the unveiling of the spectacular tree, magically decorated by heavenly angels. This glorious tree surpassed all expectations. Flames flickered from ornate steel candle holders attached to the branches. The light bounced brightly off flowing reflective tinsel. The branches hung richly laden with beautifully wrapped *szaloncukor* sugar fondant candies, and disk-shaped honey and sugar cookies. But before we could run over to sample these sweet delights, we circled the tree and sang Christmas carols.

Mennyből az angyal lejött hozzátok,
Pásztorok, pásztorok,
Hogy Betlehembe sietve menvén
Lássátok, lássátok.

Nagypapa gave each grandchild a small gift. After that, since this event took place in the Vietorisz's first floor apartment, we watched them celebrate their Christmas. The angels were scheduled to visit our apartment downstairs the following morning on Christmas. With growing envy I watched my cousins open gift after gift of clothes, games, and candies.

The next morning, the unveiling of our tree was much less impressive. The tree was shorter and its branches held far fewer sweets. When we opened our presents, I received clothes but no toys. I didn't say anything directly to my parents, but I wore my extreme disappointment like flashing lights. I barely comprehended that there was a war going on. I didn't understand that Józsi-*bácsi* was in a position that gave him access to goods that none of the other families had. Given that lack of perspective, I felt wronged. I only saw injustice and discriminatory inequities in this gift situation.

A few weeks later, still upset because we had not received as many gifts as our cousins, Laci and I approached Father to plead our case. The Vietorisz girls had all sorts of board games, but we didn't have a single one. Our situation constituted one of the greatest wrongs ever inflicted on humanity. When we finally finished our diatribe, father silently studied us.

With a disgusted guffaw, he threw some money down on the table saying, "Take it. Go buy yourselves a bloody board game." We eagerly snatched up the money and raced down the hill to the toy store. With the amount given, rather than buying one higher quality game we opted to buy two cheaper games. However, they turned out to be disappointing. We quickly lost interest in both of them and hardly ever played them after the first week. Because I based my expectations on what the Vietorisz girls received, I was never satisfied. I had no concept of how distorted that reality was.

Father was not miserly or ungenerous. Though ardently ascetic and non-materialistic, he was thoughtful and kind. One day, he took me and Ilonka down to the ice cream store. We met up with a group of young girls all wearing similar white dresses. Father called them over and bought each of them ice cream. We were puzzled by this. He rarely even bought ice cream for his own children. Why would he suddenly buy it for a group of complete strangers? Only later did he explain that these girls came from a nearby orphanage. They lived much more difficult lives than we.

He taught me the importance of fairness, giving, and selflessness. That one's self-interest was also important, but it should never come at the expense of depriving someone else of their right to live.

8

Hungary Enters the War, 1941

Hungarian Prime Minister Pál Teleki desperately sought to right his past mistakes. To leave a legacy that, on balance, would portray him as doing right for Hungary. His first big mistake occurred twenty-one years earlier, when he resigned in disgrace from his first term as prime minister after his secret attempt to restore the incompetent King Charles to the throne was exposed. His second mistake was pushing the 1939 Second Anti-Jewish Law through the Diet. However, he never acknowledged that as being a mistake. His third mistake was falling to temptation and making a deal with the Devil. It became immediately obvious to Teleki that whatever he had gained by negotiating with Hitler paled in comparison to the cost of eternal damnation. Realizing his mistake, he took urgent steps to steer Hungary away from this pending disaster.

As late as November 1940, Hungary had resisted fully committing to Germany's war effort. We refused to send troops to support Germany's first attack on Poland. We even went so far as to forbid German troops from even crossing over Hungarian soil. But Teleki's resistance collapsed when the Devil offered him Transylvania. Because of its abundance of natural resources, its half-Magyar population, and the critical role it played in our history, this former-kingdom region was seen as one of the greatest losses imposed by the Treaty of Versailles.

Sweet-talking Hitler only wanted German troops to cross Hungary on their way to occupy Romanian oil fields. Only that, and for Hungary to sign the Tripartite Pact, the military alliance between Italy, Germany, and Japan. In exchange, he promised to return 40% of Transylvania back to Hungary, an area larger than the combined States of Maryland and Connecticut.[24] Strategically, this seemed like the perfect window of opportunity to take advantage of a weakened Rumania. It had lost its "Little Entente" defense against Hungarian expansion when, on June 22, 1940, France shockingly-quickly surrendered to the invading Germans.

Immediately after accepting Hitler's offer and signing the Pact on November 20, 1940, Teleki tried to undo the damage. He again continued to refuse to commit troops to the Nazi war effort. Despite being under constant surveillance by Hitler's Gestapo, he sent an envoy to America with five million dollars to prepare for Hungary's government in exile. His ensuing conflict with Hitler came to a head when Teleki refused to allow German troops to cross Hungary to invade Yugoslavia. In December of 1940, Teleki signed a Treaty of Eternal Friendship with Yugoslavia. Allowing German troops to cross Hungarian territory would betray that

---

[24] This return was called the Second Vienna Award

treaty and lead the Allies to declare war against Hungary. He predicted that Germany would lose the war and that Europe would once again fall into chaos. If allied to the losing side, Hungary would again suffer needlessly. He also believed that after Germany conquered Yugoslavia, the Nazi wolf would come after Hungary next. There was no upside to his deal with Hitler.

Hitler was ready to launch Operation Barbarossa, Germany's secret plan to invade the Soviet Union. But before he could launch that invasion, Germany needed to ensure that its southern flank was not vulnerable to counter attack. The weak point of that flank was Yugoslavia, which was indecisive about joining Hitler's Tripartite Pact. Both Germany and Italy put heavy pressure on Yugoslavian regent, Prince Paul, who finally agreed to join the Pact on March 25, 1941. The regent's capitulation was not well received by Yugoslavia's mostly anti-German population. Just two days after the signing, an outraged Serb-dominated military officer corps launched a *coup d'etat*. Ousting Prince Paul, they put seventeen-year-old King Peter on the throne. The new government refuted the Tripartite Pact and accepted a counter British offer of security.

A furious Hitler demanded an immediate invasion of Yugoslavia. But Prime Minister Teleki refused to allow German troops to pass through Hungary or Luftwaffe planes to launch from Hungarian airfields.

"Teleki must get out of my way!" He shouted as he slammed his clenched fist down on the table.

A desperate Teleki reached out to Western Allies. He relayed messages to Britain and America stating his intention to honor Hungary's Friendship Agreement with Yugoslavia and to forbid Germany from crossing our borders. He cautioned that Hungary could only hold out if it received support from the West. The West offered no support in reply. The only response he received was a telegram from London threatening to cut all diplomatic ties if Hungary permitted Germany to cross.

Recognizing Teleki's intransigence, Hitler redirected his devilish cajolery towards Regent Horthy. He sent Hungary's ambassador to Germany, Döme Sztójay, back with an offer Horthy, himself, would find impossible to resist: the Yugoslavian territory that would restore Hungary's former access to the Adriatic Sea–the same lost land that had caused Horthy to lose his admiralship.

"The annihilation of Yugoslavia is inevitable," Sztójay explained. "So why not allow German troops to pass through Hungary?"

To Teleki's dismay, a bewitched Horthy consented to Hitler's demands. On the night of April 3, Teleki passionately argued his case before the Cabinet, only to learn that Hungary's military chief of staff, German-descended Hungarian General Henrik Werth, had already worked out arrangements for the transport of the German troops across Hungary.

"This is treason," Teleki shouted. "You have committed to the German war effort at the expense of Hungary's best interests."

A fruitless debate continued for hours in which cabinet members quietly abandoned Teleki's side. Crestfallen, Teleki left the Hungarian Ministry of Foreign Affairs and returned to his apartment in the Sándor Palace. At around midnight, he received a call that is thought to have informed him that the German army had just started its march into Hungary. Teleki sat at his desk and wrote a letter that in part stated:

"We broke our word... out of cowardice ... The nation feels it, and we have thrown away its honor. We have allied ourselves to scoundrels ... We will become body-snatchers! A nation of trash. I did not hold you back. I am guilty."

He then put a pistol to his head and pulled the trigger.

The invasion of Yugoslavia and Greece began on April 6 and lasted twelve bloody days. Horthy dispatched Hungarian military forces to occupy former Hungarian lands in Vojvodina. After the successful campaign, Germany did not occupy Hungary as Teleki had feared. But Hitler soon reneged on his promises to return the Banat and Muraköz regions back to Hungary. Hungary's land grab had come to an end. However, the resentment Hungary had caused with its three neighboring countries continued to fester. Croatia, Slovakia, and Romania attempted to revive the "Little Entente" and initiate military action against Hungary. Tensions escalated until Ribbentrop intervened to end this squabble for the benefit of Germany's bigger war. Hitler still needed Hungary.

When Germany attacked the Soviet Union on June 22, 1941, Hungary did not send troops in support. Hitler may have had the audacity to completely renege on those promises to cooperate with the Soviet Union codified in the Molotov-Ribbentrop Pact, but Hungary did not want to risk angering the sleeping bear. Hungarians insisted that "we" were not at war against the Soviet Union. However, a little bit of Hitler trickery quickly reversed Hungary's stance on the war. The scheme was simple. Hungary would be obliged to respond to an unprovoked Russian airstrike on Hungarian soil. If the Soviet Union attacked Hungary first, then the pro-Nazi faction in Hungary could claim that a declaration of war was a necessary act of self-defense.

That is exactly what took place on June 26. Unidentified aircraft struck the industrial city of Kassa[25]. Even though Russia denied any involvement with the attack, the Nazi propaganda machine told a much more compelling story. Though they never definitively proved it, Hungarians believe that this attack was staged by Nazi supporters. Hungary officially entered the war on false pretenses.

By July 9, 1941, only eight days after joining Germany's Operation Barbarossa, Major General Béla Dalnoki-Miklós had already begun to worry about the fate of his *Kárpát* (Carpathian) Group. In concert with the German 17th Army, they drove the Soviet 12th Army out of the Carpathian mountains and pushed the Front seventy miles back into Russian territory toward Kiev along the Dniester River. The 40,000 strong *Kárpát* Group fought bravely, but its casualty count climbed rapidly even in that first week of fighting. Dalnoki-Miklós recognized that the odds were against his *Kárpát* Group.

The first problem was that his mechanized unit, the *Gyorshadtest* (Rapid Corps), were using obsolete light tanks that were extremely vulnerable to new Soviet anti-tank weapons. Even though the Rapid Corps was Hungary's best and most modernized mechanized group, it was only "modern" in comparison to other Hungarian units. Compared to Soviet-fielded quick strike units, Hungary's equipment was sadly outclassed.

---

[25] Kassa, then in Hungary, today is Košice in Slovakia.

The second problem was that the *Kárpát* Group's two infantry brigades were advancing on foot and unable to keep up with the Rapid Corps. Soon the infantry brigades were sent off to police occupied territory in the Ukraine. The Rapid Corps charged ahead without infantry to protect its flanks and rear.

His third problem was that the *Kárpát* Group was fighting against much larger Soviet forces. Even though they fought bravely and successfully, they took heavy losses. Like a gambler, if he stayed too long at the table he would eventually lose everything.

But his biggest problem was that the German Army was using his Rapid Corps as a sacrificial, dispensable unit. This realization became undeniable in Uman on August 3, when Germany used the Rapid Corps as one-half of a pincer action with the German 17th Army to envelop the Soviet 12th Army. This victory cost the Hungarians dearly.

The Rapid Corps grew weaker and weaker, while the retreating Soviet armies seemed to grow stronger. By September, four million Axis soldiers had crossed into the Soviet Union and Hungarian troop casualty reports startled Budapest leadership. Regent Horthy visited Hitler in Germany's East Prussian Operation Barbarossa headquarters to request the release of our battle worn *Kárpát* Group. But Hitler refused to withdraw the Rapid Corps unless Hungary replaced them with an even larger force.

By the time the first snows fell and more than 3 million Soviet soldiers had been captured or killed, the 17th Army and the Rapid Corps captured Kiev. Between Kiev and their next objective of Voroshilovgrad stood the Soviet 18th Army. German Field Marshal von Rundstedt ordered the Rapid Corps to launch a suicidal frontal assault to break through these Soviet defenses blocking their way.

Dalnoki-Miklós knew that a frontal assault would be sending his Rapid Corps men to their slaughter. His Rapid Corps had been whittled down to six battalions. Soviet defenses had already repelled a German attack consisting of forty battalions.

Instead of making the ordered head-on breakthrough, the Hungarian general performed a flanking maneuver that encircled the Russian defenses. The superior Soviet force was neutralized and the road to Voroshilovgrad was opened up for the continuation of the German advance. Though Dalnoki-Miklós had disobeyed Field Marshal von Rundstedt's direct orders, the German General Staff heaped high praise on the Rapid Corps for their outstanding tactical victory. Dalnoki-Miklós was just glad to have avoided the complete slaughter of his men.

After five months of continuous fighting, the Rapid Corps limped back to Budapest. One-third of its soldiers were dead, wounded, or missing in action. Also gone were personnel carriers, airplanes, artillery pieces, and nearly all of their L3 tankettes, Toldi tanks, and armored cars. Not only had these victories been too costly for the Rapid Corps itself, but the whole Hungarian army had lost its best trained men and equipment.

Operation Barbarossa's massive blitzkrieg assault was designed to quickly overrun Soviet defenses. But as winter spread across the vast Russian plain, Hitler realized that this invasion was far from meeting its objective. Germany was not logistically prepared for a drawn-out battle. Chilling rains around Moscow turned fields into wet mud that swallowed their vehicles. By mid-November, temperatures dropped and the mud froze. The Germans renewed their assault on Moscow, but their equipment failed to operate in the extreme cold. By December, the temperature at the Moscow Front fell to a shocking minus 30°F. Frosty winds covered freezing troops and equipment in deep snow drifts. In the midst of a blizzard, Soviet ski troops, camouflaged in white, counter-attacked.

Only eleven miles away from the Moscow city limits, Germany called off its attack to wait for spring and warmer weather.

Before year's end, Hungary officially broke off diplomatic relations with the United States. In January of 1942, the Devil sent Foreign Minister, Joachim von Ribbentrop, to Budapest with a promise of additional territory in Transylvania and a demand for additional Hungarian forces for Germany's spring offensive. Pro-German Prime Minister László Bardossy (appointed after the suicide of Pal Teleki), immediately agreed. A flabbergasted Horthy fired Bardossy for driving Hungary to its doom. However, Hungary's fate had already been sealed back when Teleki and Horthy had succumbed to temptations and entered into their first deal. There was no turning back on Hungary's obligation to send more troops to the Eastern Front.

Our family, 1941

9

Anti-Semitism Home and Abroad, 1941-1942

One of my best classroom friends suddenly stopped attending school. I later came to understand that she was partially Jewish. We believed her family had successfully fled to the West. No one spoke of her. So it was. People didn't know how to talk about the Jews.

Our next-door neighbor, Révay Jozsefné, the ex-wife of a successful publisher, was aged, cadaverous, and frail in those years we played in our garden beneath her overlooking window. She threw down elegantly-wrapped yellow candies to us. But we refused to take them. The common lore among us cousins was that she was an old witch and that the candy was poisonous, a tale akin to *Hansel and Gretel*. We found it strange that we never saw her leave her villa, and that she lived alone in a house nearly as big as the Kelenhegyi house, which so many of us occupied. The other thing said about her was that she was a Jew.

I was not consciously anti-Semitic, but I took my cues from the surrounding adults, who held a variety of opinions even among our small cadre of aunts and uncles. Nagypapa was politically conservative but socially tolerant. Father was extremely progressive. József-*bácsi*, who had to work on a daily basis with the Germans, needed to espouse pro-Nazi beliefs. But I don't really know where he stood on the issue of the Jews.

Hungary's 1941 census estimated that 861,000 citizens were at least half-Jewish, which meant that they were considered and treated as Jews. In the newly conquered territory of Ruthenia, anyone who could not prove legal residency dating back to 1850 was deported to Poland or handed over to the Germans. Some of the deported families had lived in the area for generations but lacked paperwork. In some cases, applications for residency permits were allowed to pile up without action by Hungarian officials until after the deportations had been carried out. The vast majority of these 20,000 deported Jews were massacred at Kamianets-Podilskyi by the end of August.

On August 8, 1941, the Hungarian parliament enacted its "Third Jewish Law," which prohibited intermarriage and penalized sexual intercourse between Jews and non-Jews. This law defined a Jew as anyone with at least two Jewish grandparents.

I had no idea that I was one-eighth Jewish on account of Nagypapa's mother being a Jew. Even if one claims to be irreligious, Judaism can still be in their blood. How close did I come to being victimized for a heredity over which I had no control?

Late in the summer of 1941, the Nazis started to annihilate the Jews. As they would later do in Hungary, the Germans worked from the outside in. Jews were still somewhat safe in Berlin. But a special SS *Einsatzgruppen* (task force) led by Reinhard Heydrich traveled in the wake of the German blitzkrieg assaults in the Soviet Union to round up Jews for placement into ghettos. Soon their mission changed from deportation to extermination. Between September and December hundreds of thousands of Jews were massacred in places like Babi Yar on the outskirts of Kiev, Soviet Ukraine, Vilna, Odessa, the Slobodka ghetto, Bolekhiv, and the Bogdanovka concentration camp.

In January of 1942, at the Wannsee Conference in Berlin organized by Reinhard Heydrich, the Nazis formalized their "final solution" plan for extermination of the Jews. Many historians regard Heydrich as the darkest figure within the Nazi regime. Even Hitler described him as "the man with the iron heart." Heydrich had been one of the organizers of the November 1938 Kristallnacht pogrom. He also had masterminded the fake Polish attack on the German radio station at Gleiwitz that justified Germany's attack on Poland. It was probably fortunate for all of humanity that Czech and Slovak agents assassinated him in May 1942. Sadly, another man immediately stepped in to take the baton.

Adolf Eichmann had been Heydrich's chief assistant at the time of the assassination. If Heydrich was the architect of Nazi genocide, Eichmann was its engineer. Before working his way up the Nazi ranks, Eichmann was an unsuccessful salesman who lost his job during the Great Depression. Eichmann, the son of a bookkeeper, looked like a bookkeeper. Diminutive and slender, he had a hooked nose, and wide protruding ears. He actually looked Jewish. As a child, other children teasingly called him "little Jew." Eichmann would manage the genocide until the end of the war. He would come to play a key role in the extermination of the Hungarian Jews in 1944, and later became known as the "world's most notorious Nazi."

Also in January, a group of pro-Nazi Hungarian police officers rounded up 1,200 predominantly Jewish Serbians in the town of Novi Sad, marched them to the Danube River, shot them, and dumped their bodies into the frozen waters. This act shocked the Hungarians in power at the time. The officers were sentenced to prison terms. However, two years later, their convictions would be reversed. This style of execution of Jews, along the banks of the Danube, would later be repeated countless times–right in the heart of Budapest.

10

Béla Goes to War, 1942-1943

Father spent his first few months of 1942 back in uniform traveling up the Danube to the large training camp in Szentendre, where he trained the rank-and-file recruits. He was one of the reservists that comprised a significant portion of the 209,000-man-strong Hungarian 2nd Army that was mobilizing to the Eastern Front He was called back into service with the promise of a "quick victory." A promise that he would be back home with the family for Christmas.

In deference to his age and prior military service at the Battle of Isonzo—Hungary's bloodiest battle of World War I—Father held the rank of *Főhadnagy* (First Lieutenant). Because of his training as a surveyor and civil engineer, he led an Engineering Field Team, which facilitated troop and equipment movement across rivers and rough terrain.

New recruits received only eight weeks of training before being sent to the Front. There was no time for any tactical field training. No time to plan for the 1,200 mile journey. No time to prepare to mobilize men, horses, vehicles, weapons, food, and materiel.

In mid-April as the 2nd Army loaded troops and equipment into railcars, mobilization quickly devolved into a logistical nightmare. Soviet partisans attacked and destroyed 19 of the 822 railway trains en route. Even before their first battle, the 2nd Army suffered 27 combat deaths and 83 wounded. The army's best equipment had been lost during last year's deployment of the Rapid Corps, and the 2nd deployed with out-of-date weaponry. There weren't even enough rifles to equip the rifleman battalions. The railways only got them part of the way. Hungarian tanks had to be driven long distances to reach the front. A majority of them broke down before they even reached the Front.

Father's field team included a work crew of 35 involuntarily conscripted Jews. They were some of the 45,000 Jews called up to serve in unarmed labor service units called *munkaszolgálat*. These work units escorted wagons of ammunition and materiel. Eight workers walked alongside a wagon carrying a ton of ammunition pulled by two horses. Each worker carried a shovel used to push the wagon out of ruts or to shovel dirt in front of sunken wheels. It was a 300-mile march at a grueling pace of 18 miles a day through dry, dusty lands scorched by wildfires set by the retreating Soviet armies. This same technique had been used by Russia a century earlier against Napoleon's invading army. It left no forage for the horses. Most of his workers wore regular city shoes that left their feet bloody and blistered.

As he walked with his work crew, he passed the time in conversation. He found them to be honest, intellectual, hardworking, formerly successful business men, educators, and

Father in uniform, 1942

writers. He shared their constant worries about how their families fared back home. With them, he built bonds of trust and respect. There was an unspoken shared understanding that he held their fate in his hands. There were some Hungarian officers and soldiers who were more brutal toward the Jewish workers than the Germans. Some tried to beat his men for infractions as minor as resting their shovels on the supply carts. Father brandished the pistol, which had been assigned to him to shoot deserters, to scare off these internal attackers.

His most challenging logistical issue en route was keeping his team fed. The personal provisions each man carried ran out in the first few weeks. Soon after, the unit's food supply ran out as well. The Army handed Father a wad of Hungarian Korona currency, with which he was expected to buy food at any opportunity. Even if Ukrainian villagers had been willing to accept this foreign currency–which they were not– there was nothing to buy. The deeper they pressed into Ukraine, the worse the food situation became. Father used these funds to bribe Hungarian and German soldiers for food. In some instances, payments were made between family members back home, and food was provided only after receipt of transactions back home were confirmed. This led to days of waiting without food.

In late June, Father and his work crew arrived at the Front just as Hitler launched his 1,370,287-man summer offensive, code named Fall Blau. By July, the various Axis armies began to align along the Don River, while Germany's 6th Army marched toward Stalingrad. The Hungarian 2nd Army controlled a 125-mile riverside stretch and occupied the towns of Voronezh, Svoboda, Pavlosk, and Liski. To prevent in-fighting among the Axis armies, the Italians were positioned directly south of the Hungarians. They served as a buffer between the Hungarians and the Romanians who were still at odds over Hungary's reclamation of Transylvanian territory.

Father spent the next four months along this stationary battlefront with plenty of time to assess his chances of survival and to notice the changes in weather. He was well aware of his good fortune that the Red Army had been too preoccupied with German advances to launch any counter attack along the Hungarian controlled stretch. Unquestionably, the Hungarian 2nd Army was outclassed, poorly trained, and poorly equipped. Lacking anti-tank weaponry, they sat defenseless against a pending Soviet tank assault. Germany had promised a hundred anti-tank guns, but ended up shipping only twelve. Germany also failed to provide vehicles needed to move the anti-tank cannons. The 2nd Army still relied on horses, but insufficient fodder forced them to pull the starving horses back from the Front. This left them with immovable cannons. This shared realization of their vulnerability badly affected soldier morale. Father was not alone in feeling no commitment to Germany's war effort. He was just one of thousands of Hungarian men being sent off to participate in a war for a cause in which they did not believe.

Despite its ever-present influence on our lives, war was not a topic I discussed with my father. However, my opinions were heavily influenced by his first-hand experience of its futility and senseless suffering. Even as a child, I considered war a silly game played by men who somehow rationalized its terrible consequences. One story he did share was how during the Great War, because of strong swimming skills developed as a child, he was able to rescue three drowning men from the freezing Isonzo River. But this story always left me feeling a bit uneasy. The way he talked about it, there seemed to be some sort of rationalization going on in his head. Some sort of balance of Karma. I wondered if, in his mind, saving those lives had somehow offset other lives he had taken as a soldier. But regarding his time along the Don River Front, he shared that his primary objective in this war was to get his men back home physically and emotionally intact.

Even before directly engaging in battle, Father's men suffered due to the 2nd Army's lack of logistical infrastructure to sustain itself for an extended period. The logistical transportation supply chain collapsed, leaving front line units without basic necessities such as food, clothing, fuel, and building materials. Before Father had left for the Front, Mother had sewn together two bedsheets to fashion him pillow-feather filled undergarments. His sisters had knitted him scarves, a hat, and gloves. But his fingers still froze and frostbite permanently scarred his exposed skin. He tried in vain to stuff pieces of paper into his boots to insulate his frozen toes. Having been advised that they would be back home before winter, many on his work crew failed to bring along adequate winter clothes. The men regretted this miscalculation as September evening temperatures dropped to freezing. October evening temperatures were so low that a man left exposed for several minutes would likely die. Workers hurriedly waded through waist deep snow to fell trees for firewood. Scraps of cloth covered frostbitten faces. Frozen fingers stuck to the metal saws as starvation-weakened men dragged tree stumps back to camp.

I can only imagine how he longed to return to the sheltered warmth of our Kelenhegyi house nestled on Gellért Hill.

In mid-November, the long-dormant Front suddenly came alive. The million-man strong Soviet "Operation Uranus" drove through the Romanian Army and encircled and entrapped the Germans in Stalingrad. Sixth Army General Paulus sent a telegram to Adolf

Hitler requesting permission to retreat. Hitler denied his request and all subsequent requests to retreat. At one point, Hitler even promoted, in abstentia, General Paulus to Field Marshall. Paulus understood the implication of this promotion. Hitler expected Paulus to fight until no man was left standing.

Gruesome urban combat ensued in which more than 750,000 Soviet and 850,000 Axis soldiers died in the battle for Stalingrad. The half-million civilians of the city were also nearly exterminated. More civilians died in Stalingrad than in the atomic bombings of Hiroshima and Nagasaki combined. By Christmas, the Italian Army was limping back to Italy. But Hitler demanded that Hungary's 2nd Army stay behind to hold the line to create a safe exit path for Germany's still surrounded 6th Army.

On February 2, in complete defiance of Hitler's unyielding order to continue the fight, General Paulus officially surrendered. Two-thirds of his men were dead. The Battle of Stalingrad was the first time a German Field Marshal had surrendered to the enemy. This was also the first time the Nazi government publicly acknowledged a failure in the war effort. Families finally learned of the deaths of their sons and fathers. More importantly, historians cite the Battle of Stalingrad as the turning point of the war for Nazi Germany. It was the start of a slow retreat that led all the way back to Berlin. It emboldened the Russians and revealed Germany's vincibility. It also exposed the horrors and costliness of modern urban warfare.

Only then did the Soviets finally turn their attention back to the Hungarian 2nd Army stuck in Voronezh like a sitting duck. In short order, they mowed down 40,000, wounded 70,000, and sent the rest running in a chaotic retreat. Father and his men avoided the initial slaughter. They regrouped in a small village he called "Iliana" (I can't find that name on the map). Entering a church to shelter from the cold, they met up with a group of German soldiers already holing up. The exhausted Germans allowed them to stay.

Slightly warmed inside the church, Father soon fell asleep. In a dream, he had a premonition that would save his life. Mother spoke to him and warned him to run away at once from that church. He woke with a start, roused his men and fled the church. He later learned that the Germans who had stayed behind in the church had been slaughtered by the Russians.

Father urged his exhausted men onward to keep ahead of the westward drifting battlefront. As if time was turning back on itself, the Red Army recaptured towns and villages taken only months before by the Germans. The sequence of battles replayed in reverse order. First they liberated Rostov-on-Don. Two days later, they reconquered Kharkov. Onward and south toward Bucharest, Father herded his starving, scared, and frozen work unit.

One day in late March of 1943, my emaciated father reappeared at the Kelenhegyi house. His bearded face was badly scarred from frostbite. Having survived Hungary's bloodiest battle of World War I, he now had also survived Hungary's bloodiest battle of World War II, the annihilation of Hungary's 2nd Army at Voronezh. Miraculously, he had returned with every one of his 35 involuntarily conscripted Jewish workers still alive. This was no minor achievement considering that 90% of the 45,000 *munkaszolgálat* workers perished on the Front. Ironically, he would never see those men again. They survived the battle only to lose their lives in their own hometown of Budapest. Or, maybe they survived? One can only hope. He would never learn of their fate.

But we do know that shortly after my father returned, Hitler's foreign minister, Joachim Ribbentrop, returned to Budapest to pressure Regent Horthy into joining the Nazi pogrom to deport our Jewish population to the death camps. We also know that Horthy demurred. Hungarian Jews were given a temporary reprieve.

11

Laci, 1943

Even though his body showed signs of recovery, my father was a changed man after returning from the war. His joyful sparkle had diminished. He was quiet, serious, and sober. Having taken part of the two worst battles in Hungary's recent history, he was a changed man. He kept to himself and seldom joined the other adults congregating up in Nagypapa's salon for tea or cocktails, cards, and lively discussions. He may have held philosophical differences with certain people but that was something I can only now speculate about. Jozsef Vietorisz still held his directorship at the Nazi controlled Metal Works. But what I can say for certain is that the dynamics of the Kelenhegyi household changed after he returned.

As he pulled away, the cousins also pulled away in return. This carried down to the children. I was never satisfied with the amount of play time I had with my Vietorisz cousins, and now they appeared to be even less available. What a conundrum! We all lived under the same roof. Why were there any limits on access?

One benefit of getting less play time with my cousins than desired was that I became much closer with my older brother Laci. On the other hand poor Laci and Béla were surrounded by a house full of girls: Kato, Zsuzsa, Éva, Klára, Ilonka, Margareta, and myself. While Laci probably craved playtime with other boys, he always let me into his world. Maybe it helped that he was delicate and I was a tomboy. Whatever the reason, he was certainly my best friend.

On the morning of April 12, my great aunt, Klari-*tanti*, met me on my way home from school. Klari-*tanti* was my Grandmother's sister. She was the most elegant woman I had ever met. Impeccably attired at all times, she epitomized high culture that could only come from extended continuous wealth. She and her husband Brozi-*bácsi* had no children. But she showed, more than any adult, that she truly adored me. And I, in turn, adored her. She exuded a warmth that my departed grandmother had lacked. She always came with small gifts– candies and such–that delighted me. She was quite old by this time and would soon fade out of my life. But at that moment, she was my favorite of that generation. That is probably why she volunteered to go find me that day.

She found me after school standing in front of the candy store where I often lingered with my friends before parting ways for my solo climb up the hill. What good fortune, I thought. Good chance that she would escort me into the candy store to select a delicious sweet. Unfortunately, she expressed no interest in entering the candy store. She was unnecessarily stern and serious, telling me not to lollygag and linger. I needed to immediately come home with her. When we arrived to our apartment, the priest who had delivered Laci's blood-soaked backpack was still sitting with my parents. The three adults raised their grieving silent stares from the floor to greet me in the doorway.

Earlier that morning, Laci had been stressed that he was running late. He didn't want to miss that day's rare school field trip for the boys, attending the Pesti Piarist Order Catholic School. Afraid that he would miss the trip departure, he raced out of the house and ran down the hill to the trolley stop located in front of the Gellért Hotel. The rest of the class was already on the opposite side of the tracks and were in the process of boarding a different trolley. Laci jumped aboard a trolley but quickly realized he had boarded the wrong train. He ran to the door and jumped off. In that instant, the trolley lurched forward. He lost his balance and fell backwards. The back of his head struck the edge of the platform. The shock of the blow caused his legs to shoot out straight under the wheels of another moving trolley in front of him. The rolling wheels severed his body through his upper thighs. When describing the event, the priest opined that the initial blow to the back of his head, knocked him out before he suffered the pain of his legs being severed.

Time stopped as those words formed meaning in my consciousness. My older brother. My best friend in the entire world. Laci is dead. Laci is NO MORE.

Incomprehensible. Impossible. I could not have so suddenly lost my best friend, my brother, my primary playmate. The one who invited me to join in play even when it was a group of boys. The one who was so much smarter, more creative, more considerate and empathic. One who patiently explained and involved me in his schemes.

I am unable to recall anything about those days that followed. Of course, the entire family was devastated by his death. My grandparents, aunts, uncles, and cousins. But most of all, my parents. My father hired a well-known artist to paint Laci's portrait from a recent photograph. But after it was completed, he could not bear to look at the painting. He stored it out of sight. Years later I retrieved that portrait and brought it back to America. That portrait of my best friend still hangs in our Northfield house.

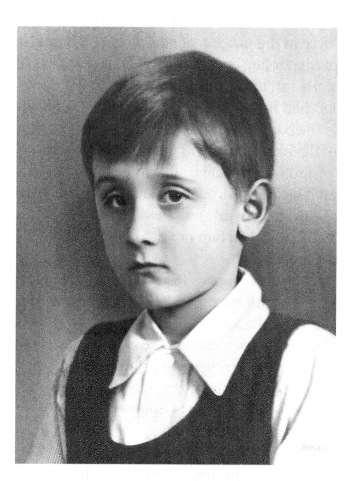

Laci

12

Germany Invades Hungary, 1944

The ringing telephone upstairs in the Vietorisz apartment broke the early morning silence of the Kelenhegyi house on March 19, 1944. Someone had called to share the news. The Germans were occupying Budapest. We raced over to a vantage point on the hill. Looking over the city, we saw hundreds of troop-filled trucks and tanks towing wagons of equipment rumbling over cobblestone streets. The procession led over the bridges and up toward the *Vár* (Castle). Without firing a shot, Germany now occupied Budapest.

Up until that fateful day, I was living a fairly normal life. I was regularly attending school. People on the streets behaved ethically and civilly. Rights were respected and criminals were held accountable. A month earlier, the Hungarian courts had sentenced Sandor Kepiro to ten years in prison for his part in the

January 1942 killing of 1,200 Serbs in Novi Sad, Serbia.[26] Though there were rabid Germanophile newspapers spewing national socialist and anti-Semitic propaganda, they were counterbalanced by conservative, liberal, and social democratic newspapers, which still printed blatantly anti-Nazi opinions. Recently published books and staged plays dared to espouse anti-Hitlerian ideologies. And, despite a persistent anti-Semitic tension, the Jews of Budapest were relatively safe.

The day before launching "Operation Margarethe," Germany's occupation of the city, Adolf Hitler had summoned Admiral Horthy to Austria. On previous encounters, Hitler had behaved extremely respectfully toward Horthy on account of the Admiral's military achievement and bearing. But now Hitler was the aggressor. He knew that Horthy was making overtures to the Allies and would no longer tolerate Horthy's equivocal commitment to the war effort and to the Jewish pogrom. Like a cat, Hitler toyed with his prey. As discussions continued late into the night, he allowed Horthy to think that the regent still had some say in the matter. In the early morning hours, Hitler informed Horthy that German tanks were rolling into Budapest at that very moment. The situation was eerily similar to how Hitler had toyed with Czechoslovakian President Hácha in 1939.

After Operation Margarethe, *SS-Brigadeführer* Edmund Veesenmayer became the Reich Plenipotentiary of Hungary. The Nazis called the shots. Veesenmayer maintained ultimate control despite appearances of a civilian government. Veesenmayer allowed Horthy to continue serving as regent, but Horthy was directed to replace moderate Prime Minister, Dr. Miklós Kállay de Nagykálló with Hungary's Pro-Nazi Ambassador to Germany, Döme

---

[26] He would be freed later that same year by the new fascist leadership.

Sztójay. Horthy hoped that Prime Minister Sztójay still felt some loyalty to Hungary. Unfortunately, he completely underestimated the extent to which Sztójay had fallen under Hitler's spell during his seven years as ambassador. Sztójay wasted no time in implementing a fascist agenda. He legalized the Arrow Cross Party and put these pro-Nazi, Jew haters in charge of the Ministry of the Interior. He sent Hungarian troops back to the Eastern Front. He dissolved labor unions, jailed political opponents, and cracked down on left wing activists. And most significantly, he started to deport Hungarian Jews. Horthy was appalled by Sztójay's actions and demanded his removal as prime minister, but Reich Plenipotentiary Veesenmayer sternly refused to even consider it.

How strange it was to wake up that one March morning to find myself in a land that would so rapidly descend into unfathomable depths of cruelty, indecency, and horror. Suddenly, those ruling over us had little regard for our safety or our lives.

I was walking home up Gellért hill when I came across several teenagers beating up an older gentleman. His grocery bag had been knocked from his hand. I watched his apples roll back down the hill. He was a Jew and the youths were followers of the Arrow Cross. I was horrified. Nobody in the family had explained to me this Jewish situation.

Like one of the Four Horsemen of the Apocalypse, the engineer of the Holocaust, Adolf Eichmann, swept into Budapest in the wake of the invading army. With him, he brought his staff of Gestapo henchmen and Security Police. The fate of Hungarian

Jews suddenly became precarious. Eichmann and Prime Minister Sztójay immediately began to coordinate the "Final Solution." He came with time-tested strategies, lessons learned, and experience gained during prior mass exterminations in other countries. His experience enabled Eichmann to implement the "Final Solution" in Hungary with deadly efficiency.

To limit exposure to worldwide condemnation, he strategically assumed a more administrative role in Budapest. He let his Arrow Cross Party collaborators implement the dirty work. He encouraged Jewish leadership to form the Budapest Jewish Council, which gave them a false impression that they still had some control over their fate. He kept the rest of the world as uninformed as possible about the pogrom. He kept the Jews unaware of their impending fate. Even this late in the war, many Hungarian Jews refused to believe that a place as evil as Auschwitz could really exist. The Arrow Cross men who rounded up the Jews frequently promised them that they were being sent to work camps. Perhaps, believing those lies was more palatable than facing the harsh reality.

In March, the Sztójay government ordered all Hungarian Jews to wear yellow stars. In April, the government placed 300,000 Jewish laborers at the disposal of the German Army. These forced labor teams dug most of the anti-tank ditches in Budapest. By mid-May, the Eichmann Arrow Cross team began rounding up Jews in the countryside. They quelled Jewish unrest in the capital by completely controlling the flow of information. Jews were forbidden to travel. Their vehicles and radios were seized. Policemen stationed at all train stations arrested thousands of Jews attempting to travel. The countryside Jews were ignorant of the pending roundups, and the city Jews knew little of what was occurring throughout the countryside.

On May 16, the first 12,000 of what would eventually total over 180,000 Hungarian Jews arrived in Auschwitz. As planned, Jews in the countryside were caught unaware and had no time to flee. Even the concentration camps were designed to prevent Jews from knowing their fate until the last minute. Eighty percent of those who disembarked from the cattle cars at the camp were murdered within hours of their arrival. The rate of killing overwhelmed the camp crematoria. The Nazis brought in Jewish laborers to the camp to dig large pits into which piles of corpses were covered with fuel and burned.

In May, the Arrow Cross walled in the city's seventh district to create Budapest's first Jewish ghetto. Using a Budapest census, they identified 184,000 Budapest Jews and 80,000 Christians of Jewish descent. As a whole, these Jews were much wealthier than the average citizenry. As the Arrow Cross moved them into the ghetto, they plundered this wealth, confiscating clothes, jewels, and other valuables. If the militia suspected that Jews were withholding valuables, they tortured them with electric shocks applied to genitals, crushed skulls, broken bones, and ripped out fingernails.

Eichmann saw himself as a genteel, law-abiding, reasonable man. He was willing to entertain civil negotiations. On May 18, he flew two emissaries, Joel Brand and Andrea Gyorgy, to Istanbul to make a secret offer to the Allies. In exchange for 10,000 trucks to be used exclusively on the Eastern Front, plus tea, coffee, soup, cocoa, and assorted war materiel, he would spare the lives of 800,000 Jews. Britain rejected his absurd proposal and imprisoned the emissaries.

Rudolf Kasztner, a Hungarian journalist, Zionist, and founder of the Relief and Rescue Committee, did successfully negotiate a deal with Adolf Eichmann. The deal, carried out on June 30, became known as the "Kasztner Train." Adolf Eichmann promised safe passage for the train in exchange for three suitcases full of diamonds, gold, cash, and securities. Along with well-known writers, educators, and artists, the train included some of the wealthiest Jews in Budapest. Thirty-five cattle cars carrying 1,684 Jews, departed Budapest bound for Switzerland. At a fork in the tracks near the Hungarian-Austrian border, the Kasztner train was directed to stop and await further directions from Eichmann. From that point, the train could travel in either of two directions: it could continue west or turn east to Auschwitz. Panic spread through the train. Had they given up their wealth only to be betrayed before even leaving Hungary? Finally, word came from Eichmann: continue west, but not to Switzerland. Instead, they were forced to disembark in Linz, Austria, where they were stripped naked, subjected to humiliating medical inspections, and then sent to showers for delousing. These Jews were well aware of the gas chambers disguised as showers. Their eyes teared up in relief when the shower heads actually emitted water and not the deadly Zyklon B gas. After two months at a German camp in Bergen-Belsen, they were finally granted safe passage to Switzerland.

At the end of June, Veesenmayer reported to Joachim von Ribbentrop that some 340,000 Jews had been delivered to the Reich. He also projected that after the final settlement of the "Jewish question," the number of deported Hungarian Jews would reach 900,000. As the Western world started to take notice of the Jewish-Hungarian genocide, Winston Churchill sent a letter in which he wrote, "There is no doubt that this persecution of Jews in Hungary and their expulsion from enemy territory is probably the greatest and most horrible crime ever committed in the whole history of the world." Allied planes dropped leaflets threatening punishment of anyone aiding the deportation of Jews. Citizens of Budapest chased down these paper leaflets, not because of what they warned, but because they served as a replacement for the badly depleted toilet paper supply.

Horthy, however, did heed the warnings. On July 6, he issued an order suspending Nazi deportations of Hungarian Jews. His order gave a reprieve to Jews in Budapest, but it was ignored in the countryside, where another 45,000 Jews were deported. Eichmann was well aware of the advances being made by the Red Army and wanted to clear out the eastern territories while they were still under Nazi control. He succeeded. He personally made arrangements for additional trains of victims to be sent to Auschwitz. By July, 437,000 countryside Jews had been rounded up and deported to Auschwitz.

As Kelenhegyi *utca* rises up from the river, only two doors to the north of our Kelenhegyi house the road makes an abrupt hairpin turn. At the narrowest point of that curve, there is a large yellow house with a Turkish minaret-style roof. It accommodated the Swedish Embassy. Unbeknownst to me or my family at the time, in this embassy one man bravely confronted the forces of evil even when it put his own life in great peril. He was unquestionably one of the most heroic men acting during the siege of Budapest. That man was Raoul Wallenberg.

Raoul Wallenberg, a University of Michigan graduate and Swedish National Guardsman, had been recruited by the CIA via a U.S. Embassy official in Stockholm and sent to Nazi-controlled

Budapest under Swedish diplomatic cover. As soon as he arrived on July 9, he and fellow Swedish diplomats issued protective passports called *Schutz*-Passes. These identified the bearers as Swedish citizens awaiting repatriation and thus prevented their deportation. These passes also exempted the bearers from having to wear yellow stars. Although not legal, these documents looked official and were generally accepted by German and Hungarian authorities. When the officials resisted, Wallenberg bribed them using funds provided by American Jewish organizations. At one point at which Hungarian leadership declared the passes invalid, Wallenberg reached out to Baroness Elisabeth Kemény, wife of Arrow Cross Hungarian Minister for Foreign Affairs, Baron Gábor Kemény. She convinced her husband to honor 9,000 passes. Wallenberg rented 32 buildings in Budapest and declared them to be "extraterritorial," protected by diplomatic immunity. He hung oversized Swedish flags on the front of the buildings and mounted placards on the doors labeling the buildings "The Swedish Library" or "The Swedish Research Institute." He saved over 20,000 Hungarian Jews from Nazi death camps.

In mid-July, Wallenberg and Adolf Eichmann met for the first time. At this first encounter, both men quickly realized that they would not get along. Wallenberg negotiated, pled, and finally made threats. Still seething about suspension of deportations to the death camps, an intransigent Eichmann stared back at him with cold, dark, rat-like eyes that sent a chill down Wallenberg's spine. He knew that his life was in danger.

13

War Comes to Hungary, 1944

After passing the Kelenhegyi house, Kelenhegyi *utca* winds up to the Citadella, a large old fortress on the summit of Gellért Hill. Because of its strategic vantage over the eastern plains, the Germans established a key command post in this Citadella. Our house was within the high defensive line that the Germans were busily fortifying with canons and anti-aircraft batteries. Because these batteries existed, this side of the hill would become a primary target for Allied bombers.

Nagypapa converted the ground floor cellar area to the west of our apartment into a shelter. He and my father reinforced the ceiling with wooden beams and placed boards across the cellar windows. They covered the cellar floor with all the rugs from the upstairs apartments and scattered mattresses, chairs, benches, firefighting equipment, and a first aid kit around the room. Being an engineer, he knew that this shelter would protect the family from bullets and shard projectiles, but a direct bomb hit would flatten the house and kill everyone in it.

Before German military forces had occupied Budapest, Hungary had allowed British and American planes to cross Hungarian airspace uncontested. In return, the Allies had refrained from dropping bombs. But now, Allied bombs rained down on the city. The first Allied bombing strike took place on April 3, 1944. Taking off from Foggia, Italy, four hundred and fifty American B-17 Flying Fortresses and B-24 Liberators, escorted by 137 fighters, struck Rákos Airfield, the airplane factory on Csepel Island, the rail yards, and factories in the industrial ring around Budapest. They also knocked out sections of railroad track to disrupt Germany's rail-mounted mobile anti-aircraft batteries. The Allies also dropped 1,390 mines into the Danube River. Barges and other vessels struck these mines, sunk, and blocked navigational traffic. These initial air raids did not target Budapest's bridges and landmark buildings, but as the fighting dragged on those too would become targets.

Upon first hearing the wail of air-raid sirens signaling the approach of enemy planes, we ran throughout the house to open all the windows in hopes that they would not shatter from the concussions. Then everyone huddled in the shelter to wait for the "all clear" sirens to sound. Rather than crowding into our shelter, the Vietorisz family was whisked off by their chauffeur to weather the raid in the more solidly constructed factory bomb shelter.

Between bombings, life in the city returned to normal. As the frequency of air-raid sirens increased, we became complacent about the pending danger. Instead of a panicked dash, we calmly walked to the shelter. It got to the point that I could tell what type of plane was approaching by the sound of the engines. More importantly, I learned to distinguish their approach altitude. The higher altitude planes were not a concern. However, we braced during that brief silence following the deep rumble of passing low-flying aircraft for the subsequent booming explosions. We also came out sooner after the bombing to investigate. At times, I came out so fast that I could still hear the whistling of shrapnel shards as they cut their way through the surrounding bushes.

The family strayed farther away from the shelter. One night, uncles József and István were still in the casino playing billiards when the siren sounded. They were forced to spend the night there. Another night, Nagypapa went to play cards at a friend's flat in Lenke Square. When the air-raid siren sounded, he decided to walk home rather than wait out the air raid in someone else's shelter. It was a moonless night and all lights were extinguished or shielded behind thick blinds. The city was darker than he had ever experienced before. He felt as if his eyes were covered with bandages. With arms extended, he groped for obstacles and anything that might give him his bearings. At a snail's pace, he blindly fumbled his way home. After that experience, he curtailed his evening outings.

As soon as our school year ended that June, Roza-néni escorted us children to Rezi. We remained in Rezi until just before school started in September. When it was time to return to Budapest, Roza-néni was too afraid to escort us back. She never again returned to us.

Budapest felt like a different city after that summer away. Like an animal sensing a palpable threat, I closely observed the adults and zeroed in on the subtlest changes in demeanor. I understood nothing about the current political situation, but caught snippets of conversations:

"Hitler's military empire is collapsing throughout Europe."

"The German armies vacated Rome, Paris, Brussels, Bucharest, Sofia, Helsinki, Athens, and Belgrade."

"Maybe they will soon leave Budapest."

"Horthy initiated peace talks with the Russians."

"Horthy dismissed Prime Minister Sztójay."

"Himmler ordered the cancellation of deportations."

"Adolf Eichmann left Budapest."

"There is an ominous dark cloud building in the east."

"Romania has switched sides."

This last snippet was a critical turning point of the war. With the massive Red Army at its doorstep, Romanian King Michael dismissed the fascist Prime Minister Ion Antonescu, severed diplomatic relations with Germany, and joined the Red Army. Previously forced by Germany to suspend hostilities toward Hungary in favor of commitment to the greater German cause, Romania was now free to seek revenge for the taking of Transylvania. The strengthening Red Army's path to Hungary was unobstructed.

In September, schools resumed as if it were a formal year. I excitedly started my first year of middle school at St. Margit *Gimnázium* (because it went through 12th grade). In Hungary, after four years of elementary school, I was proud to take that celebrated step in our educational ladder. What made it better was that I would now attend the same school as my cousins, Kato and Zsuzsa. Some days, I got to ride along with them in their chauffeured car. What a fancy way to arrive at school! But most days I walked alone, skipping my way down the hill as I had done for years. Uniformly attired students congregated each chilly morning in the prestigious school's courtyard. Almost all of our teachers were nuns; they kept an extra strict and well-planned curriculum. The Cistercian Catholic boys school was just a few hundred yards up the street. As we were starting to take an interest in boys, their proximity added to the excitement. I still

Szént Margit Gimnázium, my school 1942-1944

enjoyed many alarm-free autumn days and spent time outside playing in the garden. However, at night, as the normal daytime bustling noise of the city died down, I could hear the rumble of artillery in the east.

Two months into my blissful *Gimnázium* school year, the school was closed and converted into a military hospital. The Russians had crossed into eastern Hungary and were rapidly heading for Budapest.

The Red Army swept across the southeastern border of Hungary between Makó and Nagyvárad heading for Debrecen. Once renowned for their superior "Blitzkrieg" warfare skill, the German Panzer divisions no longer could claim that advantage. When the two sides collided, the Red Army won out by the simple fact of their greater numbers in both divisions and tanks. It was like the board game of "Risk." Odds favor the side with the greater number. When the tank battle for Debrecen started on October 10, Red Army forces outnumbered the Germans three to one. Within ten days, the Red Army fully controlled Debrecen, and tanks were racing unchallenged across the great Hungarian Plains towards Budapest.

Hoping to avert an imminent attack on the nation's capital, Admiral Horthy sent secret delegations to negotiate armistice agreements with Moscow and the West. An infuriated Hitler kept close track of these supposedly secret negotiations through his large cadre of spies and traitors. And the moment an impulsive Horthy went on Hungarian public radio to declare an armistice with Stalin, Hitler pounced. Nazi operatives kidnapped Horthy's son. Using his son as leverage, they forced Horthy to abdicate. Nazi operatives deported Horthy and his family to Castle Hirschberg outside Munich.[27]

On October 16, the Germans installed a puppet regime led by Ferenc Szálasi, the infamous, anti-Semitic, pro-Nazi leader of the *Nyilaskeresztes* (Arrow Cross Party). The Horthy government, which had ruled Hungary for nearly a quarter of a century, had fallen. An unlearned rabble of criminals now assumed power.

---

[27] Nazis held Horthy there until the end of the war. Hitler ordered Horthy's execution, but his Gestapo jailers fled in civilian clothes on May 1, 1945.

Szálasi's first order of business was to resume the extermination of Jews. By this point, the only Hungarian Jews left were those in Budapest. Two days after the takeover, Arrow Cross militiamen forcibly assembled the residents of the buildings marked with Stars of David in the VIII District. While the Jews assembled in the courtyard shivered in the brisk morning air, militia members went back into the buildings in search of anyone who had tried to hide. They reemerged dragging an invalid old man down the stairs by his feet. A long trail of blood pouring from his broken skull marked the course.

With their hands held above their heads, the Jews were marched to the Danube embankment, where they were lined up facing the river. Seconds before their imminent execution, a German officer arrived and directed the militia to send the Jews back to the ghetto. But this was only a temporary reprieve because that same day, Adolf Eichmann returned to Budapest.

Finding it difficult to commandeer trains to transport the Jews, Adolf Eichmann marched the "fucking" Jews the 130 miles to Vienna. Each day, some 6,000 Jews set out on foot from the Obuda brick works. Weakened by starvation, these Jews trudged a daily average of 18 miles in appalling conditions. Arrow Cross militia patrolled the routes and tortured or killed any Jew who stumbled or fell out of line. Tens of thousands marched from Budapest to Vienna.

You might wonder why people in Budapest did not put up more resistance to the Nazis' barbaric pogrom. People did resist. And, they suffered the consequences of trying to help. Signs were posted throughout Budapest that anyone helping or harboring Jews would face stiff criminal punishment, including immediate execution. Stories circulated about the brutal punishment inflicted upon those caught aiding. The wife of former Prime Minister

Count Istvan Bethlen was arrested when she tried to persuade Christian women to pin yellow leaves to their garments as a sign of solidarity after the introduction of the yellow star. Pal Tetetleni, managing director of a Bauxite company, was executed together with his pregnant wife and two small daughters for sheltering Jewish fugitives. Sister Sara Salkahazi was killed by the Arrow Cross for hiding Jews in a Budapest building used by her convent.

As the deportation of Jews resumed in Budapest, Raoul Wallenberg became more brazen in his efforts to save them. He placed seventy-two buildings near Szent Istvan Square in Pest's VI District under Swiss protection. This became officially known as the "International Ghetto." The idea was to concentrate Jews holding foreign passes in protected houses, each guarded by two police officers. But the Arrow Cross hit squads ignored these rules and raided them anyway.

One of the drivers working for Wallenberg recounted the time that Wallenberg intercepted a trainload of Jews about to leave for Auschwitz:

"... he climbed up on the roof of the train and began handing protective passes through the doors which were not yet sealed. He ignored orders from the Germans for him to get down...[even when] the Arrow Cross men began shooting and shouting at him to go away, he ignored them and calmly continued handing out passports to the hands that were reaching out for them. I believe the Arrow Cross men deliberately aimed over his head, as not one shot hit him, which would have been impossible otherwise. I think this is what they did because they were so impressed by his courage. After Wallenberg had handed over the last of the passports he ordered all those who held one to leave the train and walk to the caravan of cars parked nearby, all marked in Swedish colors. I don't remember exactly how many, but he saved dozens off that train, and the Germans and Arrow Cross were so dumbfounded they let him get away with it."

Some brave diplomats took steps to save Jews. Interior Ministry official Béla Horváth ordered Hungarian gendarmes to use deadly force against any deportation effort. There were also members of the army and police, such as Pál Szalai and Károly Szabó, who took Jews out from camps with fake papers. Some church institutions harbored Jews. But my biggest, and the least famous, hero of them all was Béla Jaszai, my father.

One day in early November, Franciska H. showed up at the Kelenhegyi house. My father introduced her to us as his new live-in office assistant. She occupied the room off our foyer vacated by our terrified maid Roza-*néni*.

Franci-*néni* arrived with only a small bag of clothes. I quickly discerned that she was of a different ilk than Roza-*néni*. She appeared to be smarter and more elegant. Something else about her also caught my attention. How could a meagerly employed office worker be in possession of three pairs of exquisite leather shoes? Fearing that we children might inadvertently spill the beans, Father didn't tell us that Franci-*néni*'s real name was Elizabeth Tauszig, wife of a leather goods merchant who had been deported to Auschwitz.

After learning of Mrs. Tauszig's plight from a fellow engineer, Father quickly took action before she was also deported. The real Franciska H. was a recently deceased maid who had been employed by Jozsef Vietorisz's brother. Officially, she never died. Like spies leaving messages in a hidden cache, Father transferred the new identity papers to her. To leave a legitimate paper trail, he placed an advertisement in the newspaper announcing an opening for an office girl in his engineering office. One could have easily questioned the timing of this hiring. His business at that time was at a standstill.

Mrs. Tauszig lived with us until April of 1945, when her emaciated husband miraculously appeared at our door. He had survived Auschwitz. After the war, the couple moved into in a nearby apartment. Unfortunately, her husband died soon after from consumption contracted while in camp. We stayed in touch with her until her death. When my father was in the final fatal stages of his battle with colon cancer, she used her connections to get him admitted to a prominent Jewish hospital in Budapest. And in the last years of her life, my sister Ilonka cared for her. Posthumously, in 1992, my parents were awarded a Certificate and Medal of Honor recognizing that they had risked their lives to save persecuted Jews during the Holocaust. Their names are engraved on the honor wall in the Garden of the Righteous at Yad Vashem in Jerusalem and on a plaque in the courtyard of Budapest's synagogue, the largest one in Europe.

The rapidly approaching Red Army only increased Nazi resolve to complete their pogrom. On November 21, Foreign Minister Joachim Ribbentrop sent a first class telegram to Plenipotentiary Veesenmayer stating that the speedy elimination of the Jews was essential to the defense of the capital.

On November 23, a column of 40 people, all dressed in white, marched down to the Danube. It was only when they got closer, did one realize that they were in white because they had been stripped down to their underwear. White shirts and petticoats and bloody red bare feet from walking over broken glass. When an old woman stumbled and fell, one of the teenaged Arrow Cross boy-soldiers beat her with the butt of his rifle. A Hungarian soldier approached and scolded the boy. "Haven't you got a mother, son? How can you do this?" To which the boy replied, "She is only a Jew, uncle."

This time, there was no reprieve for the Jews. To save on ammunition, the soldiers tied three Jews together, shot the one in the middle, and let that corpse pull the other two down into the freezing Danube River waters.

As the Arrow Cross continued this mass execution along the Danube embankment, Raoul Wallenberg stationed himself downstream with a few strong swimming Hungarian volunteers. As the drowning chained trios drifted by, volunteers desperately tried to fish them out of the water before they were overcome by the freezing temperatures. The volunteers managed to save several groups, but the vast majority were beyond their reach. Tears clouded their eyes as they helplessly watched the current carry the victims downriver.

From the perspective of the Arrow Cross rulers, executions along the Danube were a beautifully efficient way to dispose of bodies. If corpses started to pile up on the streets, it might induce the population to take pity on the plight of the Jews. As Police Commissioner Pal Hodosy put it, "The problem is not that the Jews are being murdered. The only trouble is the method. The bodies must be made to disappear, not put out in the streets."

If you visit the banks of the Danube today, you will find bronze shoes attached to the quay wall. A monument to the 15,000 Jews executed there between November 1944 and the end of the war.

14

The Red Army Ties a Noose, 1944

By October's end, in the intervals between air raids, I heard the constant thunder of guns. At first, we thought these were anti-aircraft guns, but soon realized this was ground artillery, Soviet units had reached the southeastern edge of Budapest. The battlefront was that close.

As Soviet leader Joseph Stalin implored Rodion Malinovski, Commander of the 2nd Ukrainian Front, to take Budapest as soon as possible, Hitler did everything he could to drag the battle out. He issued a directive that no house in Budapest was to be abandoned without a fight, regardless of civilian losses or material damage. Hitler soon followed with a second directive declaring Budapest to be a "fortress" city, meaning that it would be defended to the last man. It was painfully clear that Hitler and

Stalin were playing a chess match which gave no regard to the fate of the Hungarians.

On November 3, the Red Army launched its Budapest Offensive. They approached on two Fronts: Rodion Malinovsky's 2nd Ukrainian approached from the east and Fedor Ivanovich Tolbukhin's 3rd Ukrainian circled from the southwest. The Soviets and Romanians outnumbered the Germans and Hungarians four-to-one in both manpower and weaponry. Everyone already knew how this offensive would end.

Recognizing that the Arrow Cross Party had lost favor with the city's population, Prime Minister Szálasi tried to distance himself from the inevitable. He sent an official statement to the highest authorities blaming the Germans for not replacing the previous Horthy regime sooner. He added that "at this point, his present government can only engage in damage limitation in an attempt to prevent the collapse of the nation." Realizing that Szálasi was not even attempting to defend Budapest, thousands of Hungarian soldiers, officers, and civilians went into hiding rather than follow the directives of the Arrow Cross.

Nagypapa was our shelter commander and also master block commissioner for the residents of Gellért Hill. He conducted briefings for other block commissioners and facilitated preparation of an action plan for the pending siege. In the afternoon during one of his meetings, we heard a sudden booming explosion. The sound came from much closer than any battlefront. It came from the river below. We raced out to witness a terrible sight. Two arches of the Margit Bridge had collapsed. Shattered streetcars jutted out of the water. Moans of the injured blended with the murmurs of the stunned crowd. Bodies hung from the railing. Others floated below. Cars and people had fallen into the river. Boats raced toward the bridge to save whomever they could. German soldiers had been installing primed charges on the bridge as an "exercise." A spark from a passing vessel accidentally lit the fuses. Of the 600 victims, 40 had been the Germans who were fitting charges.

This was also the last day I would see my cousins Kato, Zsuzsi, Éva, and baby Lenke until we reunited in America over a decade later. Jozsef Vietorisz sent his chauffeur back to the Kelenhegyi house to evacuate his family. He also sent a truck onto which they loaded mattresses and suitcases full of valuable silver, bed linens, and clothes. Erzsébet and her four girls climbed into Jozsef's Mercedes Benz and headed toward Györ. As they left Budapest, low-flying allied bomber aircraft appeared on the horizon. The chauffeur quickly pulled the car off the road. Erzsébet and girls jumped out of the car, hid in a ditch, and held their breath as the planes flew over without incident. When they arrived in Györ, a factory manager had arranged two rooms for them. The truck, with all their belongings never arrived.

Klára-*néni*'s husband Laci-*bácsi* was also notably absent for the rest of the siege. He had been called back into military service and stationed in Pest to help defend the capital.

The Germans established three defensive rings around Pest called Attila One, Two, and Three. By the morning of November 5, the Red Army had crushed through Attila One, the outermost ring. Soviet T-34 tanks easily cut through demoralized, under-equipped German and Hungarian defenses, and then paused just outside of the northeast districts of Isaszeg and Hatvan to wait for ground troops, ammunition, and supplies to catch up. Malinovsky was careful to avoid penetrating too deeply with his spearhead assaults at the risk of getting flanked by Germans. Urban warfare was a tactically slow event.

The Arrow Cross government was shockingly unprepared for this inevitable assault. Other than putting up posters encouraging civilians to leave Budapest, the regime made only nominal efforts to evacuate the city. Besides, how could people leave? Civilians alone were powerless to implement a mass exodus. When orders were given for the evacuation of the Pest districts of Kispest, Pestszenterzsébet, Pestszentlőrinc, and Soroksár, the residents who complied and moved to the city center found that no accommodations had been arranged for them. Rather than solving the lodging issue, the government just rescinded the evacuation order. A later, second evacuation order was canceled after saboteurs attacked the MÁV railway. Only 35 of 353 passenger cars earmarked for the evacuation could be delivered.

Efforts to improve city defensive structures were also ineffective. At one point, the government rounded up and assembled fifteen thousand people in Kispest only to see air raids, artillery fire, and a complete lack of organization lead the crowd to disperse before any work was even started. Government orders could no longer be enforced because the police and gendarme officers had either been transferred to fighting units or chose to sabotage the pointless orders. The day after his inauguration, Arrow Cross Lord

Mayor of Budapest, Gyula Mohay, issued an order that all men in the city born between 1912 and 1923 were to report to the earthworks. From the thousands in that age group, only 500 men showed up. Most of the population was now openly defiant.

Meanwhile, the Arrow Cross party members fled like rats from a sinking ship. By mid-November, the majority of the Arrow Cross cabinet had fled westward toward Germany. But the contingent of the Arrow Cross committed to completing the "Jewish solution" stayed behind.

The Arrow-Cross walled in the Erzsébetváros district and established one big Budapest ghetto with four continuously guarded gates. Six Thousand Jews were packed into apartments, sometimes 14 people to a room.

Food supplies quickly became a critical problem. At first there was an official daily food ration of 900 calories a day, even though the five soup kitchens could provide barely 790 calories. But food carriers were often robbed or hit by shells. Those in the ghetto went without food. By the end of December, eighty ghetto Jews died each day from starvation. Enfeebled men with drooping heads pushed wheelbarrows mounded with naked yellow waxen corpses and dumped them on the growing mound in the courtyard of the Kazinczy baths.

In mid-November, Tolbukhin's 3rd Army crossed the Danube at Kiskőszeg and approached Budapest from the southwest at a daily pace of 6 to 12 miles. Malinovsky's Army crushed the Attila Two line, the second ring of defenses around Pest. Simultaneously, in a bloody battle in which the Red Army sacrificed hundreds of troops by sending them directly into German lines of defensive fire, the Soviets established a foothold on Csepel Island.

By the end of November the upper-level residents of the Kelenhegyi house permanently resided in the ground level cellar.

Up the hill, above us, a huge anti-aircraft cannon battery was constantly firing. The repercussions felt like earthquakes. The frequency of bombings increased. The windows of the house had shattered. We tried to cover the gaps with the large plat maps and engineering drawings salvaged from the office. Articulate renderings and drawings and hours of meticulous work was sacrificed to no avail. The paper also couldn't withstand the shocks, over-pressures, and the freezing wind. The glued edges gave out, the paper tore; tatters flapped in the cold wind.

It was miserably cold. As long as we could, we kept the central heating system running. But wisps of the precious warmth flowed out of the open windows. Soon we ran out of coal and resorted to little bonfires and the warmth of dense proximity. It became hard to get out of bed in the morning.

Since we already lived on the ground level, my immediate family (and Franci-*néni*) did not vacate our apartment. However, because the windows along the eastern side of the apartment were blown out, we moved into our tiny interior kitchen, the safest and warmest spot. Ilonka slept in a drawer. For my bed, my father attached a board to the wall. The others slept on the one mattress dragged in from a bedroom.

My father broke a hole through the wall of our pantry and cleared an opening large enough for an adult to crawl through on his hands and knees. This enabled us to pass back and forth to the shelter without exiting the house. It also gave our family an emergency exit should someone try to enter our apartment.

By December 4, German Army Group South had evacuated all civilians and all German female assistants. The Arrow Cross ordered the evacuation of Csepel Island, but local residents ignored the order.

The Red Army launched a suicidal attack near the village of Ercsi along the Danube south of the city. Anticipating attack in this area the Germans and Hungarians had prepared strong defensive positions. Without any supporting artillery, the Russians attempted a night river crossing. Under heavy fire, they lost 75% of their boats mid-river. When the Russians attempted to disembark from the few boats that finally reached the opposite shore, German machine guns mowed them down. One Hungarian commented, "Lieutenant, Sir, if this is how they treat their own men, what would they do to their enemies?" But the unrelenting Soviets eventually established seven bridgeheads on both sides of the river.

Hungarian soldiers felt that it was pointless to continue the struggle. But they had no good options. They could surrender to the Russians and be placed in a Siberian prison camp, where they would likely die. They could defect and fight alongside the Soviets, where they would likely die. Or, they could continue to fight with the Germans, and likely die. All conceivable options ended in death.

After a battalion surrendered and crossed over to the Soviet side, Hungarian Major-General Kornél Oszlányi issued an order stating "Incitement or conspiracy to desert will be punished by hanging. Commanders must use their weapons against deserters. Military police are to comb the woods and shoot any soldiers hiding or deserting. Those captured alive will be court-martialed, their property confiscated, and reprisals taken against their families."

Hitler assigned *Obergruppenführer* Karl Pfeffer-Wildenbruch as commander of all Budapest forces. This new commander was a pedantic rule-follower who had cruelly demonstrated his willingness to suppress civilian resistance in both Poland and France. He was willing to deploy lethal force against Hungarian civilians. But Pfeffer-Wildenbruch lacked the courage to speak the truth about Hitler's outrageously bad leadership and decision-making, unlike the previous commander, Otto Winkelmann, who had resigned in protest after Hitler refused to allow German troops to abandon Pest. On December 6, *Obergruppenführer* Pfeffer-Wildenbruch called Hitler to ask for permission to retreat to Attila 3, the innermost defensive ring.

"No," Hitler responded. "Retreating only deprives the German defense of necessary operational depth." But Hitler's refusal soon became a moot point. Attacking from the northern village of Vác, the Red Army wiped out 70% of the Hungarian defenses and opened a huge defensive gap. Even after pulling troops from Csepel Island to fill this gap, German defenses had no choice but to quickly retreat back to the last Attila 3 ring.

Obergruppenführer Pfeffer-Wildenbruch was not a leader of men. He was a bureaucrat who maintained strict protocols of anterooms, secretaries, and fixed office hours. He seldom left the safety of his office in the Castle shelter. He lied in his reports to ensure that he lacked any culpability. His subordinate officers disrespected and distrusted him. When they tried to offer helpful suggestions, he arrogantly dismissed them.

Pfeffer-Wildenbruch also ignored input and had a strained relationship with the equally incompetent leader of the Hungarian Army in Budapest, Colonel-General Iván Hindy. Hindy had assumed control over the military in Budapest during the October 15 Arrow Cross coup after he arrested his own commander, a loyal Horthy supporter. Pleased with this betrayal, the Arrow Cross leadership assigned Hindy full authority for Hungarian affairs of the capital. Hindy's prior military experience had been limited to a desk job in which he had attended to military personnel administration.

Many of Hungary's more battle-tested and loyal military leaders had defected to the Soviets after the coup against Horthy. One of those, Colonel Otto Hatszeghy-Hatz, Hungary's VII Army Corps former Chief of Staff, now flew to Szeged to deliver to General Tolbukhin detailed sketches of the Margit Line defenses, which ran between Lake Balaton and Budapest. Eagerly pointing to his sketches, Hatszeghy-Hatz explained that only 2,250 German troops defended a twenty-two mile section of this line between Lake Velence and Budapest. Any sizable Soviet thrust could easily penetrate this weakness.

On the morning of December 20, Tolbukhin's 3rd Ukrainian Front overwhelmed German Margit Line defenses with five times the artillery and infantry and 3 times the number of tanks. Two days later, after bloody street fighting and significant losses on both sides, Tolbukhin took control of the city of Székesfehérvár. After that assault, Soviet tanks slowly and steadily advanced, taking control of villages west and north of Budapest. They captured the town of Dorog, where several hundred goods-laden wagons stood stranded at the railway station. When they reached Esztergom, the Red Army had methodically slung a noose around the neck of the capital. The encirclement of Budapest was complete.

15

Christmas, 1944

Adolf Eichmann was still overseeing the burning and destruction of incriminating records in the offices of Department IV-B4 when the clock struck midnight the morning of Christmas Eve. He would not allow the German tendency for meticulous recordkeeping to lead to his downfall. Knowing that the game was over, Eichmann needed to destroy the paper trail that led straight to him. A few hours earlier, at the Jewish ghetto, he had given his final, unequivocal order to German General Gerhard Schmidthuber: massacre all the Jews in Budapest.

Associates woke Swedish diplomat Raoul Wallenberg before dawn with news of Eichmann's last order at the ghetto. For the past month, Wallenberg had been sleeping restlessly in a different house each night, anticipating a night visit by Gestapo assassins, and listening to the approaching thunder of artillery. The Nazi's hastily concocted annihilation plan was simply to march the ambulatory Jews on one final death march and then blow up the ghetto to kill all who remained inside.

As the morning sun breached the horizon, Wallenberg bribed Arrow Cross Party member Pál Szalai to deliver a note to General Schmidthuber which stated, "Eichmann boarded a flight to Berlin and fled under the cover of darkness. General, what happens from this point forward will be on your head." The message had its desired effect. Fearing that the impending carnage would mark him as a war criminal, the worried-eyed general cancelled Eichmann's orders. The last Jews in Budapest lived another day.

I decorated our apartment with collected shiny aluminum anti-radar strips dropped by British and American planes. All morning, Radio Budapest broadcasted Christmas carols and organ music. The radio announcer calmly explained that, on account of the curfew, midnight mass would be celebrated at two in the afternoon. The adults barely paid attention to the announcement. None of us planned on attending.

Only Father left our compound that Christmas Eve, in search of bread. Skulking between trees and buildings with two fresh loaves under his jacket, he came across an unexpected man dragging an impressive Christmas tree down the street.

"I got it for only 10 Pengő," the man proudly proclaimed. "Never cheaper, even in peace time. Just take it the woman says to me. It doesn't matter. The Russians are already in Budakeszi, she says. Naturally, I didn't take her seriously."

However, the saleswoman had been correct. Tank treads clattered on cobblestones as Soviet tanks slowly rumbled down Budakeszi Road toward the castle. Neighbors spotted Red Army troops hurrying past their garden fences. These soldiers wore padded suits and carried odd looking submachine guns with round cartridge drums.

Hearing news of this Christmas Eve assault, the adults in the cellar express a confusing mix of joy and fear.

"We will be liberated from the Nazi and Fascist dictatorship."

"Quick, we must dismantle our Christmas tree and decorations so as to not offend these godless Russian invaders."

"He has brought us bread!"

Recognizing that the starving crowd would not tolerate waiting, Father broke off pieces from the loaves and handed a piece to each person in the cellar. What burned this moment into my memory was when my younger brother Béla tearfully complained about the disparity in bread portions. He demanded that he receive a share that equaled Father's. It reminded me of how ravenously hungry we all were.

In a separate shelter in Buda, my starving cousin Éva (Margit-néni's daughter) found it impossible to feed her newborn infant. She clutched her baby to her breasts so that he might at least enjoy the comfort of a warm human body before fading away.

Jozsef Vietorisz had arrived to Győr in time to spend Christmas with his family. The children decorated a small tree using a box of old Christmas decorations left in the apartment. Each daughter received books, clothes, and a nightgown. In a humorous moment that highlighted their inexperience in the kitchen, Jozsef purchased five small piglets from a villager who also, mercifully, killed the animals. But Jozsef and Erzsébet did not know how to prepare the animals. When the water came on that evening, they dropped the carcasses into a large cauldron. They tried to boil off the fur. But fur, skin, and meat sloughed off the piglets into an inseparable glop. They resigned to eat the pork full of fine hairs. After dinner, the Vietorisz family listened to the large Phillips radio, which reported that the Russians had surrounded Budapest. No one could get in or out of the city.

The relentless Soviet artillery barrage that began on that Christmas Eve evening marked a turning point in the siege. From that day forward, the ever-present danger kept us confined us to our shelter. The Kelenhegyi house sheltered one small part of the nearly one million civilians who remained trapped within the capital.

Had we known how bad it would get, we would have seized the window of opportunity to flee Budapest. But we were like someone watching a distant storm approach. It's not until the storm is already upon you that you realize how fast it is actually moving. Then it's too late. The storm is above you. You expect it to pass through as quickly as it came. But this storm stalls over the city and inflicts its unrelenting wrath. Urban warfare is slow and incremental. It lingers in one area long enough to inflict maximum suffering. Budapest was the only city, apart from Stalingrad and Berlin, where the largest armies in the world grappled in house-to-house combat.

Renewed shelling woke us on Christmas morning. Surprisingly, electricity, water and gas, and telephone service still operated. The Arrow Cross newspaper stopped publishing on Christmas Day.[28] Shelling halted operation of street car lines near Széll Kálmán Square. Down below us, a few ferry boat captains still bravely crossed the Danube River.

Our cellar was never designed for a long siege. Nor was it ever intended to hold the forty-two people now sheltering in the ground floor of the Kelenhegyi house. In addition to the Szesztay families who normally lived in the house, we were joined by Szesztay, Koranyi, and Vietorisz relatives who had fled Nyíregyháza and other eastern villages after the Red Army invaded in October. So many people breathing in the confined space left the walls and ceiling dripping with condensation.

I don't even remember all of the names of those sheltering with us, but I do remember the children. Tamás Vietorisz, 18, bookish and pleasantly handsome, came over to our apartment to study in the brighter light. I adored him. He was supposed to be taking his high school final exams and never gave up hope that they would

---

[28] Two other papers, Uj Magyárság and Osszetartás would continue printing for two more weeks.

take place. While we still had power, he studied while playing Beethoven's 5th and 7th symphonies on the record player. This planted the seeds of my lifetime love for those classical pieces.

Laci and Feri Szlávik, 12 and 13, filled an important gap left by my brother's death. They helped turn an otherwise frightful situation into an exciting adventure. The scariest moments were when we heard the increasing rumbling volume of approaching low-flying bombers. But immediately after they passed, the Szlávik brothers and I rushed out to spot the changes.

16

Unrealized Endings - New Year's Eve, 1944

The New Year's Eve night sky was again alight with deadly fireworks. Despite the relentless bombing, the air-raid sirens no longer sounded. That didn't matter because it was too dangerous to venture out. We remained captive in our shelter.

Even though the Soviets were just over a mile away from the Hungarian and German headquarters hidden in the Castle tunnels, the underground phone lines between Budapest and headquarters of the German Army South still functioned. Pfeffer-Wildenbruch called high command to report that his only remaining hope was that German forces outside of Budapest would come to the rescue. If that relief did not come soon, Germany would not be able to hold both Buda and Pest.

Adolf Hitler, who still directed operations down to individual battalion level, tended to stay up most of the night and start his days late morning. From Berlin to the Front, he issued his irrational orders late at night after the fighting had died down. More self-reliant generals took advantage of this conundrum. They acted on the assumption that the orders they wanted would arrive after the event. But Pfeffer-Wildenbruch was not that type of commander. He lacked the confidence to disobey the *Fürher* in even the minutia. His indecisive leadership doomed both his men and the civilians. When they did come, Hitler's belated orders were predictable. German troops were categorically forbidden from attempting to break out of Budapest.

Soviet commanders Malinovsky and Tolbukhin fought in and suffered through the siege of Stalingrad. They knew that urban warfare was unavoidably costly for both sides. Unlike open field battles, in which greater strength quickly decided the outcome, urban conflicts dragged on for weeks and months in the confusing maze of streets and buildings. Tanks, which could effectively cover long distances in open terrain, now struggled to maneuver in narrow streets. Central control disintegrated into a multitude of small scale actions. Heavy artillery was replaced by hand-held weaponry. The only way to win was to fight street by street, house by house. Even with their overwhelming forces, the Russians knew that an urban siege would cost many Russian lives and take time that they did not have. They had no interest in being bogged down in a protracted battle in Budapest. Their real objectives were Vienna and Berlin, not Budapest.

With Stalin's approval, the Soviet commanders prepared a peace offering. The German garrison could surrender under remarkably generous terms. Food and medical attention would be provided. The Hungarians would be released "forthwith." The Germans would be repatriated to Germany immediately after the conclusion of the war. All officers would be allowed to keep their uniforms and medals. Officers could even keep their sidearms. Two Soviet captains led simultaneous, but separate, parley delegations.

Miklós Steinmetz, who led the Pest parley team, fluently spoke Hungarian because his family had emigrated to Moscow after the failed 1919 Bolshevik revolution. German and Hungarian soldiers watched in stunned silence as Steinmetz drove a jeep toward the German lines along Üllői Avenue in the neighborhood of Pestszentlőrinc. He aide sat next to him in the passenger seat and waved a white flag on a stick. Observers could not believe that this vehicle dared pass this way. Their disbelief was substantiated when a loud explosion followed by a whitish-gray cloud of smoke cleared to reveal two dead bodies slumped motionless against each other in the wrecked jeep. Steinmetz never made it to the German front line in Pest. The jeep had triggered a land mine, which had been placed along the Avenue to slow the advance of Soviet tanks.

On the Buda side, Ilya Afanasevich Ostapenko did reach the German side. The Germans blindfolded him and his aide and drove them to the citadel command post on Gellért-*hegy* hill. After a polite introduction, Ostapenko, who spoke perfect German, handed the written ultimatum to the senior officer–who immediately contacted Commander Pfeffer-Wildenbruch. While they waited for the commander's reply, the Germans offered the two Soviets a gladly accepted glass of soda water. After receiving

Pfeffer-Wildenbruch's negative reply, the two Russians were blindfolded and driven back to the front line. Blindfolds removed, the two Russians rapidly walked across the neutral zone toward the Russian line. About halfway across the neutral zone, Ostapenko turned to his aide and commented, "looks like we have made it. We've been lucky once…" But his sentence was cut off by a loud crack. Bomb fragments whistled by the two men. Wild-eyed, Ostapenko turned to face the German line, and then fell to the ground, dead.

According to a Soviet postmortem, two splinters and four bullets were lodged in Ostapenko's back. It may have been the shelling from an uninformed Soviet battery, or errant shots from the Hungarian anti-aircraft guns stationed up on the hill. But one thing was certain: neither of the two dead Russian captains were deliberately killed by the Germans. The Russians, however, did not see it that way.

Radio Moscow described the deaths and expressed outrage at the murder of their peace delegations. Meanwhile, on the German side, the cowardly Pfeffer-Wildenbruch denied even the very existence of any official Soviet delegation. He knew that delegates were protected by international law. Any blame for harm done to them would be on his shoulders. So he lied to his superiors. He sent a false report to Berlin stating "the Russian did not send Soviet Officers but rather four German prisoners of war who were handed over to the secret field police in Vienna." This would be the last Soviet peace offering.

Vowing bloody revenge, the Red Army launched a new barrage. On the ground, a thousand guns battered German defenses. From the sky, bombers relentlessly dropped their deadly loads. The bombardment continued for eight hours each day for the next three days. Nearby houses received direct hits, killing everyone inside.

In January, Hungary became Hitler's main theater of war. The Wehrmacht's last attempts to reverse forward progress by the Red Army included Panzer Corps operations originating in Tata, Esztergom, and an attempt to retake Székesfehérvár. They equipped their tanks, for the very first time, with infrared sights to enable nocturnal operations. They staged hundreds of tons of food, medicine, and ammunition that stood ready to be transported to Budapest. However, the Germans never got close enough to make a difference to those trapped within the capital. Battles dragged on to the west of Budapest until long after there was no one left in Budapest to save.

17

Surviving the Squeeze

Father returned to the shelter one day rolling an empty wine barrel. "We will use it to store water," he announced. It gave the water stored inside an unappealing red tinge, but worked well as cooking water. While taps still flowed, he filled every available vessel and had built up a decent reserve when the water service stopped on January 10. When that reserve ran out, he fetched water from the medicinal springs feeding the Gellért Baths and from a slowly leaking water tank in a nearby park. After it snowed, Father fetched water while wrapped in camouflaging white sheets. But eventually he relented and allowed the women to take over water duty. The thinking was that a woman venturing out at dusk with armloads of bottles and pitchers was less likely to be shot at than a man. The women had to pass directly past the German snipers ensconced as sentries in the upper floors of the Kelenhegyi house.

When the water service stopped, the toilets also stopped working. Unfortunately some hopeful residents continued to use the toilets until the indoor plumbing started to reek. Dried out drains discharged a suffocating stench. The men dug a trench in the back yard that would serve as our "outhouse" for the rest of the war. They covered the trench with boards to stand on. But there were no walls. No privacy. I did my best to hold my bladder until the cover of darkness. I also was tasked with taking out the *Bili* (chamber pot) for those too feeble to venture out to do their business.

Cooking gas service also stopped. For the rest of the war we cooked over small fires, burning wood that Father had stockpiled. Finally, a mid-January bombing barrage knocked out our electricity and telephone service. Ironically, in the moments before the electricity went out, we were listening to the radio. Arrow Cross propagandists touted the ultimate victory of the Germans. Their unrealistic propaganda was an awfully sad joke. By this time, only 5% of the Hungarian army officers supported the Arrow Cross regime.

For light, we made "blinkers," which were small bottles filled with benzine and stuffed with now worthless 20 Filler bank notes wrapped around a piece of twine. The faint illumination only outlined the shapes of nearby people.

Nagypapa, as area shelter commissioner, was the focal point for information dissemination. The two Szlávik brothers and I served as couriers of small cryptic messages to other nearby shelter commanders. These notes spoke mostly to meeting basic needs, such as which bakery had bread, or when and where water was available. But despite our best efforts at maintaining a communication network, useful information became sparse.

By the end of January all central food supplies had been exhausted and food delivery for the civilian population ceased. Work animals had all been slaughtered for their meat and their feedstock consumed. Many people went without food for the remainder of the siege. Fortunately, Father and Nagypapa had the foresight to stockpile food for this moment. Father kept well hidden bags of corn and wheat berries and a grinder. Each day, he only ground as much as we would use, mixing the ground grains with water, salt and honey into a gruel. He hoped that soldiers, unable to make easy use of unground grains, might not take our food supply from us. We were also blessed by two miraculous events that introduced some variety into our diet.

The first occurred at four in the morning under cover of darkness on January 26, 1945. On the adjacent hilltop west of the castle in Vérmező meadow, German soldiers cautiously waved flashlights into the night sky to guide the last aerial supply gliders in for landing. A month earlier, Germany had formed the "Budapest Supply Group" to perform aerial resupply of food and ammunition intended only for German soldiers. Two hundred salvaged aircraft of various types, piloted by swashbuckling kids aged 16 to 18, attempted these dangerous, low-success-rate missions. When they could not land on German controlled airstrips, the pilots dropped food canisters suspended by hard-to-see red parachutes.

On this particular morning, Soviet troops controlling the streets adjacent to the meadow blasted the approaching planes with a barrage of gunfire. The parachute of a container released from one of these diverted planes failed to open. Rather than slowly drifting down through the night sky, it quickly plummeted until it violently slammed into the playground of our compound.

Forbidden on penalty of death to touch one of these dropped canisters, we snuck out to find the contents of this canister spread across the lawn. The adults quickly cut off and hid the telltale red parachute fabric. During the night Franci-*néni* and Klára worked for hours scratching out meat and sardines from the smashed, flattened cans. These meager salvageable food scraps were a godsend. Luckily, the Germans never came looking for this errant canister.[29]

A second miracle occurred when fighting was at its peak around our compound. The house shook from a loud explosion directly below us on Kelenhegyi *utca*. It was followed by a loud crash in my father's office. When the sounds of fighting grew safely distant, we went to investigate. To our amazement, the back half of a horse had been blown up into the air and through our large front office window. Because of the extreme cold, the carcass quickly froze. The women were able to produce several days of stew from the meat sliced off the carcass.

While we luckily kept ourselves fed, the Jews in the ghetto starved. Arrow Cross Prime Minister Szálasi rejected an International Red Cross food aid offer valued at 50 million pengős because it came with the condition that part of the food must be delivered to the Jewish ghetto. Instead, he demanded help from the German Army Group South stating, "...it is not possible to guarantee food supplies. The capital's own stocks are catastrophic. The number of deaths by starvation is already alarmingly high, particularly among children." Hungarian commander Hindy also sent a dispatch stating "food supplies to the army and civilian population in January will be dreadful. I have been informed that supplies to the ghetto, which now contains 40-60,000 Jews, have ceased completely and the Jews are restless." While those Jews began to succumb to starvation, a train

---

[29] Several months after the end of the war, we felt safe enough to pull out the sturdy red parachute fabric, from which we sewed children's clothes.

laden with stolen gold pulled out of the Nyugati Train Station and headed west.[30]

---

[30] In May 1945, US Army officers and troops plundered a "gold train" in Austria on its way to Germany from Hungary that carried gold, jewels, paintings and other valuables seized by the Nazis from Jewish families. A 2001 suit filed in Miami said the Army falsely classified it as unidentifiable and enemy property, which avoided having to return the goods to their rightful owners. The suit alleged that the US made no effort to return the goods and lied to Hungarian Jews who sought information about their property after the war. In 2005, the US government reached a $25.5 million settlement with families of the Hungarian Holocaust victims.

18

Pest Falls

On January 10, as Soviets captured the Nyugati Train Station and Kálvin Square, Hungarian Infantry Captain, László Majaross (Laci-*bácsi*), gathered his men into the cellar of a Pest Credit Bank building where he announced that he was going home. For the past few weeks he had done his best to keep his team away from pointless combat. But now the noose had been slung so tightly around the city that he could no longer avoid engaging the enemy. Defection and desertion were punishable by death, but what did he have to lose at this point? He just wanted to see his wife, Klára-*néni*, and their two children one more time. He spoke of how he missed seeing the rapid development of his 18-month-old son, Peter. Those precious moments lost.

He left his stunned men in the cellar and strolled to the square in front of the Vigadó Concert Hall. The sight before him was reminiscent of Nero watching Rome burn. With the backdrop of

Buda shrouded in darkness, the hotels in the foreground situated along the Danube embankment glowed from the amber flames of their destruction. A Soviet incendiary bomb had set the roof of the Parliament Building alight. Its flames burned an unearthly shade of blue and green due to its copper and lead covering. City streets were covered in a jumble of broken glass, torn overhead streetcar cables, and toppled lampposts. Houses were aflame. A blueish-yellow gunpowder vapor lingered in the air, mixed with the stench of mountains of uncollected foul-smelling refuse. Corpses punctuated the rubble. Bodies were contorted, blown into unnatural postures, with missing or mangled limbs. Wide-open eyes stared up from waxen yellow faces and lines of dried blood ran from noses and ears. The pockets of their torn, soiled, and bloodstained clothes were turned out by those searching for identification or valuables.

A loud explosion from the river interrupted his contemplation. Retreating Germans had just blown up the Horthy Miklós (Petőfi) Bridge.[31] As Laci-*bácsi* approached the Central Market, he watched Germans soldiers desperately fighting off a Soviet unit trying to trap them on the Pest side of the river. Alone, but still wearing his military uniform, he stepped onto and started to cross the Ferenc József (Szabadság) Bridge, when Soviet troops abruptly accosted him and took him prisoner.

---

[31] That evening, the Ferenc József Bridge also collapsed. The Germans claimed it was hit by a Soviet bomb. But the Hungarians knew that the Germans had blown it up.

Like a falling house of cards, German defenses in Pest rapidly collapsed. Anti-aircraft defenses no longer existed. Russian fighter-bombers flew low over rooftops and strafed anyone foolish enough to be seen on the streets. Soviet reconnaissance patrols entered Pest's inner districts via the culverts, squeezed through narrow passages, and surfaced under the cover of night among the ruins behind the front lines. Soviet aircraft dropped small tactical bombs intended for lines of tanks. However, these bombs errantly struck and destroyed homes and apartments. One round struck a six-story building on Klotild *utca* in central Pest that was being used as a military hospital. Ammunition stored in the mezzanine exploded and the entire building collapsed burying 300 patients and staff.

When, on January 17, German commander Pfeffer-Wildenbruch finally received Hitler's approval to evacuate Pest, only two of six bridges still reached across the Danube River. Thousands of people flooded over the badly damaged Erzsébet and Chain bridges and log-jammed the narrow approaching streets. In the slowly moving parade, women wailed and children cried as orange cinders from a burning palace rained down on them. There was no room to maneuver to evade the radiating heat. Hungarian and German profanity filled the air. Military units attempted to march between the vehicles. Motorized German military police fired guns into the air in useless attempts to control the unruly crowd. Inching forward through the gridlock, they finally reached the square on the Pest side of the Chain Bridge. A veritable firework display of explosions brightly lit the bridge. When unimpeded Soviet planes strafed the bridges, those crossing midspan had no way to seek cover. Shrapnel fragments ripped through them. Vehicles thudded over abandoned corpses but steered to avoid the gaping holes in the bridge that looked directly down onto the frigid waters rushing below. One German jeep fell nose first into one of these holes. Its tail end up in the air and its dead occupants teetering inside. Thus, the exodus continued through the night.

Two sixteen-year-old boys, Ambrus and Tivadar, loitered street-side, watching the slowly passing frantic crowds attempting to leave Pest. Both were skinnier than any teenager should be. Both were dressed in scrounged-up parts of military uniforms. With the clothing, they had tried to create the impression that they were affiliated with a militia group. To avoid having to join ranks and fight with one of the Arrow Cross militias, they cleverly concocted a story about being on special assignment from another one. So far, their outlandish ruse had worked.

Both smiled sardonically at the chaos unfolding before them. For these two mischievous friends, the breakdown of societal restraints during the siege had opened a window of opportunity for outrageous shenanigans. They salvaged, stole, and sold on the black market. With preoccupied parents, the two were free to roam the streets of Pest unsupervised. Most of their adventures occurred in the evenings, like this, when most of the population were safely hidden away in their basements and shelters.

But the two boys were caught off-guard when a jeep filled with German soldiers suddenly pulled up in front of them. The soldiers grabbed and squeezed the boys into the already crowded vehicle. The jeep then made its way across the Erzsébet Bridge. Upon reaching the Buda side, the jeep approached the Gellért Hotel and then abruptly turned up Kelenhegyi *utca*, passing alongside the damaged baths. The soldiers were trying to reach German headquarters located at the Citadel and needed the boys to navigate for them. In his best broken-German, Ambrus convinced the soldiers that the road they were on terminated at the top of the hill. All the soldiers had to do was stay on Kelenhegyi utca. Satisfied, the soldiers let the boys out of the jeep directly in front of our house and drove off up the hill.

From their hillside vantage point, Ambrus and Tivadar were able to look back across to the apocalyptic scene on the Pest side of the river. An ocean of flames surrounded the Margit Bridge. The iron facade of the Nyugati Train Station was glowing red. It looked as if all life had perished and only the raging fires were left to rule over the ruins. They suddenly longed to rejoin their parents in their basement on the other side of the river. But that would not happen this evening. Bridge traffic was only moving in the Buda direction. With nowhere to go, they sat down on the curb in front of our house and shivered in the cold night air.

Father, who was returning from a reconnaissance, noticed the two boys shivering outside of our house. Taking pity on them, he invited them into the apartment. When the Germans blew up the bridges the next morning, Father told the boys that they were welcome to stay with us until they could find a way to return home to Pest.

There was no room in the kitchen. My parents gave the boys blankets and allowed them to sleep in the bedroom we children used to sleep in. The windows had been blown out and that room was bitterly cold, but the hardy boys made the best of the arrangement. We fed them something each morning. The boys ventured off during the day. I was surprised and relieved each evening to hear them return to the bedroom. They stayed with us in our apartment for the remainder of the siege.

That same day of January 17, the Swede Raoul Wallenberg mysteriously disappeared. It wasn't the Nazis or the Arrow Cross who finally got to the meddlesome Swede. Suspecting that Wallenberg was an American spy, Soviet Counter Intelligence Agency agents took him into custody. The Soviets eventually divulged that this man, credited with saving tens of thousands of Jews, died on July 17, 1947, in Moscow's Lubyanka prison. Details pertaining to Wallenberg's arrest, imprisonment, and execution remain the subject of continued speculation.

The Red Army reached and liberated the Jewish ghetto, but the slaughter of Jews continued on the Buda side. Surprisingly, the most egregious Arrow Cross death squad was led by a Roman Catholic priest of the Franciscan Order. Father András Kun wore a belted pistol holster strapped around his clerical white and black Roman collared cassock. First, he and his Arrow Cross gang murdered 170 patients hiding in the Jewish hospital on Marcos *utca*. Next, he ordered the arrest, torture, and execution of Jewish author Ernő Ligeti, his son, and his wife. Then he slaughtered 90 people at the Jewish Almshouse on Alma *utca*.

Two days later, on January 21, Father Kun and his gang murdered 149 people in the Jewish hospital on Városmajor *utca*. At this hospital, he told patients and staff that they would be taken to the Jewish ghetto in Pest. This was a lie. With the bridges gone and the ghetto in Soviet hands, it was already impossible to reach the ghetto. Nonetheless, the innocent hospital residents obeyed his orders to line up. Kun's militia then gunned them down. Afterwards, the militia went back into the hospital wards and killed those patients unable to walk, along with their nurses.[32]

---

[32] Kun was arrested that same day. Fellow gang member, Peter Szabo, kept a diary detailing their crimes, including the rape of nuns. Found by chance, the buried diary with identification papers provided the evidence for the People's Court to sentence and execute Kun.

19

Battle in the Buda Hills

I n early February, the siege had closed to within a mile of the Gellért and Castle hills where the Germans were making their last desperate stand. Papal Nuncio Angelo Rotta paid a visit to Pfeffer-Wildenbruch's command post located deep inside a Castle bunker. As the Vatican's ambassador made his way to the Obergruppenführer's office, he passed lice-infested wounded men lying in the corridors.

"The Pope urges German Supreme Command to end the suffering and ultimate destruction of the civilian population."

"Fürher's orders remained unchanged," Pfeffer-Wildenbruch responded to Rotta.

"Can you not ask the *Fürher* again?"

"Every day, I ask him. I beg him to allow us to break out. Each time, he tells me that Budapest must be held to the bitter end."

Sensing their impending doom, German Officers presented Pfeffer-Wildenbruch with a breakout proposal.

"Soviet commander Malinovsky, who controls the west and north has given us our opportunity to escape."

"There is a one-mile gap in the northwest quadrant of the encirclement. We must leave immediately!"

"No, we must await the *Fürher's* orders," the Obergruppenführer replied with a dismissive wave.

"But we know what his orders will be. He will tell us to stand our ground until relieved. He always says that."

"This is pigheaded madness," an officer shouted.

"You are out of line."

"Now I know that our men are meant to be sent to the slaughter."

This was truer than they realized. By this time, German command determined that a breakout was hopeless and had written off Budapest. For Hitler, prolonging the siege by even a few more days was worth more than the possible success of a breakout. What would he gain if he rescued a few thousand men? They were unarmed and in need of immediate hospital treatment. Rather, he derived maximum benefit by dooming Budapest's defenders.

German snipers positioned in the rooms above our heads thwarted Soviet attempts to take Gellért Hill. We dared not leave the shelter all day. To pass the time, my brother Béla and I played a game to see who could count the most dead bodies. At first the game was amusing. We were like two kids trapped in the back seat of a car on a long drive playing "I spy a...." We spotted corpses along roadways, hidden in bushes, and behind buildings. We even had a corpse in our front yard. Then I spotted a truck coming down our street from the Citadel above. The truck bed was piled so high with corpses that I could not count them. The lifeless bodies were covered with a white lime powder which gave them a ghostly pale hue. Some had open eyes that stared vacantly back at me. I was sickened by the sight. After that truck, I refused to play our count-the-bodies game. The ghastliness of close quarter combat dispelled any thoughts of play, even for an eleven year old.

A stray Soviet artillery shell intended for the hilltop battery landed on the nearby Mon Reve Villa and completely leveled the building. We did not know how many had been hiding at the now silent property. But we needed to go there. In the villa's garden was a pond that still held water, and we were running out. The problem was that this property was located on the southern facing slope, which was completely exposed to continuous bombardment from the Russian Army unit positioned below at Albertfalva. Whenever we ventured out, the sounds of cannon fire scared us away and we eventually abandoned attempts to reach the pond. We went to sleep that night with our water supply completely expended. The next morning, as if God had heard our prayers, we awoke to find the ground covered in deep snow. Our water supply dilemma was temporarily abated.

Close quarter combat broke out in a hillside villa near ours where my uncle Géza, Father's brother, was holed up with his wife's family. After one occupant took a bullet in his shoulder, the others laid flat on the ground, covered their ears, and prayed. A German threw a hand grenade down a staircase. A Russian responded by filling the hallway with flames from an automatic flamethrower. The deadly gel stuck to the German victims' bodies and burned them alive.

The evening of February 10, a sudden drop in temperature following a brief snowfall created very heavy fog that blanketed Gellért Hill. In that dreamlike haze, the German units made their last stand. As if in slow motion, soldiers emerged as ghostly apparitions and then fell to the ground. They fought valiantly and died. The next morning, we heard only sporadic gunfire on the hill to our south. Below us, at the Gellért Hotel, Colonel József Kozma, commander of the Hungarian antiaircraft artillery, raised the white flag of surrender.

20

The Germans Break Out

U p in the Buda Castle that February 11 morning, Pfeffer-Wildenbruch called his final war council to announce that he finally received the green light from Hitler. He laid out plans for the breakout. The Germans would leave all tanks and heavy weaponry behind. In small groups of about 30, they would travel through the woods. Each group would be led by a Hungarian familiar with the territory. The groups would then reassemble on Remete Hill, located about 2.5 miles to the northwest of the Castle. The reassembled larger group would then make the final journey west through the low hills and forests until they reached the German lines. The first group would leave that evening at 20:00.

This "top secret" breakout plan was a disaster from the onset. Divisional commanders only received their orders at 14:00, regimental commanders at 16:00, and the rank and file and Hungarians were only told of the plan at 18:00. Learning of the plan only two hours before it was to start, Hindy complained that

Pfeffer-Wildenbruch should have discussed it with him beforehand. But the German disdainfully brushed him off one last time, contending that Hungarian divisions were subordinate to his divisions.

Secret or not, the breakout was no surprise to the Soviets. In the days preceding the breakout, the Russians had established three encircling rings spreading to the northwest: The innermost at Széll Kálmán Square along Margit *körút*, the second belt near St. János Hospital, and the third along the Danube at János Hill. They evacuated houses along anticipated routes and filled them with snipers.

The breakout was also no surprise to Buda citizenry. By the time the first wave was scheduled to leave, over a thousand people had assembled in the dark. Women pushed baby carriages. Old people dragged children in tow. The crowd was so thick that soldiers assigned to lead the way couldn't push their way to the front.

Then all hell broke loose. Flares lit the sky. Searchlights lit up the crowd. Mortars began to land. Grenades exploded. Panicked shouts were drowned by the rat-tat-tat of gunfire. The Russians lying in wait at every window fired on the crowd. People scrambled for doorways but there was no escape. Pre-positioned machine guns on both sides of the street trapped people in the crossfire. Like cornered animals, maddened people scrambled, elbowed, pushed, kicked, and trampled fallen bodies. Abandoning all self-discipline, the panicked crowd rushed down the road directly into the line of fire and headlong into disaster.

Russian tanks appeared and shot into crowded buildings. The dead piled up in the street. Moans, profanity, and pleading filled the silent gaps between gunfire. One man shouted "Please, shoot me because I can't myself. Both my arms are gone." A German

Cavalry Division commander lost his leg in an explosion and then turned his gun on himself.

Those who did make it to the woods found themselves trekking through eight inches of snow. The wind and sleet soaked their clothes and chilled them to the bone. Their numbers continued to dwindle as snipers picked them off. Soldiers' rations for that day had been a piece of chocolate, a hard candy, and a small cube of bread. Consumed by frostbite, fear, and starvation, the escapees operated from the reptilian portion of their brains. Dragging themselves through the snow, one group came upon a Soviet bread cart. Rather than sharing, the starving fugitives shot each other. The victors disappeared laden with bread, while the vanquished lay dying in the snow.

Pfeffer-Wildenbruch and selected German commanders stayed back in the castle headquarters until 23:00 and then escaped via a different route through the Ördög-árok culvert. But their escape route was also blocked. After leaving the culvert, they emerged to face a surrounding attack. They hid in a villa on Budakeszi *utca* and were quickly captured the next morning.

The slaughter of the German garrison trying to escape from the Castle that day was bloodier than the first waves of the U.S. landings on Omaha Beach in Normandy. In less than six hours, thousands of people were killed over a two mile section of the front line. The morning of February 11, before the attempted break-out, Pfeffer-Wildenbruch had 44,000 soldiers. By February 15, only 3 percent (785 German and Hungarian soldiers) made it through to the German lines. Of the original 44,000, 17,000 died and 22,350, many badly wounded, were captured.

Nearly 5,000 soldiers had remained in the Castle either because they never received the orders to break out or because they were too injured to move. The chief medical officer and his staff had fled, abandoning patients to their fate.

A young non-commissioned officer discovered General Pfeffer-Wildenbruch's unlocked and evacuated bunker. It was still full of supplies and clothing that the General had hoarded for his personal comfort. The young officer decided to exchange his ragged uniform for one of the General's abandoned uniforms. As he walked out of the General's quarters, one of the wounded soldiers lining the tunnel mistook the young officer for the General, pulled out his pistol and shot the well-dressed officer dead before others could intervene.

21

Ambrus and Tivadar, 1945

Emerging from our shelter on the morning of February 12 to an unfamiliar silence, we gave respectful distance to a large unexploded artillery shell sitting only three yards from the southwest corner of the Kelenhegyi house.[33] We had survived in proximity to the last of the German holdouts, in the epicenter of the bloodiest last battles of the siege. Now, we walked down the hill and then parallel to the river in the direction of the Castle. We passed a burnt out tank, a damaged supply cart, and a stiff, frozen corpse with one arm sticking out from the snow reaching toward heaven.

The sight of this corpse caused my normally calm and confident role model, Klára-*néni*, to break out in uncontrollable sobs. She had expected her husband, Laci-*bácsi*, to have returned home by

---

[33] The Hungarian military came and diffused it and removed it a few days after we gave them notice of the bomb.

now. But she had not heard from him or a word about him for more than two months. Perhaps, she was imagining that his corpse similarly lay somewhere else in the city.

As we continued on, a couple of German soldiers, half-demented from hunger, instinctively tried to hide as we approached. Oddly, we saw no Soviet soldiers on the street.

Across the impassible river, the once grand hotels and palatial buildings lining the quay walls were now piles of rubble. The city had been decimated. Seventy percent of all buildings were badly damaged. Nearly every window was broken.

Inside the Castle walls, the royal palace, a beautiful Baroque building, was still aflame. The corner that housed the Prime Minister's residence was now a pile of rubble. Through a gate in the courtyard, the door of the coach house was ajar. Inside, a carriage that once transported the visiting King of Italy was smashed to bits.

As we returned home, the adults spoke with aghast sadness. "For the past 500 years, we have been on the losing side of every war. But this?"

"Remember that we all survived."

"Let us say a prayer of thanks."

"The worst is over."

"Yes, the Soviets have freed us from the tyranny of the Arrow Cross and Nazism."

"Soon, life will return to the way it had been before the siege."

The adults were naively mistaken. We had only exchanged one terrible occupancy for another. One deranged megalomaniac for another.

"*Kogda my smozhem pereyti rekul?*"

"Again," Father demanded.

"*Kogda my smozhem pereyti rekul?*" The Szlávik boys and I repeated.

This was the first of several Russian phrases that my father had pieced together using a Hungarian-Russian dictionary and that he was training us to memorize.

Word had reached the Kelenhegyi house via the shelter commander communication network that Soviet soldiers were grabbing unsuspecting adult males off the streets to meet their prisoner quotas. Men should not leave their homes. Russian commander Malinovsky had reported capturing 110,000 prisoners of war during the Siege. The problem was that he only had 60,000 in hand. He sent his Red Army troops out to find more prisoners. At first, they captured anyone wearing a uniform, including police officers, postmen, and fire fighters. Still falling short of their target, they searched municipal records for German sounding names and seized people from their homes. Even that was not enough. So they positioned troops at highly trafficked intersections and grabbed unsuspecting passers-by off the street. Besides, we still had received no news about Klára-*néni*'s husband, Laci-*bácsi*, and she was losing her mind with despair.

Father, however, desperately wanted to learn the fate of his two brothers living in Pest. So he concocted this plan to teach me and the Szlávik boys a few questions in Russian that we were to ask the Soviet soldiers occupying the Gellért Hotel at the bottom of Kelenhegyi *utca*. This first question translated to "when will we be able to cross the river?" Other questions included "Will they construct a pontoon bridge?" and "When will the ferry service be restored?"

Holding hands the three of us entered the hotel lobby. An echoing cacophony of unintelligible Russian babble filled the air. My terror subsided when I realized that the soldiers were indifferent to our presence. We approached a small group of men who glared at us with tired annoyance.

"*Kogda my smozhem pereyti rekuI?*" we recited in unison.

They only shushed us away, giving no indication that they comprehended our terrible Russian. We approached another soldier sitting alone. But again received no response. We eventually gave up and walked home, never knowing if they misunderstood us or simply had no information to share. We were very relieved that we would not be required to memorize their Russian responses.

Father sternly admonished us children not to go near the pile. On the street in front of our house was one of the last uncollected piles of surrendered German and Hungarian weapons. I don't know why the Red Army had yet to collect those surrendered weapons on Kelenhegyi *utca*. I studied this mound of ammunition belts, holsters, rifles, and pistols, but obediently did not touch it. However, the temptation was too great for two teenage boys like Ambrus and Tivadar.

Though I barely knew them, I had grown fond of Ambrus and Tivadar and grateful for their company. Despite being trapped on this side of the river with us, they still maintained positive attitudes. They were respectful to the adults. They were quick to give me a pat on the head or a wink and a smile. They reminded me of our missing Laci-*bácsi,* oozing of testosterone and invincibility, and making the most of their circumstance. Had they not survived this siege in part because of their cleverness and opportunistic thievery?

Ambrus and Tivadar still slept in the children's bedroom huddled in blankets against the cold night air that freely entered through the paneless windows. The rest of us slept in the kitchen that stayed the warmest in our heat deprived apartment. Father, who clearly had also taken a liking to these boys, checked on them every morning to make sure they survived the cold nights. He also always made sure that Ambrus and Tivadar got something to eat for breakfast even if it was their only meal of the day.

The next morning, when he went to the bedroom to rouse the boys for breakfast, he found them nervously standing at attention looking like new cadets in assembly getting chewed-out by a cruel drill sergeant. Only then did he notice the three Red Army soldiers in the room. Guns pointed, the soldiers had been equally startled by and displeased with Father's untimely intrusion. He held his breath and his ears throbbed as one of the soldiers approached and patted down his pockets and legs.

At first Father assumed that this was a simple robbery. Stories of such soldier robberies were already spreading. Maybe this soldier was searching him for valuables. But the soldier didn't make him empty his pockets. Only then did father noticed the two German Luger pistols laying on the bed.

Though the fighting had stopped, Russians and Hungarians still viewed one another as the enemy. Soviet soldiers were on guard for reprisals or revenge attacks from both soldiers and civilians. Any Hungarian with a concealed weapon could inflict significant casualties. A teenage boy might attack to avenge the loss of a parent. Even as a child, I recognized the palpable antipathy between the soldiers and the citizens of Budapest. Some 50,000 Soviet soldiers lost their lives in the liberation of Budapest. That was more than half of all Soviet solders killed in Hungary during the entire war. Possession of a weapon was punishable by death.

Out in the kitchen with mother, I heard the "pop pop" of a fired gun. The door opened and the soldiers emerged from the bedroom. Averting my stare, they silently walked down the hall and out of the apartment. An eternal minute after the soldiers had disappeared into the morning light, my pale and shaken father also emerged from the bedroom. Without uttering a word he hugged Mother and cried. Father buried the wrapped bodies of Ambrus and Tivadar in a shallow grave under the apple tree.

Several months later, when he was finally able to cross the Danube, Father finally reconnected with his two brothers in Pest. They had survived unscathed. He learned that the siege experience had been much different on the Pest side. The main difference was that the Red Army did not linger like they were continuing to do around Gellért Hill. Pest was only a milestone in their quest for the Castle. But after they took Buda there was nowhere for these soldiers to go. Father also located the families of Ambrus and Tivadar and shared the tragic news. The families eventually came to the Kelenhegyi house to exhume the bodies for reburial.

Pest recovered much more quickly than Buda. The fighting had ceased there by mid-January, while it had continued to rage for another month in Buda. We in Buda suffered the longest even after the fighting stopped. Our house was repeatedly occupied and looted by Russian soldiers. We continued to live in the cellar long after the last battle.

After the Germans vacated the upstairs floors they occupied during the siege, we found used razor blades, combs, and squeezed out toothpaste tubes. In comparison, after the occupying Russians left our house, we found filthy rags, empty bottles, and piles of excrement. These were two notably different armies.

Entrepreneurial Hungarians distilled homemade *Házi Pálinka* a strong fruit brandy, which they exchanged for food with Soviet soldiers. Some Soviets were so desperate for drink that they poisoned themselves on colognes containing lethal ethyl alcohol. Jeeps of drunken soldiers careened wildly through the narrow streets with little concern for the pedestrians. One could comprehend and somewhat accept war casualties. But it was hard to stomach the senseless deaths that occurred during the unpredictable lawlessness that followed.

These soused Russian soldiers lingering in Budapest after the siege clearly were not the buff handsome communist workers portrayed in the more frequently appearing propaganda posters. These men had come from a countryside ravaged by passing armies. They had left families struggling at home. They had starved and marched across freezing winter plains. In contrast to the westernized Germans, the Russians were like a Mongol horde emerging from a wild hinterland that lacked flush toilets, large libraries, eyeglasses, watches, and other luxuries that we took for granted. For most of them, Budapest was their first exposure to a western-style metropolis with its bourgeois culture and material amenities. And though Moscow claimed to be our liberator, we were the reluctant conquered enemy, ripe for victimization.

One night several angry drunk Russian soldiers returned to the Kelenhegyi house. They herded us into the largest cellar room, where most of the other household members still slept. Their first order of business was the perfunctory confiscation of gloves, boots, and wristwatches.

Next, waving pistols and shouting in intelligible gibberish, they lined us up for inspection. They slowly walked down the line and evaluated each of us. Dirty as I was, with short hair, they mistook me to be a boy. Ironically, further down the line, they assumed that Feri Szlávik, with his longer curly blond hair and delicate facial features, was a girl. He vehemently protested and finally pulled down his pants to prove that he was a boy. Laughing, the soldiers continued down the line.

The older women, including my mother, wrapped in babushkas looked weathered well beyond their age. They, fortunately, did not appeal to these men. But the soldiers zeroed in on Gyula Vietorisz's seventeen-year old maid Julia, who was, unfortunately, quite attractive. They dragged her over to Bálint-*néni*'s room, a corner cut out of the larger cellar room we occupied. They laid Julia down on the bed and then took turns climbing on top of her. My mother told me not to watch, but she was too overwhelmed and scared to enforce her command.

With naive and scientific curiosity, I watched the rapes. I was surprised that the soldiers didn't even take off their pants. They simply opened their zippers and mounted poor Julia. As the men traded places, she just laid there and cried. Though we all longed to rush over to her rescue, no one dared move. When finished, the men simply grunted at us with eyes averted and walked out. Tens of thousands of such rapes occurred during this period. They dragged mattresses from nearby houses into the churches and turned them into rape factories. And, like poor Julia, many got pregnant and underwent subsequent abortions.

Several times after that night, Russian soldiers returned to the Kelenhegyi house in search of any yet undiscovered valuables. Having heard that angry soldiers sometimes set houses on fire, we tried to be as non-confrontational and inconspicuous as possible so as to not aggravate these men. They were as unpredictable as the chaos that still reigned in the streets. These soldiers were never held accountable. When confronted about the behavior of the soldiers, Stalin simply responded that "a soldier who has marched thousands of miles through pools of blood and through fire and water will want to have a little fun with a wench or steal a trifle."

We just took it for granted that it was not safe to walk the streets after dark. The police, who might have enforced the laws, had been rounded up to fill quotas as prisoners of war. This lawless chaos lasted for a year after the siege. But in many other ways the circle of life continued, and our lives returned.

22

Hope and Recovery

Eighty miles west of Vienna, just outside of the Krems railway station, my aunt, Erzsébet Vietorisz, and her four daughters huddled this bright brisk morning awaiting their rendezvous. Since fleeing Gyõr on December 29 to Sopron and then to Vienna, she had hardly seen her husband Józsi. She spent a few nights at Reisnerstrasse #9, and then boarded a train just before the Red Army took Vienna. Having left the Kelenhegyi house with a truckload of household goods, all she now carried were some clothes, four small Persian rugs, and some bedding. There were very few private vehicles on the road that morning. She and the girls easily spotted her husband's Mercedes approaching in the distance. As it neared, she recognized Józsi's chauffeur. But when the vehicle stopped in front of her she sadly realized that Józsi was not inside.

Józsi's luck had run out. The train carrying the mechanical equipment from the disassembled weapons factory sat idle on a side rail track guarded by Russian soldiers. Up until the last minute, he had been committed to his assigned mission of finding a suitable location to reestablish the factory. He had identified an ideal location along the French/German border in Rothau. However, before they began to offload there, it became clear that Rothau would soon fall to the Allies. So the train headed back east into the arms of the Russians. The train had been sitting in the warm sun so long that one railcar filled with potatoes began to rot and ooze a liquid that smelled of cheap vodka.

Józsi-*bácsi* burnt those papers signed by Hermann Göring that allowed him to travel anywhere within German controlled territories. He eventually worked his way around checkpoints and reunited with his family in Liezen, Austria. The family settled there long enough for their fifth, and last daughter, Erika, to be born. In 1950, they boarded an ocean liner and sailed to America. They settled in a town that reminded Erzsébet-*néni* of Budapest: Pittsburg.

A canary flew into our apartment through the still pane-less window. Father caught the pretty little bird. It was scared and nearly frozen from flying through nippy spring air. We brought it into the warm kitchen and nursed it back to health. After several months, Father took the canary to a village and exchanged it for a goose, which we ate.

A hopeful Hungary rose like the Phoenix from the ashes of the lost war. A primary post-war concern was keeping the population fed. Hungary's Provisional National Government, which had been operating out of Debrecen since December of 1944, established emergency food kitchens and directed factories to feed their workers. Budapest Mayor Zoltán Vas introduced food coupons. The rations amounted to 500 calories thru March, and 1000 calories after that. Though it constituted only about half of the 2000 calories considered the minimum daily requirement, it ensured a minimum survival. We supplemented our rations with vegetables grown in our yard.

The second most critical concern was restoring transportation. Nearly all working vehicles had been confiscated by the Soviets, so we relied on the rebuilt rail lines to get food from the countryside to the capital. Once again, the railroad became the circulatory system that revived our economy. Work crews cleaned up the streets. Horse drawn cabs reappeared on streets until the trolleys started to run.

Other essential governmental services slowly returned including trash removal, electricity, telephones, radio broadcasts, and mail service. However, water and gas remained erratic. We still did our laundry in the hot springs.

After April 4, 1945, which was declared "National Day," marking Hungary's official liberation from Nazi occupation, I returned to school. The majestic school building rising out of the side of Gellért Hill had been used as a military hospital during the Siege. Despite sustaining bullet damage, the building was surprisingly structurally intact. Only a few of our teachers returned. Those teachers who did return tried very hard to bring normalcy back to our disrupted lives. They could not, however, squelch the disturbing ghost stories spreading among the students about the

197

dead soldiers who had been buried under our very feet on the school grounds.

The free market entrepreneurial spirit rose like weeds between the cracks of bureaucracy. Down on Béla-Bartok Street, Klára-*néni* and Laci-*bácsi*'s sister, both still mourning the disappearance of husband and brother, set up an espresso coffee stand. Klára's sister-in-law was also a clothing designer. They leveraged Klára's seamstress skills to make pretty children's dresses and clothing repairs to earn additional income. Out of other paneless shop windows, vendors sold lard, plum jam, ground copper vitriol used as a fungicide, rucksacks, and shirts sown from German parachutes, winter coats sown from horse blankets, jackets from tent canvases, and grain mills from engines of destroyed vehicles. They fashioned footstools from the seats of abandoned tanks, tool lubricant from drained engine grease, and rainwater barrels from empty oil drums.

Before the war, Father had employed four men in his survey and engineering business. Immediately after the war, these men still looked to him for employment. There was no survey work to be had. So, they started repairing houses. The first and most pressing task was to repair damaged roofs with salvaged shingles from destroyed homes. Next they worked on replacing windows. This was more challenging because construction materials were outrageously expensive–if found at all–and unbroken window panes were rarely found in the destroyed buildings.

One afternoon after the frozen earth had thawed, my aunt Gizela-*néni*'s good friend, a neighbor woman, came to the Kelenhegyi house to demand that my father return her treasure. Before the siege, she had presented him with a steel box and asked for his help in hiding it from the Russians. Without ever opening the box to see its contents, Father dug a three-foot deep hole next to the house and buried the box.

This warm spring afternoon, I sat and watched Father commence digging. This woman also stood over him as he labored away with his shovel. His shirt was soon drenched with sweat as he struggled to remove rocks and other debris that had sloughed off of the house. When the hole reached a depth of three feet, Father stopped. He looked perplexed.

"Where the hell is my box?" The woman impatiently demanded.

"It should be right here," Father replied.

"Are you sure? Maybe you have dug in the wrong location."

"No, this is the correct location. I had carefully paced off the spot from the corner of the house."

"Well then, where is my box?" She was irate and seemed to have no consideration that Father had been doing her a favor.

"I don't know."

"You are a thief! I should have known." With a few added obscenities, the woman marched home in a huff.

The sun set. Father returned to the hole and dug by the light of a lantern. Finally, his shovel pinged against the metal box. It had turned out that so much additional earth, rock, and debris had blown up against the house that the box was much deeper than he originally buried it.

The next morning Father and I walked to the neighbor woman's house. We watched her carefully open the returned box. It was full of gold coins and jewelry. She reached into the box and pulled out a tiny necklace and handed it to me. The golden chain was so thin and delicate that it felt like it would come apart in my hand. The pendant was a gold heart no bigger than my small thumbnail.

"For you," she said.

"You mean I can keep it?" I asked with joyous surprise. I looked over at Father, to whom she had given nothing.

He was disappointed that this miserly woman did not repay him for taking the effort and personal risk to protect her treasure. But when he saw how happy I was to have received the heart necklace, he chose to say nothing. He simply smiled at me. Wearing my shiny new necklace, I happily skipped the entire way back to the Kelenhegyi house.

When our unusually short school year ended in June, I did not travel to Rezi, but stayed in Budapest for the summer. We were in recovery mode, rebuilding our lives as one would do after a long illness. We cleaned the Kelenhegyi house from top to bottom and then started on the exterior grounds.

Father had to rebuild the office wall that had been destroyed by a grenade blast. One reason the Kelenhegyi house did not sustain more damage was that the massive pillars that surrounded the property below us shielded us from the trajectory of artillery fire. Those stone columns took the brunt of the assault and were now piles of rubble. When he rebuilt the wall, he mortared in two metal shell casings into the wall. Those shells are still there today.

Summer faded into autumn and I returned to school. Then one fall day, a ragged, emaciated man appeared at our door looking for Klára-*néni*. He had just been released from a gulag prison camp in Foksany, Romania. His good friend at the camp was Laci-*bacsi*. This in itself was good news because Laci was not in Russia. Those taken to Russia remained there for years, or never returned.

The man had other good news to share. The day he left the camp, Laci was still alive. Many of the prisoners died, mostly from dysentery. Laci remained healthier than most. This was due, in part, to the excellent shape he had been in when he was taken prisoner. But also, because he never smoked, he was able to trade his ration of cigarettes for food. To lift spirits and pass the idle time, this man and Laci had organized a theater group. Being the one with the handsome face, Laci often played the woman's part in the play. He played his parts with great humor. He distracted others from their constant preoccupation with their misery. He had a wonderful attitude and this worked in his favor. Even the guards enjoyed the performances. The man assured Klára-*néni* that her husband found ways to survive the hardship and that he would return to her one day.

Klára-*néni*, who had believed that her husband had long before died, was speechless. She dumbfoundedly stared back at this man, who kindly smiled at her and quietly departed. Several weeks later, Klára-*néni's* bearded and unrecognizably emaciated husband returned to the Kelenhegyi house.

In sharp contrast to Poland, Romania, and Bulgaria, where he immediately installed communist governments, Joseph Stalin strategically established a semblance of parliamentary democracy in Hungary. To appease the West, the Provisional Government was comprised of the same political parties democratically elected just before Hitler took over the country, including the Small Holders, the Social Democrats, and National Peasants. He called Hungary his "Polish trade-off." A broadly represented government flourished.

His only caveat was to insert two "Muscovite" communists. These Muscovites were Hungarian communists in exile who had lived in Moscow since Hungary's failed 1919 Soviet revolution. They had successfully navigated Moscow's treacherously unstable political environment in which established politicians suddenly fell out of Stalin's favor and were purged overnight. Béla Kun, the leader of Hungary's 1919 revolution, was one of those unlucky ones who fell victim to the purges. Accused of being a Trotskyite, he was executed at the Kommunarka firing range.

Despite the tremendous recovery that still lay ahead, there was optimism and hope that strong leadership and a true interest in the common good would prevail. In November 1945, Hungary held its first post-war national elections. The Communist Party (HCP) called for this election believing it would win by a large majority and thus be positioned to legitimately control Hungarian politics. But the greatly disappointed communists ended up only garnering 17% of the vote. The population remained anti-Soviet and skeptical of HCP motives. The Smallholders Party received 57%, Social Democrats 17%, and the National Peasant Party 7%. Zoltán Tildy, leader of the Smallholders party replaced Béla Miklós as prime minister.

The Soviet-controlled Allied Control Commission, which still maintained oversight over Hungary, accepted the results under the condition that the Muscovite and General Secretary of the HCP, Mátyás Rákosi, be named deputy prime minister. The year of 1945, which had started during the peak of the siege, ended on a promising note with the overall acceptance of the new government. The minor inroads made by the Communist Party were little cause for concern. However, we should have been more worried about Mátyás Rákosi.

23

The Rise of Soviet Hungary

Short, fat, and bald, a disproportionately large head, no neck, hunched shoulders, and a pallid bloated face, Mátyás Rákosi lacked the looks of a leader. But his looks belied his clever rise to power. When he was twelve, his father, a Jewish grocer, *magyarized* their family name from Rosenfeld to Rákosi. A precocious learner, he was sent to the elite Budapest Oriental Academy and would eventually learn to fluently speak eight languages. Serving in the Hungarian Army during WWI, he was captured on the Eastern Front. During his several years in a Russian prisoner of war camp, he came to embrace communist ideology.

Rákosi commanded the Red Guard during the 134-day, 1919 Hungarian Soviet Republic. When that collapsed, he fled to Moscow. In 1934, Stalin sent him back to Hungary to reestablish the Hungarian Communist Party (HCP). He was arrested in 1937 and sentenced to life in prison. In 1940, Stalin negotiated Rákosi's release in exchange for the return of highly-prized historic Hungarian flags stolen by the Russians when they crushed the 1848 Hungarian Revolution.

Like any surviving Muscovite, his loyalties were aligned with Joseph Stalin and the Party, not with the Hungarian people. From the start, he emerged as the leader of Muscovites and held firm control over the HCP. He was a pillar of Bolshevik rectitude with no exploitable personal vices. He cleverly used people of all capabilities in fulfillment of Sovietization. He was eloquent, charming, witty, and had a phenomenal memory. He outmaneuvered, confused, and divided his enemies to achieve his objectives. He would become the most hated man in Hungary.

Realizing that the Party would never win the popular vote, he started to implement what he, himself, coined "salami tactics." As if he were cutting thin slices off a log of salami, he methodically eliminated opposition to communist rule. In March 1946, he united the Communist, Social Democrat, and National Peasant parties to form a "left block" coalition. This block organized demonstrations and attacked the reputations of deputies from the right-wing Smallholders Party. Using blackmail and false accusations, they forced the Smallholders Party to expel 23 of its most courageous and outspoken leaders. However, Rákosi's most effective tool for eliminating opposition was the establishment of the secret police.

Rákosi relied on members of his own clique for active leadership positions, never willingly surrendering one iota of control to a "local" communist. But he made a notable exception to his rule in March, when he replaced a Muscovite with László Rajk as Minister of the Interior. A man of comparable ability and determination,

Rajk became one of the few non-Muscovites to be assigned a significant government position.

Rajk had never lived in Russia. He was the product of the communist influence on Budapest college students. A former student leader and veteran of the Spanish Civil War (1936-39), he led a small communist cell that existed in Hungary throughout the siege. Leveraging his considerable charm, he assembled a notable following consisting mostly of fellow students from Eötvös College. He was popular with a wide faction of national communists ranging from extreme left-wing industrial workers to former Arrow Cross members who admired that he was notably a non-Jewish Party leader. He also inspired the admiration of youth and intellectuals who had taken part in the resistance.

Rajk nearly lost his life in the last month of the siege. In December of 1944, the Arrow Cross captured and sent him to the Sopronkőhida prison to await his execution. Rajk's brother, Endre Rajk, who was a Fascist Party under-secretary at the time, was able to postpone his brother's execution until the end of the war. Released in May of 1945, László Rajk returned to Hungary and immediately returned to politics. He soon returned his brother's favor by securing Endre's release from the communists who had rounded him up for having been an Arrow Cross Party member. Rajk was an outsider who was eager to prove his value to the Muscovites insiders controlling the Party.

To non-communists, Rajk was an anathema. He was unscrupulous in his efforts to intimidate any real or perceived enemies of the HCP. Rajk established the secret police, the

Államvédelmi Hatóság (ÁVH), State Protection Authority.[34] Rajk tagged another ambitious non-Muscovite, Gábor Péter, to lead the ÁVH.

Péter was a short man with rodent eyes and a neat, trimmed mustache. Born as Benjámin Eisenberger in Újfehértó, Péter quit working as an apprentice in his father's tailor shop to serve as an NKVD (People's Commission for Internal Affairs) agent. Once and always a tailor at heart, he invariably wore impeccable suits and silk ties. In 1945, he served in the Hungarian Provisional Government's Secret Police where he proved to be cruelly effective in rounding up enemies of the state. He carried this culture into the ÁVH, in which political "reliability" took precedence over training or professionalism. Péter rehired the same thugs who had worked for the former Fascist Arrow Cross Party. These unprofessional, undereducated, and brutish careerists rose quickly to high positions. The ÁVH operated without civil or parliamentary control. Sentences were suspended for criminals who agreed to become informers.

He was a heavy drinker and had a string of mistresses. In 1931, he had a love affair with the Austrian communist Litzi Friedmann, who later became the wife of the famous Soviet spy in Britain, Kim Philby, of the Cambridge Five. He later had an unconventional and scandalous marriage to the beautiful, but terrifying, Jolán Simon, who was both a KGB agent and Rákosi's personal secretary. They lived a decadent life of luxury, surrounded by servants in their Rózsadomb (Hill of Roses) villa with its sweeping view of the Danube and city below.

---

[34] Originally called the Hungarian State Police Protection Department (Államvédelmi Osztaly - ÁVO), but renamed ÁVH in September of 1948. In this story I will only refer to them as the ÁVH.

The ÁVH moved into the same–already publicly feared–building at 60 Andrassy Boulevard (later renamed Stalin Boulevard). This was the same building used by the fascist Arrow Cross Party as its prison and interrogation facility. The elegant facade looked as innocuous as the other buildings that faced the Boulevard. Black-curtained Poboda sedans never pulled up in front. They always decamped at the side street entrance off Csengory *utca* where a machine gun tower, manned 24-hours a day, watched prisoners being led into the expanded basement full of dank holding cells and torture rooms.[35] Arbitrarily arrested captives were shut into dirty, lice-infested cellar blocks for days without food or water only to be dragged out for torture and interrogation. An endless parade of politicians, professors, writers, businessmen, religious leaders, and even loyal communists were subjected to whips, truncheons, nail presses, alternating boiling and freezing baths, electrodes, and drugs. Eventually, even the innocent pleaded guilty. Those that didn't survive the torture were placed in the *lefolyo*, an acid bath that dissolved their remains, which were then flushed into the sewers.

A rapidly expanding cadre of ÁVH officers fanned out throughout the country. Their surveillance system blanketed every aspect of public and private life. Their informant network was twice the size of their officer staff. This nationwide organization of social controllers reported on happenings everywhere from Budapest down to small villages and neighborhoods. Both apartment janitors and tenants recorded the comings and goings, activities, and conversations of the other tenants. Twenty-seven thousand "peace committee" members

---

[35] It was later converted to a museum named the "House of Torture."

spied on farms, factories, schools, offices, restaurants...
everywhere. We lived in constant fear that any conversation we
had might have been spied upon.

All of the information gained from eavesdropping was fed back
to the ÁVH who subsequently made arrests from which there was
no appeal. At its inception, the ÁVH primarily arrested outspoken
anti-communists and Nazi collaborators. Many of the 40,000 who
had been accused by 1948, had legitimately been supporters of the
Arrow Cross movement. But the rapidly expanding and
unchecked ÁVH had an insatiable appetite. It hunted out anyone
who even vaguely threatened Party rule.

Rákosi became ever more brazen in his implementation of
"salami tactics" to marginalize opposition. Non-communist
politicians were discredited as "anti-democratic," removed from
government, or jailed on trumped-up charges. He was infinitely
cruel and fascinated by terror. He was careful never to get blood
on his own hands, but loved to hear grim details recounted by his
thugs.

Top politicians began to fall as popular leaders of opposing
political parties were inevitably key targets. Former Prime
Minister István Bethlen, who was an outspoken conservative and
anti-fascist, disappeared into a Gulag prison. Béla Miklós, Horthy's
popular former commanding general and the first prime minister
of the post-war provisional government, tried in vain to stay
engaged in politics. He was elected to parliament as a
representative of the Hungarian Independence Party. But due to
his broad popularity, the ÁVH harassed him and his family. They
forced his son to resettle. Realizing he could not overcome the
pressure, Miklós retired from politics. When he died, the
government denied the General the customary military funeral
honors. The secret police also forced Prime Minister Ferenc Nagy

into exile. His replacement, Dinnyés Lajos, served as the last non-communist prime minister of Hungary, until he too was purged. The intimidation inflicted by the ÁVH was unbearable. Even my innocent family and friends got caught up in these politically driven purges.

East and West political rhetoric inflamed Cold War tensions. On February 9, 1946, Stalin gave a speech to the Soviet Congress in which he implied that East-West conflict was inevitable. "The unevenness of development of the capitalist countries could lead to violent disturbance." War was inevitable as long as capitalism existed. Supreme Court Justice William Douglas called Stalin's speech the declaration of World War III. Winston Churchill made his prescient "Sinews of Peace" speech in which he said "from Stettin in the Baltic to Trieste in the Adriatic an *iron curtain* has descended across the Continent. Behind that line lie all the capitals of the ancient states of Central and Eastern Europe. Warsaw, Berlin, Prague, Vienna, Budapest, Belgrade, Bucharest and Sofia; all these famous cities and the populations around them lie in what I must call the Soviet sphere, and all are subject, in one form or another, not only to Soviet influence but to a very high... measure of control from Moscow."

In 1947, the *Szabadság* (Liberty Statue) was unveiled atop Gellért Hill. It instantly became a prominent landmark. It portrays a woman with her arms raised to the sky holding an outstretched palm leaf. The statue towers over the city and is visible from any point on the Pest side. On the statue pedestal, a placard reads "To the memory of the liberating Soviet heroes [erected by] the grateful Hungarian people." Adjacent and below the woman is another statue of a Red Army soldier. This Liberty Statue was unveiled just as we were realizing that not only had the Soviets taken our civil liberties, they also were destroying our livelihoods.

Enormous sums of money went to western allies, but a pittance went to communist block countries. When the U.S. Congress passed its heavily debated July 1946, $3.75 billion American Treasury loan to Britain, congressional leaders justified it as a declaration of the "*Cold War*." The world was half free and half communist. Speaker of the House Sam Rayburn argued that the United States must support its longtime ally in Britain, since the bipolar division of the world was inevitable: "I do not want Western Europe, England, and all the rest of Europe pushed toward an ideology that I despise...." In 1947, in response to attempted Soviet-backed communist rebellions in Greece and Turkey, America's Truman Doctrine provided military assistance to any country in which an armed minority or foreign power was trying to take power. A year later, the Marshall Plan provided economic aid to help countries recover from the war before those countries collapsed and became easy targets for Sovietization.

In contrast to the West, the Soviets cut corners wherever they could. Their lack of investment drove Hungary into insolvency. The opening of Kossuth Bridge, the first permanent postwar bridge across the Danube, was a major Soviet propaganda event. They touted its early completion, the culmination of seven months of twenty-four hour non-stop construction. But it was so poorly constructed that its bearing capacity had to be limited from its opening day. Bigger buses were not permitted to cross. Vehicles were required to maintain a speed of less than six miles/hour and a

65 foot safety gap. It turned out that the bridge had been built out of recycled war debris; it started to fall apart soon after it opened. It was condemned and demolished by 1957. Most bridges stand for a hundred years or more. This one lasted one decade.

The biggest post-war economic issue, however, was the insanely rampant inflation of Hungary's currency, the Pengő. Prices spiraled up out of reach as the Pengő underwent the highest rate of hyperinflation ever recorded. New currencies kept getting introduced with ever higher denominations. Milpengő. Bilpengő. A trillion Pengő! To help people keep such large numbers straight, each new denomination was printed in a different color. By the summer of 1946, Hungary's hyperinflation peaked at 42 quadrillion percent a month.

The neglected retired elderly were most dramatically impacted by hyperinflation. No longer engaged in the economy, they helplessly watched as their life's savings withered away like desiccated flowers. Nagypapa was one of those who lost the fortune he had so diligently spent his life accumulating. He had no earnings or wages that kept apace with skyrocketing prices.

While Father frequently traveled out to buy food before it became unaffordable, Nagypapa could not spend his money fast enough. Each day he paid ten times more than he would have paid the day before. The balances of his bank accounts evaporated into thin air. By August 1, 1946, when the Forint replaced the Pengő at a rate of 400,000,000,000,000,000,000,000,000,000 (400 octillion = 4×10^{29}) to one, Nagypapa was as poor as the rest of us. At least he still retained the Kelenhegyi house. But the communist government would soon expropriate that as well.

24

Illona Jaszai, 1947

Returning to my routines at St. Margit Girls *Gimnazium* on Villányi Street, I eagerly jumped back into my studies and continued to excel. Before the war, our maid would do the ironing. Now my mother rose early every morning to iron my white blouse and navy blue school skirt. The cheap hand-me-down skirt lost its pleats whenever I sat down. We no longer had any domestic help. We had no money. Father was always looking for work and even had resorted to selling Mother's jewelry for food.

Every morning we were required to attend mass in the school's chapel. Stuck in the church pews, my mind wandered in all sorts of directions. Why did my strict homeroom teacher Sister Donatila become a nun? Had there been a love affair that went wrong? She was dour and humorless all four years I attended that school. What made her that way? That led me to think about my own parents' relationship. What kept their bond so strong? Men and women. I had lots of time to ponder these questions.

I was very religious and strongly believed in the supreme power of God. God did send Jesus down to remind us that we needed to treat each other with kindness and compassion. Jesus's message sounded a lot like the advice Father gave me, but Father rarely went to church. He insisted that I attend and always quizzed me afterwards about the underlying message of the priest's sermon. He seemed most interested when the sermons spoke of sacrifice, such as John 15:13 *"Greater love has no one than this, that someone lay down his life for his friends."* Wasn't this the underlying story of Jesus Christ?

My after school routine also remained the same. My girlfriends still rarely ever came to the Kelenhegyi house. I cherished the part of the walk we made together. But there was always that point where I found myself walking up the hill alone. One day, returning home from school, I ran into my godfather, Jenő Prettenhofer, who was also on his way to the Kelenhegyi house. He handed me a small candy, kissed my cheek, and we engaged in small talk as we trekked up the hill. However, as soon he got to the house, he and my father disappeared into Father's office for a clearly heated discussion. I did not know it at the time but my godfather was in serious trouble.

Prettenhofer had once saved Father's life by carrying his flu-weakened body to the hospital at that Italian prisoner of war camp during WWI. They had been best of friends ever since. Written over a photo depicting the two of them in military uniform was the word *csalad* (family). I suspect that one reason he and my father were so close was that they were ideologically aligned. Having survived together the horrors of WWI, they both were pacifists. They opposed Nazi rule but were not inclined to take up arms against them.

Prettenhofer was a hard-working metallurgical engineer who had worked his way up to become the director of the Győr steel mill. The Nazis took control of the factory during the war and redirected its output toward the war effort. He could have resigned his position in protest, but jobs were hard to find. He stayed on, and kept a low profile. Because of his position at the factory, he walked a delicate line. The Nazis were paranoid about subversives who might attempt to disrupt factory production. Like so many people caught in this superpower chess game, he tactfully avoided talk of politics and survived the Nazi ordeal. He kept his nose to the grindstone, and performed his job as any competent technician would.

Ironically, avoiding conflict with the Nazis made him appear disloyal to the Soviet cause. Because his factory made armaments for the German war machine, Prettenhofer was implicated in being part of an underground collaboration against the Hungarian communist government. Just when it seemed that he had safely navigated his delicate wartime predicament, the ÁVH went after him.

He had given me no indication on that sunny May afternoon as we walked up the hill, that he had fled his office at the Győr factory and was on the lam. He stayed with us for several days. Both he and Father were visibly agitated. They spent most of their time locked away in Father's office engaged in deep discussion. Prettenhofer's predicament became my father's.

One of those mornings, while the two men were once again locked behind closed doors in Father's office, Mother began to have terrible stomach pains. She was fully aware of Prettenhofer's plight and, thus, chose not to interrupt their meeting. The intensity of her pain increased. By the time Jenő and my father emerged, she was deliriously shaking from stomach pains. We could not tell at the time, but she was bleeding heavily internally.

Father rushed down the hill and hailed a taxi. By the time he got his pale wife to the Rokus Hospital in Pest, she was fading in and out of consciousness. The doctors immediately brought her into surgery and determined that she was suffering from an ectopic pregnancy. This is when an egg attaches to the fallopian tube rather than the uterus. The embryo grows into a mass that often kills the mother. The only way to save her would have been to immediately conduct abdominal surgery. But they did not operate They could not because the hospital did not have her blood type.

From atomic science to medicine, Hungary has been a fount of scientific discovery. A Hungarian discovered blood typing at the turn of the century. But scientific knowledge has little benefit during the devastating deprivations of war. The siege had already ended two years ago. We had already counted our blessings for having survived. But the siege continued to steal away victims long after the fighting had ended. In addition to the hundreds of thousands killed, Budapest was left with innumerable casualties and an unsupportable demand for blood. The apologetic doctors could do nothing but help to ease her pain. My father desperately raced around town visiting hospitals and clinics in a futile search for her blood type.

Everyone back at the Kelenhegyi house was engaged in agitated and helpless discussion about Mother's state. From my aunts, I came to understand that the doctor advised Mother and Father that another pregnancy would put her at extreme risk and that that they should not have any more children. Armed with this new information, I was able to visit my mother once at the hospital before she died.

"Why did you let father do this to you?" I angrily asked, referring to her pregnancy.

She stared deeply into my eyes with a look that told me she fully understood my feelings. After a moment, she responded, "Imagine that you are holding a pitcher of water in your hand and a thirsty man asks you for a drink. It is with such joy that you share that water. So it is with love for a man."

It was hard to comprehend that she was gone. It all happened so fast. In the months before my mother's death, I had been totally absorbed in my own self-centered teenage rebellion. I still feel shame and regret when I admit that I had not been on the greatest of terms with her. I can't even recall any specific root of our conflict. There was so much that I needed to learn from her. But at that stage of my life, I had not been ready and willing to listen. Suddenly, she was gone. Though I would miss her tremendously, I quickly leveraged my anger at Father to build a protective wall around my emotions, blocking out thoughts of her. She faded from my memories much too fast.

I couldn't see the pain Father felt. Rather than feeling pity for him, I felt sorry for myself. I forgot about their strong, deep love, their profound connection, and their bond built around their love for their children. Forgot about the societal gaps that they bridged in order to be together. Forgot that she visited his dreams at the Eastern Front and warned him to flee the church. Forgot that they had already shared the tragic loss of their eldest child. I didn't think about how the loss of both his son and his wife must have trampled his spirit.

My aunts also showed him no sympathy. They chose to blame him for Mother's death. Logically, we all may have known that he was not to blame. How could he have done anything differently? It was so unexpected and sudden. But it was easier to hate him.

They were openly and deliberately cold and distant. The atmosphere at the Kelenhegyi house was never the same for Father. It didn't matter that he was clearly devastated by her death. My aunts were united and unrelenting in their frosty neglect.

Father was terribly lonely and needed someone to console him, but lacked the luxury of time to wallow in his self-pity. Being a typical man of his era, he had no experience in the kitchen. He struggled to shop, cook, clean, feed, and care for three young children while still looking for work in the postwar recession. He once tried to cook us cream of wheat, but had no milk and added way too much sugar.

My aunts, who continued to blame Father for Mother's death, found many subtle ways to remind us that we were pariahs. They refused to share their food with us. I remember this vividly because one evening stands out, when Gizella-*néni* relented and invited us children to dinner. But even that dinner was only canned tomato soup. I also felt alienated, but for my father, it must have been much worse.

Though they successfully excommunicated us, my aunts didn't have the authority to physically expel us from the house. Nagypapa was still the patriarch of the family and the only one who could ask that we leave. This he never did. He was the only person who expressed compassion for our situation. Despite losing his daughter, he remained a good friend to my father. I imagine that was the primary reason why we still resided at the house. But Nagypapa could offer little help. He no longer employed the extensive domestic support that existed before the war. Our great household patriarch was now in his late 70s, aging rapidly, and as penniless as the rest of us.

I was the oldest living child–almost fourteen years old–but I was ill-equipped to help my father. The lifestyle I had grown up in taught me little about self-sufficiency. I never learned to cook. If I had, it wouldn't have been my mother who taught me. Rather, I would have had to reach out to one of our live-in maids. And I wasn't interested in learning a maid's job. I was equally ill-equipped to shop–another task delegated to the hired help. The one way in which I did help was to baby-sit for my nine year-old little sister, Ilonka.

My father's sisters came from Rezi to help. Each sister took a turn staying with us. But they also found it hard to manage the household. They were now old and accustomed to their simple routines and a slow village pace. The complexities of Budapest overwhelmed them. They lacked the health and physical stamina to haul groceries and household necessities back up the steep Gellért Hill and to cook and care for three needy children. Father greatly appreciated their valiant efforts to help, but he saw their exhaustion. He knew this was an unsustainable situation. His sisters knew it as well. They proposed that we all move to Rezi. But the tiny Rezi house was already crowded with just the three spinsters. Besides, my father would have found it nearly impossible to find work in that tiny village. We had to find another solution.

My Mother, 1919

25

Emilia Csukly, 1947

I n late October, an old army friend invited my father to attend the Tata *Szüreti Mulatság* (annual grape picking festival). In the four months since Mother died, Father had done nothing but work and care for us. Even now, he was reluctant to take a break, but his good friend insisted that a short reprieve in the beautiful historic town of Tata with its forested hills and abundant springs would be best for all of us.

Miklós Kovats would be remembered as a modern day martyr who gave his life to protect the lives of other Tata townspeople. In the years leading up to the Second World War, he supervised the maintenance of the exquisite Eszterházy English gardens that surrounded Lake Tata, with its 600-year-old castle rising majestically upon a rock outcropping jutting into the shoreline. Next to the castle stood the Eszterházy Palace which had served as a popular retreat for Hungarian royalty for over five-hundred summers. Generations of heirs of this most affluent of Hungarian aristocratic families added their own touches to this Baroque summer palace. Its walls were covered with paintings from Europe's renowned artists, including works by Leonardo da Vinci. A castle theater, added in 1888, hosted divas from Budapest and Vienna. A stunning horse racetrack featured the world's first automated starting gate. But for the masses, these renowned surrounding gardens built around a series of natural springs and ancient ruins gave the most pleasure.

For a peasant girl like Emilia Csukly to marry a man like Miklós Kovats, it felt like she herself was marrying into royalty. He was such a kind, trusted, and well-respected man. They had two sons, Arisztid Géza, born in 1931 and Miklós, born in 1932. But then the war came and even this idyllic town of Tata experienced its share of tragedy. The Germans used Tata as a strategically significant command post from which to launch Konrad I, one of Germany's last major counter offensives. When that collapsed in March of 1945, the Red Army swept into Tata to seek revenge on the town for having unwittingly supported the Germans.

Red Army soldiers scoured Tata in search of Count Eszterházy. Not only was he suspected of supporting the Nazis, he was also one of the richest men in Hungary. What a perfect communist propaganda coup it would have been to capture the epitome of western opulence and decadence. But despite their efforts to scare information out of the local residents, the Count was nowhere to be found.

However, the Soviets did capture a few Hungarian soldiers who had been hiding in the Eszterházy stables. So they arrested the Count's grounds superintendent, who had loyally stayed on to keep watch over the estate. First reported as missing, Miklós Kovats was later found floating in the lake with a bullet hole in his head. Killed for harboring a few innocent, frightened men.

This was the story that Emilia Csukly, the widow of Miklós Kovats, related to Father on that lovely warm Indian Summer day in 1947 at Pista Pluha's *szüret* in Baj located three miles from the center of town. She also explained that she continued to maintain her husband's vineyard just down the road. Her teenage sons, Arisztid and Miklós, ran around with friends snatching sips of wine and teasing the girls. Enhanced by the stunning scenery, the joyous ambiance, and an abundance of food and wine, the two recently widowed parents instantly connected.

While my father deeply loved my mother, there was always an underlying tension in their relationship stemming from her upbringing as a rich, sheltered, city girl, and his coming from a poor family. Their mutual love was strong enough to bridge these two worlds. But when she died, he was quickly reminded that he did not belong in her world. It must have been so different meeting Emilia. She came from a similar upbringing. It was so easy to talk with her, to open up, to be himself. They both were lonely, struggling to raise their children with limited support from others. It must have rekindled his spirit to have a woman speak so kindly to him after the hostility he had endured for the past four months. Already 49 years old, he must not have expected to find a new partner. Especially with three young children, no permanent employment, and frightfully little money to his name.

After that trip to Tata, Father was smitten with Emilia. Returning to Budapest, he immediately wrote telling her that she had rekindled in him emotions that he thought were permanently buried with my mother. His longing for Emilia was physical as well as emotional. Every day, he wrote another letter, in which he expressed his newly rekindled passion. He intimately described his longing in language that surprised me when I read the saved letters many years later. He implored her to come to Budapest. To come meet his darling children. He suggested they could live for a while together in the Kelenhegyi house. With great hesitation, Emi finally came to visit my father in Budapest. Her visit was a disaster.

First, the "darling" children that Father had described to her failed to warmly embrace her. I was not ready for my father to be happy again. I thought that it was too soon after my mother's death for my father to be with another woman. It was not a respectable way to behave.

Second, my aunts made it clear that she would not be a welcome addition to the household. Gizella-*néni* wanted Father to marry her friend whose jewelry box father had buried in our yard. This woman continued to make advances on Father even though he bluntly told my aunts "I would not marry her if she were the last woman on earth."

Third, Emi was not a city girl. She felt much more comfortable among gardens, orchards, and vineyards. Discouraged, she returned to Tata. She made it clear that she would not return to Budapest. But father continued his relentless letter-writing campaign. He could not live without her. He could wait no longer. By New Years, he opted to move to Tata and quickly married Emilia Csukly.

However, it was not so easy to move the family to Tata. In addition to the logistics of leaving the Kelenhegyi house, he also had to deal with a reluctant child—me. How could he get me to be a bit more enthusiastic about the idea? He begged assistance from my school principal who sat me down and tried to make me understand that the decision had been made, and that I ought to make the best of the situation. Father agreed to wait until my school year ended before the entire family would move in with our new step-mother and her sons in Tata. I finally relented, but still Father's plans did not play out as envisioned.

In February, an ÁVH officer and several secret police henchmen showed up at our Kelenhegyi apartment.

"My condolences regarding the untimely death of your wife," said the nasally officer. He was delicately boned, while the brutes who accompanied him clearly provided the muscle.

"Thank you for your sympathy," Father replied.

"Oh, I almost forgot to mention," the officer interjected with feigned insignificance. "We have captured Jenő Prettenhofer."

"Oh?" Father asked, not quite sure how to respond.

"Yes. Poor man. His execution is already scheduled. Imagine, leaving such a lovely wife and those two children alone. Such a pity."

"Yes it is." Father agreed trying to conceal his rising heart rate.

"And that bring us to today's business. You see, we also know that you harbored him when he was a fugitive."

"I most certainly did not," Father lied as he tried to confidently look the officer in the eyes.

"Oh that's good for you," The officer replied with a thoughtful pause. "But you see, when we were hunting for Jenő, we thoroughly searched his brother's apartment. And what did we find? A letter written by Jenő while he was on the run. We know that because Jenő dated his letter."

The ÁVH officer paused, pulled out a handkerchief to wipe a sniffle, and then continued. "There was something very peculiar about this letter. It was a typewritten letter. Normally, that would make it very difficult to trace. However, the typewriter used to compose this letter had a slightly bent letter "T" key. Every time that letter was used, it printed out slightly askew."

He paused again at looked silently at Father whose face was beginning to redden. "You wouldn't mind if we examine your typewriter, would you?"

That very same day, the ÁVH imprisoned Father in the infamous dank cellars of 60 Andrassy Street.

26

Tata, 1948

Even though Father was still in prison, my aunts were committed to executing the plan for us to leave the Kelenhegyi house. In June of 1948, after completing my fourth year under the nuns at the Catholic school, they escorted Ilonka, Béla, and me to the Kelenföld Train station and put us on a train bound for Tata. Without adult supervision, we sat amongst our luggage and nervously watched the city pass into the distance. Emi-mama, driving a horse and buggy, met us at the Tata station. We silently rode to meet the rest of the family, with whom we would now share her tiny apartment on Varalja *utca* 2.

I quickly realized that Emi-mama was a good woman for Father, and for us children as well. She proved to be a pillar of strength. She taught me practical skills needed for daily survival in our new environment. She was fair, kind, and treated us as equals to her own sons. However, she was emotionally reserved and not outwardly affectionate.

That emotional gap was filled by Nagyi, Emi-mama's mother. Nagyi was outgoing. She embraced us with love, hugs, and kisses. She filled the motherly gap we children badly needed at that point in our lives. Nagyi, who had grown up in Germany, still had a strong accent. She was the primary cook for the household and tried to teach me, though I remained uninterested. She was the person whom I sought out when I needed someone to talk to. She quickly became my favorite. We became instant friends, and remained close until her last breath.

One day, I was riding bicycles with my friends heading out toward the vineyard when I collided with one of the boys. The bike went down. My buttocks skidded hard on the rough dirt and sustained a large bloody scrape the size of an open hand. Being a young teenage girl, I felt unnecessarily embarrassed and didn't want to draw any additional attention. I chose not to tell anyone about my wound, except Nagyi. She cleaned it, put antiseptic powder on it, and checked it daily until it fully healed. In those days, we girls only wore skirts, which was fortunate because a loose skirt never irritated the wound and it healed nicely. She was the kind of person who knew how to nurture and coddle me when I most needed it. I trusted her with my secrets. I still feel the warm glow of her love when I think about Nagyi.

It took a little longer to get used to my new brothers. When I first arrived they both decided to harass me by silently staring at me. I refused to be unnerved by their little game and stared back at them until they tired of the silly game. Neither boy was ever outwardly mean to me, but I sensed that they were not interested in having the sort of relationship I had had with Laci. My new older brothers would not become my best friends. Ari was only two years older and Miki only one year older. Our friendships developed slowly.

Ari is short for Arisztid–a name meaning "best." A Christian name commonly used by Hungarian nobility. He was outgoing and athletic. He was a strong swimmer and also the springboard diver for the team. Once when doing an inward dive, his head collided with the board. For the rest of his life, he was left with a scar on his forehead in the shape of the letter "A." At least the scar matched his name. However, soon after the accident, Ari decided to go by his middle name, Géza. Having a name implying nobility was a major disadvantage during the communist era. I tauntingly continued to call him Ari until, years later, he went back to that name.

Ari was a wild boy. He frequently got into trouble at school. Exasperated, Emi-mama sent him to stay with his uncle in Pannonhalma. As a result, Ari and I lived together, in total, for less than one year. I didn't really get to know him well until he came to visit Ricsi and me in America many years later. From that point forward, we remained extremely close. Ricsi and I tried to spend time with him and his wife Zsuzsi whenever we returned to Hungary.

Like his brother, Miki was handsome and athletic. He was popular and sought after by the girls of Tata. But unlike his brother, Miki was not vivacious. He was indecisive, quiet, and introverted. Even though we spent more time together, his detached nature made it harder to feel close to him. Miki was also better at staying out of trouble. One notable exception was the time he brought home a pheasant and proudly presented it to Emi-mama declaring that he had shot the bird with his BB gun. When Emi-mama started to prepare the bird for dinner, she observed that this bird had been killed by a much larger gun than a BB gun. It turned out that Miki had been hiding a gun. Emi made him fetch the gun at once. When he produced it, she immediately threw it into the water well. That was the only time I recall him getting into any trouble.

Miki and I lived parallel, but separate, lives. Our groups of friends didn't overlap. Though we were both at that hormonal youthful age, neither of us harbored any romantic interest in each other. I know this because we later discussed it. Miki left to study forestry engineering at Sopron– the same subject Father studied and at the same college Father had attended years before.

One funny thing about Miki was that even though we had no blood relation we actually looked like siblings. We had similar color hair and eyes. But it was our prominent noses that fooled everyone. Those who didn't know our family situation always assumed we were born of the same parents. One time, a girlfriend of mine went to Sopron for a college dance and afterwards reported to me that she met my brother, whom she instantly recognized because he looked so much like me.

Those first few years in Tata, my sister Ilonka was very reliant on me. She seemed in need of constant attention and care. With all that she had gone through, caring for her felt like the right thing to do at the time. I did her laundry. We slept together in the same bed. I helped her with homework. Little things like that. I did it unconsciously and had little memory of it. But Ilonka remembered it well and mentioned it later. But it was Ilonka who later became the true caretaker for Father, Emi-mama, her own husband, and her mother-in-law. She emanated a kindness to which young children instinctively gravitated. I realized that this was behavior learned from our birth-mother: Her empathy and her instinctive sacrifice for the welfare of children.

Me in 1948 in Tata

27

Béla Jr., 1948

My little brother Béla had been a cheerful, untroubled child until our mother died. After her death, he became withdrawn. But after we moved to Tata, he seemed to be returning to his jovial self. He quickly became best friends with a boy who lived two houses away. The boy's family operated a funerary services business on the same property on which they lived. Rather than remaining confined in our small crowded apartment, he spent most of his time on their large working compound. The boys rode the elegant black horses that hauled the hearse carriage. They assembled flower arrangements and wreaths. There was abundant activity to entertain two young boys.

Béla was especially fascinated by the masks that the funeral home made for some of the bereaved families. These masks hailed from ancient Carpathian traditions and were believed to represent the borders between life and death. Béla begged and the family consented to make him a death mask. To make this mask, they pressed soft clay over his face and then used that as a mold to create a plaster mask in his likeness. He happily brought it home to show us. I found the mask a bit creepy. A pale white resemblance staring back at me.

This was about the time that we started to notice that Béla's joints were starting to swell. Before we had left Budapest, he had struggled with earaches that never seemed to heal. He quietly sat holding his hands over his ears. But one might have mistaken his silent suffering for withdrawn sadness. We certainly did not consider those earaches as indicative of a much more serious issue. And who would have noticed it anyway? Mother had died. Father was in jail. I was trying to make sense of the transition from a privileged life in Budapest to now living dirt poor in Tata. But it wasn't just my life that seemed to be on a downward spiral. The communist economic model was driving the entire population's standard of living to a common denominator barely above starvation levels. In sum, we were distracted.

Emi-mama struggled to keep the family fed. That first year in Tata, we took advantage of a bumper crop of fruit. I loaded wheelbarrows of apples and flowers to sell at the market. The flowers were a great example of Emi-mama's industrious inventiveness. We didn't own a plot of land ourselves, but she noticed an underutilized garden at the adjacent convent. It was directly outside of our window. To reach the garden, we climbed out through our apartment window onto a ladder placed against the wall. There she grew and harvested beautiful bouquets for market.

Emi-mama insisted that I take piano lessons. She said that a refined child needed to play an instrument. Since she had no money to pay the teacher, she paid for the lessons with fruit.

These piano lessons were fun, but they lasted for only my first eighteen months in Tata. Not long enough to become proficient. Emi-mama also believed that a young woman needed to know how to knit and crochet. She started to teach me, but, fortunately, a much more patient Nagyi took over the knitting instruction.

Emi-mama was also in the late stages of a pregnancy. Because she was naturally pleasantly plump, people did not even notice that she had been pregnant until her last few months. When we learned of the pregnancy, Nagyi led us all in a frenetic campaign to sew (by hand) diapers and baby clothes.

In September, just when he should have been starting back to school, Béla became extremely pallid and weak. Emi-mama took him to the hospital. We learned that he was suffering from leukemia. Within a month, he was admitted to the pediatric ward. It was conveniently located across the street from Béla's friend's family funeral home business. I visited Béla daily. Since we had the same blood type, I twice gave him blood.

Father was still in prison when his last child was born. The birth on November 26, 1948, of Emike, my half sister, was a joyful reprieve from our incessant worries about Béla's health. By this point, his whole body began to swell. I loved to take baby Emi out for walks pushing her in the buggy on the street. But I was self-conscious, worrying that people might think that she was my baby. I thought it would have been shameful for a 16-year-old like me to have a child.

All the while that Father had been in prison, Emi-mama had been on a mission to make skinny Ilonka gain weight. Despite the extra starches and milk Ilonka received, she did not gain weight. She was still notably skinny when Father was finally released from prison. One of the first things he asked Emi-mama when he saw his daughter was "were you not feeding the girl?" Emi-mama would never let Father forget that insensitive moment.

Fortunately, Father was released in time to visit Béla in the hospital. Leukemia is a cancer that suppresses the normal development of white blood cells. A hundred years earlier–in 1848 –the medical profession had already identified and named this disease. The same year that my brother lay dying in the pediatric ward, American doctors were experimenting with the first chemotherapies. But in Hungary at this time, leukemia was an unquestioned death sentence. Father was again just as helpless as he had been when Mother lay dying at the hospital. He could only watch as infections and fungi ravaged and tortured Béla's immunosuppressed body. His only remaining son died four days before the boy's thirteenth Christmas.

28

Church and State Battle over Schools

Despite the recent changes occurring at home, my baby brother's death, our new half-sister Emike, Father's release from prison, I remained excited about starting at the renowned Piarist *Gimnázium* (High School). Originally an all-boys school run by the Catholic monastic Piarist order since its founding by Count Miklós Esterhazy in 1892, girls had only recently been allowed to attend. The school offered one of the best educations in the country. All the Esterhazy heirs attended, as did the children of many noble families. The caliber and prestige of this school was well known throughout Hungary, and I felt lucky that fate had made it possible for me to attend. However, I was sadly disappointed to learn that the Party had taken over control of the school.

Party Chairman Mátyás Rákosi renounced his Judaism and all forms of religion. More than just an ardent atheist, he saw the church as a threat to communist control over the population. He would have loved to completely outlaw the church. However, in this predominantly Catholic country, he had to settle for severe restrictions. And what better place to deprive the church of its ideological pulpit than in the school classrooms?

He attempted to starve the stubborn Church into submission. After the 1945 Agrarian Land Reform Act took away most of the Church's vast land holdings, the Church lost most of the revenue it had used to fund educational institutions. The Party offered to financially support the schools in exchange for full control of the curriculum.

The weaker Protestant churches could not withstand the pressure and agreed to a compromise with communist authorities. The state took over their schools, paid teachers' salaries, and even permitted two hours per week of religious instruction. The rest of the curriculum was completely stripped of religious content. But the Catholic Church stubbornly refused to compromise. Catholic Cardinal Jozsef Minszenty led a quixotic, courageous, ideological battle against the Party's unrelenting pressure, while throughout the rest of society political opposition was withering on the vine.

The conflict between church and state came to a head on December 26, 1948, when the ÁVH arrested Hungarian Cardinal Jozsef Mindszenty on charges of treason, conspiracy, and other offenses against the People's Republic. Anticipating his arrest, the cardinal penned a letter stating that he had not been involved in any conspiracy, and that any future confession he might make would be done under the duress of torture. As he predicted, imprisoned Mindszenty did sign a confession after being repeatedly tortured. The government sentenced him to life in prison. It was a dark moment in our history when the Party so brazenly humiliated our country's spiritual leader.

To add insult to injury, the government tore down one of Budapest's most beautiful churches, the *Regnum Marianum* located in Heroes' Square. In its place, they erected a forty foot high statue of Rákosi's "great teacher" Josef Stalin.

When I started high school, the takeover was already underway. The government had disbanded Catholic orders and forced secularization of its schools. In my first few days attending that fall, I learned that most of the Piarist order teachers had been replaced by Party hacks. The new principal, a loyal and ardent communist by the name of Antal Gergely, was short and rotund. He walked with an over-confident swagger and sneering disdain for the educated bourgeois and nobility. Even though I was now as poor as any other student, he labeled me the rich Budapest daughter of an engineer and immediately added me to his "undesirable" list. Gergely repeatedly let us know that he had been schooled in Russia. This was somehow superior to the education that this institution had offered over the past three quarters of a century.

Our classroom fell into an awkward silence when Principal Gergely huffed in and inspected the vast bookshelves containing works collected by the now departed instructors.

"This one must go," he announced holding a book that he unilaterally declared out of alignment with the new ideology. Sadly, this illiterate monster directed the destruction of hundreds of classics.

Some of my classes included senior, final-year, students who had experienced this Piarist *Gimnázium* as the high quality institution it had once been before the communist takeover. Confident that Principal Gergely would not want to hold them back for another year, they brazenly expressed their displeasure in comical battles of wits. When he spotted, hanging on the wall, an artfully framed quote from the Christian-Socialist theologist Ottokar Prohaszka which spoke of an economy based on the "truths of Christ," Principal Gergely once again said that it had to go.

"You better find more appropriate wall decorations for this room," he said as he stared disdainfully at the quote. The next time the principal entered our classroom he found the walls covered with cut-out magazine advertisements promoting everything from toothpaste to women's swimsuits.

Discomposed by the audacity of the students, he briskly sauntered over to a closed book cabinet and pointed. "Where is the key for this cabinet?" he demanded with a disgusted expression.

"It is unlocked, Comrade Principal," one student responded. When the principal opened the cabinet doors, he immediately jumped back in terror. Sitting on the shelf was a hand-grenade.

"What is this?" he cried out. The student calmly walked over and grabbed the inactive grenade and pulled out the pin. "Sir, this is the key to the cabinet."

29

Ricsi comes to Tata, 1949

Blossoming spring flowers lifted our spirits as we tried to put the sorrowful winter of 1948-49 behind us. Father used the proceeds from selling his surveying equipment to purchase a house located at Varalja *utca* 4a directly across the road from the ancient lakeside castle. The house was at least 200 years old. It had been part of the Esterhazy estate and was occupied for years by employees of the Count. This many-roomed house was gloriously spacious in comparison with the apartment we just left. Its plastered earthen walls were so thick that its wide windowsills made for comfortable seating. I often wedged myself into a window and read by the light streaming through the partially opaque glass panes. Such thick walls were also excellent insulation. The house kept cool in the summer. However, in the winter the largest rooms were too big to heat so we closed them off and stayed in the smaller rooms.

The house felt larger in so many ways. There was the large cast iron tub in the bathroom, a large kitchen, an ample pantry, and a wide concrete porch facing the street. It was wide enough that I could still easily pass by the occupied large rectangular dining table where we took our summer afternoon meals.

At that time,[36] we were blessed with an acre of verdant gardens, fruit orchards, a pigpen, chicken coop, and Father's five beehives nestled under the shade of a massive sycamore tree. His bee-keeping equipment was housed in the large shed abutting the side of the house. His honey centrifuge could spin three honeycomb frames at one time. With a special knife he sliced off the ends of the combs, and drew out the most delicious honey. Plenty to both consume and sell. Our raspberry bushes grew into thick thorny clumps. I don't recall ever emerging from a picking session without numerous scratches, but those raspberries were the best I ever tasted. I gorged on the ripest berries as I harvested the rest. We stored our vegetables, fruit, and honey in the perennially cool and dry dirt-floored cellar.

The attic of this old house was full of paper records, books, furniture, and clothes relocated from the Esterhazy palace. These records might have been invaluable for a future historian, but since we couldn't afford to buy paper, my father used the blank backsides to pen his correspondence. We also used the paper and old furniture in our fireplace. From among the attic bric-a-brac, we did find a few treasures. One was a leather-bound Latin dictionary dating back to the sixteenth century that I still have at home. However, the one item that most caught my attention was a beautiful white eyelet-laced dress. What history did this dress

---

[36] Months after the 1956 revolution, the government seized the garden part of the property to build a senior housing complex, leaving the house with only the land between house and street.

hold? Who has last worn it? For what occasion? I tried it on. It fit me with room to spare.

Right around the time Father was released from prison, most private jobs and businesses were eliminated. The government now assigned him a low-status, low-paying office job at the newly constructed metallurgical factory in the recently renamed town of "Sztalinváros," located 43 miles south of Budapest along the Danube. Commuting by rail, he was gone from early morning until late at night.

The Party proudly proclaimed that Hungary would turn into a country of "iron and steel." Now we were burdened by immense investments in industry and extraordinary defense expenditures. This factory was a model of the Soviet drive to increase heavy industry. The problem was that it didn't pencil out. The iron ore and coking needed to make metals were locally unavailable. These were purchased from Russia at outrageous prices. Lacking any local demand for its output, the factory sold its products back to Russia at reduced prices. The government reported increased industrial production. But in reality, Hungary's economy was contracting. When challenged with such statistics, Rákosi responded that the new socialist man could overcome such technical details. Meanwhile, he ordered the erection of the tangible iron curtain, a tangle of barbed wire along the western borders of Hungary.

It feels awkward to say this, but despite Father's post-prison employment struggles, the loss of another brother, and a disappointing first year of school, I felt fortunate to be spending my teenage years in Tata. The whole town felt idyllic and safe–the same way my early years felt within the Kelenhegyi house compound. Only now my world was this beautiful town plus the surrounding countryside. I wrote letters, effusing its merits to my cousins, Margarita and Klára, who loved to leave the city and spend their holidays in wonderful Tata.

I got involved in extracurricular activities including chorus, folk dancing, and gymnastics. Our school, which did not have its own sports facilities, was permitted to use the newly built Olympic Park in Tóváros located nearby at the north of the lake. This allowed us to take part in country-wide tournaments, and greatly increased the fun of participating in a sport. I also tutored a classmate in Latin and math. He was the son of a successful farmer. In exchange for my tutoring, we received half a gallon of good, fresh milk three times a week, something we had done without for several years.

Unlike in Budapest, where I rarely spent time outside of school with friends, I now spent nearly all of my time between classes, on weekends, and after completing summertime home chores, hanging out with my very best friends. Though I always was an extrovert and easily made acquaintances, throughout my life there were very few people I would call close friends. In Tata, I had three best girlfriends: the slightly butch Klára, Gabriella the *nebáncsvirág* (touch-me-not flower) who was so bashful that she blushed when spoken to, and the doctor's daughter Baba. The four of us frequently spent time with a group of four boys. None of these friendships were romantic. The eight of us were an extremely comfortable little group. However, that is not to say that I was not starting to get noticed by the boys.

Though I was ever frustrated with my stiff hair, I had blossomed into a curvaceous teen by this time. One day, several boys came to serenade me as I as sat in the wide windowsill of our old house. My brother, Miki, had warned me that they would be coming. I had prepared little lily-of-the-valley nosegays that I handed out to them through the window. Oh, how my heart fluttered with the excitement of being noticed.

In 2010, I received a book entitled *Mult Idoben* (In The Past). It was Emeritus Professor Andras Vizkelety's memoir. He described his school years in Tata. I found his book such a pleasure to read because he was three years older than me. I knew him and many of his friends. On page 201, he talked about having been an avid folk dancer. He described his dance partner, a sweet girl on whom he had a very big crush. He described how when they danced she held herself in such a way as to be the perfect dance partner. She was pliable and engaged, yet showed no sexual connection. He said she was a great partner and a good friend. "She taught me for later life that a lady can be a good friend and partner without sexual interference." That girl's name was Marika Jaszai. Me! I had no idea how seriously infatuated he had been with me. Reading it sixty years later, I was deeply touched. I immediately wrote and told him that I felt as if I had received a big bouquet of roses from out of the blue.

How different my life would have been had I remained in Budapest. I once visited the Kelenhegyi house and it was no longer the place of my idyllic childhood. Strangers loitered in the degraded gardens. The grand house had been broken up into many small apartments filled with Party loyalists. A truly unpleasant man, Mr. Bognár, now occupied our ground floor apartment.

Besides being an ÁVH informant who spied on everyone living in the Kelenhegyi house, Mr. Bognár was a liar and a thief. He fabricated stories about people in the Kelenhegyi house that got them expelled to the countryside so that his comrades could take over the vacated apartments. He sawed off the metal security bars over one of our windows, declared that he had been robbed of all of his possessions, and claimed reimbursement. Two years later, he pulled the exact same scheme. The second time around, the insurers dug deeper into his extraordinary claim. How did he manage to recover everything he owned in two short years? Also, how was it that the thieves were able to cut the bars from inside the apartment? His ashamed wife committed suicide. For years, Mr Bognar made life terribly unpleasant for my cousins still living in the Kelenhegyi house, until he too died and his daughter sold the apartment.

In its purest form, Communism envisions a better world in which the entire population is uplifted through an equitable distribution of our collective output. But human behavior fails to conform to this underlying altruistic expectation. Individuals tend to pursue their self-interests over the common good. Communist loyalists were some of the greediest people I had ever met.

Secretary General Rákosi had brutally eliminated any challenge to communist rule by the May 1949 elections. In stark contrast with the 1945 elections, these in May were completely rigged. The uncontested Communist Worker's Party won 95% of the vote. The remaining 5% went to representatives of the Smallholders and National Peasants Parties. However, even these other-party candidates were Rákosi stooges. He set the agenda, he rewarded compliance, and his ÁVH henchmen punished those who failed to comply. Unfortunately, he was more interested in protecting the regime than in forwarding national interests.

Having eliminated external threats, Rákosi now started to eliminate perceived threats within his own Party. One-third of the Party was accused of deviating from the Soviet line and purged. The most notable show trial was that for Interior Minister László Rajk, who made the mistake of being too nationalistic. This was the same Rajk who had helped establish and run the ÁVH. Convicted of treason, espionage, and plotting with Yugoslav and Western intelligence agencies to kill the Muscovite leaders in order to overthrow the democratic state order, Rajk was executed as his wife, Julia, listened to it from her own prison cell.

Fellow students and I cautiously shared our shock and repugnance over these Stalinist show trials. How could this country turn on its own communists? Many of the hundreds imprisoned were the same loyal citizens who had risked their lives in the anti-Nazi resistance movements during the war. People who had dedicated their lives to the cause of socialism. Communists who had praised the Soviet Union, praised Stalin, and dutifully supported the Party line no matter how depraved it became. By 1949, an estimated 200,000 victims had been purged. Rákosi's reign of terror was harsher and more extensive than in any of the neighboring Soviet satellite countries. Thousands died. Tens of thousands were imprisoned or taken to slave labor camps. Thousands more were deported or forcibly relocated from their city homes to the countryside.

My girlfriends' and my favorite summertime gathering spot was the famous Továrosi pool, with its warm crystal clear water constantly refreshed from a nearby spring. We would linger after our delightful swim, play countless games of Gin Rummy, and kibitz with the other teens in town who also gathered there. Everyone knew everyone else at the pool. That was why I took special notice of the new boy in town.

Like us, he started to show up every day. I watched him as he swam countless laps. He had a muscular, slender body, a handsome smile, and a quiet air of confidence that made me want to learn more about him. As a group of girls, we finally got up the nerve to approach him.

His name was Ricsi Répásy. He was four years older than us. He explained that his countless lap swimming was an effort to get back in shape for his planned return to the swim team at the University of Debrecen where he studied medicine. He had taken the semester off and was visiting his brother, Pista, a General Surgery Internist at Tata Hospital. His brother was able to get him a menial job at the hospital, and since this pool was so close, he liked to come here to swim and relax after work. Each day, our conversations got a bit longer. He opened up to us and shared more of his life story.

In early childhood, he suffered a severe case of Junior Rheumatoid Arthritis. At the age of six, he spent nearly an entire year bedridden. He had to relearn how to walk. As years passed, he exercised diligently to regain his strength and physique. But he still suffered lingering affects from this childhood disease. One of which was iritis, a fairly rare eye disease, which became inflamed during his second year of medical school. It got so bad that he could not bear being exposed to light. For three months, he was confined to a darkened room. He could not complete the semester. But now, fortunately, he was on the mend and happily enjoyed being back out in the sunshine.

One afternoon at the pool, Ricsi, looking a bit shaken, recounted an incident at the hospital that day. His brother and the only other surgeon working that day had gone out to lunch when some villagers brought in a boy. After diving into Tata Lake, the boy's stomach brushed against a sharp shell on the lake bottom. Ricsi laid the boy on a bed to inspect an 18-inch gash across the boy's abdomen. The boy suddenly coughed. The force of the cough split open the wound and the boy's intestines ballooned out. Ricsi immediately began to stuff the boy's intestines back in as he screamed for an aide to search for a doctor in one of the other buildings. The aide found another doctor. However, by the time they returned, Ricsi was well underway in closing the wound. Watching for a while, the doctor told Ricsi that he was doing a fine job and should finish. Ricsi recounted that this incident was his first real exposure to what a future in medicine would require. He found the experience exhilarating. Luckily, the injured boy was recovering well.

My girlfriends and I were all equally infatuated with this handsome medical student. However, he had politely deferred from demonstrating a preference for any one of us. We decided to force the issue. One afternoon while he swam his laps, we positioned ourselves at the four corners of the pool. Curiously, he watched our antics as he backstroked across the pool. We girls had made a pact: in whosever's corner of the pool he exited, that girl would be given the first right to date. When he emerged in my corner, Ricsi and I began our slow courtship and the next chapter of our lives.

It was customary at the time for a young suitor to be formally introduced to parents of a young woman before further courtship could occur. In Budapest in 1950, such introductions were becoming less common, but outside the capital, in towns like Tata and Debrecen, tradition prevailed. Tata Hospital Surgeon Pista Répásy was of sufficient social stature in the community to introduce his younger brother. Pista entered our house with the confidence and easy social charm of a retired military officer. My father and Emi-mama, were already quite aware of and happy about Ricsi's interest in me, but they dutifully played the role of the overprotective parents reluctant to give up their prized princess.

With introductions out of the way, Ricsi and I freely spent pleasant summer evenings strolling through town getting to know each other. He escorted me out of town to pick up our weekly allotment of milk. Never having been with a man, even the touch of our pinky fingers sent shockwaves through my body. Touches grew into hand-holding and intentional, but extremely appropriate yet heavenly, bodily contact. However, our first kiss was yet to occur.

I always admired intelligence, and Ricsi's was formidable. He was thoughtful, self-deprecating, and light-hearted. But you could tell that his mind was always working on some deep thought. He was extremely well read. It was the silver lining of having to spend

249

much of his childhood bedridden. He easily jumped subjects from art to history to music, and–of coarse–science and medicine. Since he was older, I looked up to him. Hung on his every word. But he was careful not to flaunt his knowledge. He engaged me and probed for my opinions. We agreed that the Party's new high school curriculum was dumbing down the masses. He suggested readings to supplement my education. In addition to the classics, he recommended Aldous Huxley's *Brave New World*, George Orwell's *1984*, and the encyclopedia. I read as much as I could. I loved literature and his mentorship. All too soon, those pleasant summer days came to an end and Ricsi returned to Debrecen to continue his studies. Debrecen was a world away. I wasn't sure if I would see him again. But I was at least thankful for a very enjoyable summer.

30

Back to Prison, 1950

There was a joke going around at that time about the three classes of people that still existed in Hungary: those who have been in prison; those who are in prison; and those who will be in prison.

One fall day in 1950, a fellow prisoner whom Father had befriended while in the ÁVH prison in Budapest, Géza Lőcsei, appeared on our doorstep. Father immediately embraced his young friend with a warm hug and welcomed him to stay with us, which Géza did for about a week. Both Father and Géza had been imprisoned for minor political offenses. They shared a penchant for intellectual discussion and had passed much of their time in captivity together. Father was pleased to hear of Géza's release.

Géza bonded with everyone in the household. Miki, Ari, and I were intrigued by this handsome, educated young man who was so close to our age, yet possessed a worldliness that we lacked. Since father refused to tell us anything about his time in prison, my stepbrothers took Géza aside to grill him about what it was really like. I eagerly wanted to join in on those discussions, but they locked themselves away, and ignored my persistent banging at the door.

He was considerate. He eagerly took on chores for Emi-mama and Nagyi. For two-year-old Emike, he built a swing hung from our large, wild chestnut tree out front. He walked me to school a couple of mornings that week. We took an alternative route I would never have dared to traverse alone, climbing a steep, forested hill. But with him, I enjoyed the adventurous walk. When he finally left us, my father gifted Géza one of his jackets. Cooler days were upon us and the poor man had arrived with only the clothes on his back.

There was a word frequently used in Hungary at that time, *csengőfrász*, which translates as "bell fever." It refers to the terror felt throughout the country that ÁVH officers might come ringing one's doorbell in the middle of the night. As secret police forces often do, the ÁVH goons liked to operate in the dark.

Before dawn on the second day after Géza's departure, our dog's frantic barking woke me. I looked out the window to see what was upsetting him. Dark silhouettes were scaling our fence and approaching the house from various directions. I hurriedly dressed and woke the family. There was heavy knocking at our door. ÁVH officers in their blue uniforms with green epaulettes rushed in and rounded up the household. With the exception of Nagyi who stayed with baby Emike, they escorted the entire family out of the house and on to the street. The last I saw of any other family member was when they made each of us climb into separate vehicles. Obviously, they were taking measures to keep us from being able to confer with one another. The ÁVH took me to the nearest police station, and locked me into an internal stairwell. For hours I sat alone on the cold, bottom concrete stairway step and waited. Every once in a while, a stone-faced officer came in to interrogate me.

"Where is Géza Lőcsei?" he asked.

"I don't know. He was here and then he left," I cried.

"Where is Géza Lőcsei?" he repeated. Again and again, so it went until I lost track of time.

I didn't see the other family members. The police refused to divulge any information regarding their whereabouts. Terrified that the ÁVH might resort to torture to garner information, I honestly told them everything I knew. But I feared that this officer was not believing me. Between interrogations I whimpered in the dimly lit stairwell. Then, it ended as suddenly as it began.

The officer opened the door at the top of the stairs and told me I was free to go home. Bewildered, I walked all the way home. Nagyi related that other ÁVH officers had stayed behind at our Tata house and even detained neighbors who stopped by to buy Emimama's fruit. I later learned that after leaving Tata, Géza had gone to the Kelenhegyi house in Buda. The ÁVH had anticipated this move and had set a trap leading to his capture. Cousins at the house described how one ÁVH officer had banged on the piano left behind in our apartment to drown out the sounds of other officers beating Géza. By evening of that long day, each family member eventually returned home, shaken but unharmed. Except Father.

We assumed Father would imminently also be released. But days and weeks passed without his return. Once again, his kindness had backfired on him. What crazy lesson about karma were the gods trying to teach him? We learned that Géza had not been released from prison. He had escaped. I immediately thought back on my walk to school with him. I had naively given little thought to his calm suggestion that we make our morning walks to school more interesting by finding a forested route that avoided the main boulevard. The ÁVH had known of Father's and Géza's evolving relationship in prison. When he escaped, they immediately went looking for Father. When they recaptured him, Géza was wearing the coat that Father had gifted him. Sewn into the coat was Father's name and address. Once again father was implicated in aiding and abetting a fugitive. The ÁVH kept him in prison for the next six months.[37]

Ours was just one of the many ÁVH dawn raids occurring at that time. Many bourgeois families were deported. But unlike those who emigrated, we were left to survive by sheer will. Those months Father was back in prison were the most difficult times I had yet experienced. That was when I came to truly appreciate the fortitude and ingenuity of Emi-mama.

Since the murder of her first husband, her life had been one of toil and struggle. Father brought romance back into her life, but he also burdened her with caring for five children and her aging mother. Adding to that burden, many neighbors gave our family wide berth. They were too afraid to be implicated by association. My innocent, but twice imprisoned, Father was a pariah. An enemy of the State. Fortunately, there were those who remembered her upstanding first husband Miklós. Her old friends

---

[37] Géza survived in prison until the 1956 revolution when he was released. He escaped to America where he attended medical school and became a doctor. He was one of the fortunate intellectuals to have survived the ÁVH.

respected, and stuck by her. Those who still managed the Esterhazy fisheries occasionally gifted her with fresh fish. To make it last, she preserved the fish, like sardines, in oil. We ate it cold on Fridays.

Much of our food came from our small cornfield, orchard, vineyard, and vegetable garden. When not in school, I tilled, planted, weeded, fed the pig and chickens, and harvested. I recall failing to properly hydrate while working under the hot sun, becoming exhausted, and nearly fainting.

On weekends, each child received one egg, which they could have prepared any way they wanted. I always chose to have mine soft-boiled. But my brothers chose to have their egg scrambled over sautéed peppers and onions. They cleverly got much more of a meal out of the deal.

Emi-mama was so inventive in how she kept our family fed. When we couldn't afford meat, she cleverly concocted a healthy meat substitute, a pate-like paste of yeast and sautéed vegetables, served as a spread on bread. When we had money, we purchased the readily available flour, sugar, bread, and affordable horse meat. Emi-mama was a master at making the horse meat taste like the more expensive pork and beef. Ricsi did not know until much later that he had been served horse meat when we invited him to join us for dinner.

Father was still in prison when Emi-mama decided that it was time to kill the pig that we had fattened on leftover scraps. Miki and Nagyi were tasked with slaughtering the pig. First, they had to lure the wary pig from its enclosure into the kitchen. We were officially not allowed to possess, let alone slaughter, our own pig. We could not afford to have neighbors hear the pig squeal. If they had, we would have been obliged to bribe them off with a *kostolos* (a taste of the pork). Miki recalled that the slaughter was nearly as horrific for him as it was for the pig. That one pig kept us supplied with lard, ham, and smoked sausages through the next winter and spring.

We tried to make money in a multitude of ways. Emi-mama hung a sign out on the front gate that read "Gyöngyfüző (bead maker)." She started to make and sell beautiful bead necklaces from finely sliced oak and walnut seeds. They were terrifically attractive and she actually made a small profit from her efforts. She continued to make this type of jewelry for as long as she was physically able.

I never passed up an opportunity to make money, but never made much. A couple of times that summer, my jovial uncle Feri and his wife passed through Tata on their gypsy-like tour of the countryside selling colorful headscarves and other craft goods at village flea markets. I helped tend their booth and modeled the colorful clothing they tried to sell. My future sister-in-law, Kaca, taught me how to weave beautiful scarves. But there was a very limited market for these. I eventually abandoned the effort in favor of other money-making endeavors.

I was willing to try anything. My good friend Feri, one of the four boys with whom I always hung out, got me a job helping him repair sidewalks for the village. Feri was a constant clown and a pleasure to spend time with. He pushed the heavy wheelbarrow filled with decomposed granite, while I helped shovel the gravel into the holes eroded by the winter rains. We had no other tools, so we simply stamped the gravel down with our shoes, often making the task into a silly song and dance act. Anything to get a laugh. We randomly worked our way around Tata Lake. No one minded where we went or how good of a job we performed. It was a typical communist government job: little productivity and little pay. The school even put us to work. Instead of gym class, we were sent out to work in the fields to turn hay drying in the fields.

Because Stalinist Communism pursued its self-serving objectives through intimidation, it failed to inspire people to act with integrity. This led to unanticipated societal changes. The cultural fabric of doing the right thing–of propriety–faded from mass consciousness. It was replaced by a new moral standard, whose only throttle was the risk of punishment. Children raised in this new environment lived for the moment. Since the government took everything and gave nothing back in return, why not steal it back whenever the opportunity presented itself? Without compunction, people stole from work, school, or any public institution. They also stole from each other. Until you were caught, stealing was condoned.

My strong religious beliefs kept me from stealing. The religion that Rákosi desperately wanted to outlaw, still provided that ever important and needed moral compass in this amoral environment. More Hungarians attended church during this period than they would afterwards when all restrictions on religion were lifted. After moving to America years later, I worried about hosting families immigrating from Hungary. I was always concerned that their children would unhesitatingly steal whatever they saw as desirable.

Emboldened by apparent unwavering support from Stalin, Rákosi was now in the peak of his megalomania. His face was plastered on posters calling him "Stalin's best pupil." He fanatically proved his loyalty by being more Stalinist than Stalin himself. He nationalized and renamed one of Hungary's largest wartime defense contractors, from the Csepel Island Manfred Weiss Steelworks to the *Rákosi Mátyás Vas és Fémművek Nemzeti Vállalat* (Mátyás Rákosi Iron and Metal Works National Company). He renamed one of Budapest's busiest transport hubs, from Széll Kálmán Square to "Moscow" Square. Rákosi also introduced a new Hungarian flag on which over the red, white, and green tricolor stripes a new State coat of arms featuring a red star, hammer, and sickle replaced the old royal coat of arms. It quickly earned the nickname the "Rákosi" coat of arms. The twentieth of August, the traditional Feast of St. Stephen the first king of Hungary, was now "Constitution Day." Christmas Day was now "Pine Tree Day." There was a strong undercurrent of disillusionment with Rákosi, but very few people dared to openly speak out against the government.

Out of all the tragic events that he endured, it was this last stint in prison that finally broke Father's spirit. He was notably adept at compartmentalizing his mind and blocking out memories that could otherwise lead to post-traumatic stress symptoms. He adamantly refused to talk about his time in prison. But he once confessed that the torture was worse his second time at 60 Andrassy Boulevard. While he spared us the worst, he once recalled how he was required to stand with his arms outstretched and was beaten whenever he let them drop.

When he returned home after his second stint in prison, he kept himself busy studying and writing. He tried to recall his school subjects. He studied maps, Latin, and any history he could get his hands on. He spent endless hours clicking away on his typewriter, primarily composing correspondence to friends and family.[38] "He is already so old," I thought. "Why does he keep studying?" I later came to appreciate that exercising his brain kept his mind from wandering where he did not want it to go.

Throughout my childhood, Father had been a paragon of even-temperedness and self-control. But after his prison years, he became quick-tempered. I don't remember him and my mother having fights. But with Emi-mama, the fireworks were occasionally on display. Unlike my mother, who had tended to defuse the situation, Emi-mama would not tolerate his outbursts. She fought back. And usually, she was in the right. She demonstrated the strength needed to keep the family together, while he slowly lost hope.

After his second prison stint, he lost his job in Sztalinvaros. Finding no employment in Tata, he took on small jobs in Budapest. He lived like a pauper. Feeling guilty about taking food away from the family, he only took along some bread and honey or cheese to his work. He spent nothing. When a job ended and he was back home, Emi-mama would try to fatten him back up. These were miserable times.

Mornings when he had no work lined up, Father puttered off on his small motorbike to work in the vineyard. He worked alone. The vineyard was his sanctuary. Its small two-windowed house looked out over a small vegetable garden and apple, pear, plum,

---

[38] I still have a few of his letters typed on the back of pages of Estherhazy business correspondence dating back to the 1830s.

and walnut trees, and hillsides covered with grapevines. One room contained a small bed, table, chairs, and a stove. The other room housed the winepress and gardening equipment. Stairs within the house led down to a cool, damp wine cellar dug into the hillside. Years of wine ripening in wooden barrels left an unforgettable musty, tart, and sweet aroma. However, despite the vineyard's idyllic setting and the beautiful views overlooking the lakes and Tata hills, the weight of his misfortune continued to weigh on his soul.

His life had started with such promise and good intent. He was the only Jaszai child to obtain a university education. He survived the Great War and even saved drowning men in the Isonzo River. He married into a wealthy Budapest family. He started his own business and successfully employed other men. He survived the Second World War and safely guided his entire work crew back from the Russian front. He helped a woman hide from the pogrom. Hid another woman's treasure. He was a loving husband, father, and a loyal friend.

However, despite his heroics and kind deeds, he was cursed with one tragic misfortune after another. Enduring Hungary's worst battles of both WWI and WWII left him scarred. The Spanish flu and starvation weakened him. His business became a war casualty. He lost his wife and the two sons he had fathered. He was treated like a pariah by his wife's family and his neighbors. He was twice imprisoned and tortured for doing no more than helping out good friends.

Though he rarely attended church, Father was deeply pious in his own way. He lived his life according to the teachings of Jesus. He embodied kindness, loyalty, and love. But this world broke his body, his spirit, and his faith. It was a miracle that he even

260

continued to struggle. To pick himself up repeatedly. God had tested him beyond the breaking point.

One of my greatest regrets in fleeing Hungary was not being there to help take care of him. My sister, Ilonka and her husband, Ernő, took on the brunt of Father's and Emi-mama's care as they aged. After Ricsi and I emigrated to America, Father underwent surgery for colon cancer. For the rest of his life, he required a colostomy bag. We tried to help from America but all of this was happening just as we were struggling to establish our new lives. Even with the dollars we were able to send them, Father and Emi-mama struggled for the rest of their lives with meager incomes.

In his early seventies, Father suffered a stroke. No one noticed at first, until friends came to the house and told Emi-mama that he was down at the synagogue handing out money to those who survived the Holocaust. He was trying to make amends for having allowed the Holocaust to happen. His erratic behavior worsened and he was hospitalized for eight months before the blood clot slowly dissipated in his brain and he began to function normally again. However, after he returned home during a summer shower, Emi-mama found him walking in the yard holding a garden fork up to the sky and shouting up challenges and pleas for God to strike him down with a lightening bolt. God finally relented and struck him down with stomach cancer. He died at the age of 79. He was my tragic hero.

31

Debrecen, 1951

My courtship with Ricsi evolved at a glacial pace. It was far from a hot-blooded romantic whirlwind. Without money to travel or even telephone, Debrecen could have been on another planet. In 1951, I saw him only once. He traveled with his swim team to Budapest and then popped down to Tata for a day using a train ticket purchased by his brother Pista. Postal correspondence was the thin thread that kept us connected. I was encouraged that, even though he was busy with medical school, he committed to writing to me twice a month like clockwork.

Through those letters, I began to understand his outlook on life. I recognized the differences in our personalities and imagined how we would compliment one another. He was obsessed with self-improvement, while I tended to focus on self-acceptance. He was a planner and a dreamer. I lived in the moment. He had grand ideas. I was strong on following through.

Ricsi's mother's parents, 1903

Like my parents, Ricsi's parents came from two distinct social strata. His father, István, came from poor peasantry. He was rescued from the cycle of poverty and illiteracy when Piarist Catholic priests, dedicated to educating poor children, shepherded him from his small village to Debrecen and gave him an unparalleled education. István admired these priests for roaming the countryside in search of smart and needy young students. For their virtuous vows of poverty, chastity, and obedience. He joined the priesthood after matriculation. Serving as a priest during the first Soviet Revolution in March of 1919, he was jailed because of his religious affiliation. Also imprisoned at that time were rich landowners and their families. It was in prison that he met and fell in love with pretty young Rozália Erhardt, the daughter of a wealthy miller. Her father owned much of the land surrounding the village of Egyek, located to the west of Debrecen.

István remained a spiritual man but broke his ties with the church. When he left the priesthood to marry Rozália, the church refused to recognize their marriage unless he vowed to remain celibate. That was not going to happen–at least not at their young and passionate ages. But he never gave up on the idea of one day having a church wedding. When István was 70 and in ill health, he vowed to remain celibate for the rest of his life. The church then agreed to officially marry Rozália and István.

Holding doctorate degrees in theology and literature, István quickly rose to become an officer and then Director of the Debrecen Police Department.

Their two daughters Ottilia (1921) and Márta (1922) both became French and German secondary school instructors. Their eldest son, István (Pista, born in 1924) attended the military officer academy–the Hungarian equivalent to West Point. Serving as an officer during WWII, Pista was captured near the Russian Front. His parents received a letter reporting his death. Then several months after the war ended, Pista suddenly appeared on their doorstep in Debrecen. The rumors of his death had been greatly exaggerated. He returned to school to study medical surgery. Upon graduating Pista was offered that permanent position in Tata.

Richard (Ricsi) was the baby of the family. Born in 1929, he was five years younger than Pista. Due to his childhood illnesses, Ricsi was thin, short, and frail. In contrast, his brother Pista was tall, broad shouldered, and incredibly strong. The physical differences and age gap resulted in more of a paternal than sibling relationship between the two brothers. And the sisters were more like two additional mothers. During Ricsi's childhood, his parents were living at the peak of their comfort and success. As a result, Ricsi lived a spoiled, carefree life. He grew into a handsome young man and was extremely successful in school. Ricsi planned to study abroad. He longed to live the life of a playboy in Paris, a Bohemian in Prague, and a Liberal in London. Why not do all three? The world was his oyster. That all changed with WWII.

After the war, Ricsi's father got caught up in a purge of government officials, and lost his job with the police department. Ricsi's parents fled Debrecen and moved in with their daughter Márta in a small hillside village, where her husband Berci served as the Greek Orthodox priest. The government confiscated István's large Debrecen home, turning all but one room and bathroom over to other needy working class families. Ricsi stayed on alone in that one remaining room of their Debrecen house to complete secondary school and attend medical school.

Any hope of inheritance was swept away when, in Egyek, Rozália's father's land was taken away during the agricultural reforms of 1946. Instead of traipsing decadently across Europe, Ricsi struggled to secure his daily meal. He had no money to heat his little room. Pista sent him a 300 Forint monthly stipend, enough for food. But he often ran out of money before month's end. His sisters sometimes sent him food packages. When those ran out, he went to visit those he called his "fat" girlfriends who, in exchange for kind flirtation, were willing to feed him. Whether or not his heart belonged to another, they enjoyed being courted by this cute medical student. On his worst days, he ate only scraps of dry bread. As long as he kept himself fed, he could continue his studies. Medical school was free for good students.

The problem was that he was not a well behaved student. He was clever enough to pass his exams by cramming during the last few weeks of the semester. That left him with unsupervised time to get into trouble. He was almost expelled from medical school after he and several drunken buddies broke into the morgue and took baths in the large vats used to prepare corpses. Another night he slept in the student dormitory after a night of excessive alcohol consumption only to watch his friend get up in the middle of the night, circle his bed twice, lift open the sheets as if it were a toilet seat, vomit the contents of his stomach into his bed, close the sheets, circle the bed twice, and then climb back into the very same bed. One day, when Ricsi did not arrive as expected for a scheduled dinner at the house of one of his fat girlfriends, she went out to search for him. She found him sitting on a wall in a drunken stupor saying, "There is a fence over there. And another over there. And there. And there. I am fenced in on all sides."

A lack of resources did not diminish his sybaritic confidence and sense of invincibility. Getting by was an adventure, a challenge that tested his mettle. But these were stories I learned of much later in our relationship. In his letters, he wrote about swimming, singing in a mens' choir, attending free theater, and debating philosophy in coffee houses with college buddies.

Despite my ever-present hope that this relationship would evolve, I was determined not to allow it to leave me devastated if it didn't. I kept my emotions in check. My life had already been so full of heart-wrenching losses. There was a part of me that was not fully invested. I was prepared to receive a letter in which he confessed to have fallen in love with one of his Debrecen girlfriends. Or that the burden of a long-distance relationship was too much to bear. I allowed myself to be 80% in love.

Ricsi was undeniably loyal, trustworthy, and admirable. He had plenty of opportunities to find a more suitable partner, but he had set his sights on me. What made him choose me? What made him deem me as his best option? It was not a relationship built on burning passion, but there was enough of a simmering flame to keep our long-distance relationship alive.

Répásy family: Ricsi, Rozália, Ottilia, Márta, István, Pista

32

Veszprém, 1952-1953

The crowning event of my high school graduation on May 15th, 1952, was the evening ball. I had never attended anything so elegant. This was the first time I would make use of that white dress that we found up in the attic of our new house. A talented seamstress fashioned it into a full skirted dress. The Tango was the dance of the evening and I joyfully danced late into the morning hours.

Next came the question of life after high school. Even though I was a top student in my class and earned all A's in my matriculation exam, Mr. Gergely, our bigoted communist principal, refused to recommend me for further studies. The problem was not my performance, but that my father was an engineer from Budapest. He wrote that I was a bad *Káder*–meaning from the wrong class. He only forwarded positive recommendations for those working class students who demonstrated loyalty to the

Party, regardless of their academic performance. This epitomized the decline of our schooling system.

I was so angry at Principal Gergely for denying me the opportunity to continue my studies. I refused to let him dictate my future. I would find a way to attend university. I didn't care which one or even in which subject. Father's youngest brother, Géza, his wife Trudi, their six-year-old son Andris, and Trudi's German mother now lived in our deceased Jaszai grandparents' house in Veszprém. Despite the lack of a spare room in that tiny house, they agreed to let me stay with them.

Géza and Trudi slept in one of the two upstairs bedrooms. I shared the other room with Andris. The room was not wide enough for two single beds, so we slept on divans. Trudi's mother slept downstairs in an area partitioned off of the living room.

I took my school transcripts to the admissions office of the *Nehéz Vegyipari Egyetem* (Heavy Industrial College), a well respected engineering school. All universities were free once you met the admission requirements. With my grades from my "once" prestigious high school, I was accepted.

Géza and family were no better off financially than we were back in Tata. As Father had done, Géza was selling off his wife's jewelry to make ends meet. The family made a big sacrifice when they took me in. Father occasionally came bearing gifts of food but could not give Géza any money.

From morning until about six in the evening, I spent every weekday on campus. I would return home to find a plate of food keeping warm perched on a ledge of the wood burning stove. Trudi's mother did all of the cooking. The food she prepared was distinctly German. Lots of big dumplings in delicious gravies that filled me up and compensated for the lack of meat.

Because I was so focused on my studies, the school year quickly flew by. I primarily studied mathematics and chemistry. I also took obligatory Russian language and military training classes. These two classes were such a waste of time. I was pretty reluctant to learn Russian and forgot it soon afterwards. A young uneducated soldier gave us our twice-weekly military training. I learned how to disassemble and oil a gun. But I never even got a chance to shoot one.

My only extracurricular activity was participating in the school choir, which led to one memorable event. May 1st was known as the "International Day of the Struggle and Celebration of the Workers for Peace and Socialism," a compulsory event in which we marched in mass parades past great tribunes filled with members of the Party and guests of honor. This year, local party officials invited the Hungarian composer Zoltán Kodaly to conduct his famous choral work for tenor, chorus, and orchestra: the *Psalmus Hungaricus*, Op. 13. Kodaly had composed and first performed it in 1923 to commemorate Budapest's fiftieth anniversary.

Nearly a thousand singers were assembled, pulled from every nearby school and church choir. Each individual choir had been provided the musical score in advance. We learned our individual parts well, but never practiced together before that day's performance. Only minutes into the twenty-five minute piece, it was obvious that the massive choir and orchestra were totally out of synch. A frustrated Kodaly threw up his hands and walked off the stage saying, "this just will not work." One of the music teachers stepped in to conduct the rest of the piece but everybody was quite disappointed. For me, the event was humorously symbolic of Party mismanagement.

I had little time to socialize. The one girl I did become close with was Judit Kriza. A daughter of a university physics professor, she also had a keen interest in learning to become an engineer. We preferred to forego larger study circles in favor of our hideaway in the cemetery across the street.

Though I never dated anyone while at school, two years after Ricsi and I moved to America, I received a long letter from a young man who was a senior when I was a freshman. He told me that he had his eye on me, but had not approached me because he felt that he was not yet ready to have a family. I found it strange that he knew specific details about my marriage to Ricsi and my four- year-old son Andris. He wanted me to leave my husband and return to live with him in Hungary. He guaranteed me a good life. He was fully prepared to accept and adopt Andris as his own. I barely remembered him. I could not help but laugh. It was an extremely flattering yet absurdly ridiculous offer. Receiving that letter in America, his entreaty seemed so old-world. I never responded but often smiled when I thought about it. Can't blame him for trying.

33

The Agricultural Collective, 1953

On March 5, 1953, while I was finishing up my first year of university in Veszprém, Joseph Stalin unexpectedly died. Hearing the news I was cautiously celebratory. My inclination to go dancing in the streets singing "the evil tyrant is dead" was squelched by lingering fears that my frolics might be reported to the ÁVH.

Looking back, I suspect that Stalin was losing his mind long before this final brain aneurysm killed him. His paranoia had consumed him. He had recently imprisoned one doctor who advised him to retire as mitigation for his ailing health. Though of Jewish descent himself, Stalin became irrationally suspicious of Zionist plots. The prior September he had several, mostly-Jewish, Kremlin doctors arrested for allegedly plotting to kill him. This kicked off a wave of anti-Zionist purges throughout the Soviet satellite countries.

Stalin demanded that puppet leaders in the Soviet block provide him evidence of Zionist conspiracies. To meet that expectation, leaders turned in loyal staff. In Prague, thirteen senior communist officials, eleven of them Jews, were convicted of conspiracy. In Budapest, Mátyás Rákosi felt compelled to provide Stalin with even more impressive results. He created a list that included Jewish ÁVH officers, who up to that point had faithfully executed his inhumane orders.

Most notable on that list was ÁVH Director Gábor Péter, who was arrested two days before Christmas. Rákosi invited Péter and his wife, Jolán Simon, to his hillside villa, had them arrested and detained in his damp basement. Until they were moved, Rákosi fed them only scraps from his table. On January 15, 1953, the leading communist newspaper, the *Szabad Nép*, announced that the Party had unearthed a Zionist plot supported by Israeli and Western intelligence organizations. "Had it not been discovered," the newspaper explained, "this plot would have posed a much greater threat to our noble cause than the doctor scandal in Moscow."

Under torture, Péter confessed to carrying on a conspiracy within the ÁVH, of being an American agent and an informant under the Horthy regime. Péter's arrest was not officially reported until end of January. But, by then, the rumor of it had already reached us in Tata.

It was difficult to separate fact from propaganda fiction. The purges got crazier and crazier. Even the obedient communist János Kádár, who had replaced Rajk as minister of the interior, was arrested by the ÁVH, tortured and stripped of all his privileges. Kádár's unfortunate and desperate successor, Sandor Zold, killed his wife, his children, mother-in-law, and then himself after learning that he too was about to be purged.

After my first year of university, I envisioned a future as an engineer. The deeper I delved into technical subjects, the more interesting they became. But I had other choices to make. Ricsi and I discussed a plan in which both of us would transfer to schools in Budapest. I contacted the university at which my grandfather had been a tenured professor. It was willing to accept me, but needed my transcripts from *Nehézvegyipari Egyetem* in Vesprém in order to grant me credit for my first year of study. I was once again confounded when the university in Veszprém refused to release my transcripts. I was in the midst of battling for the release of those transcripts when it became clear that Ricsi was going to finish medical school in Debrecen.

That summer, when he came to visit, our discussions turned to our pending marriage. He proposed waiting until he graduated from medical school. I started to worry about a wedding dowry. It was customary for the bride's family to provide one, but we had no money. Neither did Ricsi's parents for that matter. I decided to forego school, get a job, and earn a dowry.

I found a job in Tata at a grain *beszolgáltatás*, a collection service for the Agricultural Collective. I commuted by bicycle to the collection facility located outside of town near the many stream-fed water mills. Coming to work for the Collective in its fifth year of operation, the process ran fairly smoothly. The farmers still expressed their disapproval with the concept, but they never treated me, the cashier, unkindly. I sat at a small desk and recorded the reported weights of wheat, corn, and potatoes. I used an adding machine to ensure that I accounted for every penny. And I always showed them my calculations so that they accepted the result. Hungarian farmers surrendered ownership of land and farm equipment and then rented back that same land and equipment through "donations" of the vast majority of their harvests to the government at prices well below the costs of production. If they brought in more than the required minimum, we paid them a nominal amount.

I sympathized with the plight of these struggling farmers who fought the system by reducing their agricultural production. For the first time in history, our agriculturally rich country found itself importing grain. I came to understand that the Land Reform of '45 and the '48 Collectivization of Agriculture were two vastly different programs. Reform was widely popular. Collectivization was despised. The former had been championed by a popular Muscovite who shepherded the proposal through by building consensus and nurturing positive relationships. The latter was forced upon the population by Rákosi who applied the same threats, intimidation, and terror he had deployed when nationalizing industry, foreign trade, and banks. The resistance of these proud farmers proved to be a notable chink in Rákosi's economic plan, and marked the beginning of his downfall.

Though ever cheerful, the plump, bespectacled, professorial champion of agrarian land reform, Imre Nagy, sometimes came across as doltish. That belied his actual interpersonal intelligence that enabled him to survive the political winds in Moscow. He carefully adhered to the mantra that the only truth that mattered was Stalin's truth. That failing to follow Stalin without deviation was suicidal.

After studying Soviet agricultural economics at the University of Moscow, Nagy ran a collective farm in Siberia. There, he became passionate about ending "Landlordism" in Hungary. Hundreds of years of political chaos and foreign power occupations had perpetuated the consolidation of wealth by Hungarian nobility and the Church. Because Hungary had such a chaotic history, such concentration of wealth existed longer here than in other European countries. The top one percent of land owners owned half of Hungary's arable lands. The Eszterházy family alone owned over 400,000 acres[39].

In the post-war Provisional Government, Nagy was appointed Minister of Agriculture. By March of 1945, he had introduced the Land Reform bill that split huge estates owned for centuries by Hungarian nobility and the Church into tiny parcels. All estates larger than 570 acres were expropriated. Even livestock were confiscated with the excess land. Nearly 3 million acres of confiscated land was redistributed to 725,000 landless workers and smallholders. The new estates were limited to 8.5 acres for crops and pasture and 1.8 acres for gardens and vineyards. A 10-

[39] Hungary actually measures its land area in "hold" which equals 1.066 acres.

year moratorium was imposed on the sale of land received in the process of reform to prevent re-concentration of large estates.[40]

Even though this land reform was an ultra left-wing concept, it was accepted and adopted by a broad coalition. It was the same publicly debated prewar issue that gave birth to Father's surveying business. This was a historically significant event. It liquidated one of Europes last strongholds of mediaeval feudalism. The walrus-mustached Nagy became widely popular. He was seen as an authentic peasant. His jovial humor earned him good will. From that point on, people affectionately called him "Land Divider."

Even with Rákosi's ruthless political tactics, Communism would never have taken a foothold in Hungary if there wasn't a segment of the population who believed in its ideology. Imre Nagy was a Muscovite who believed in its altruistic potential to transform society.

After Stalin's death, Moscow was governed by committee, and no one on that committee wanted to take the blame for Hungary. Our economy was on the verge of collapse and the reprehensible unrestrained use of terror and excessive purges were reprehensible. Moscow's obvious scapegoat was the "mini-Stalin," Mátyás Rákosi. Accusing him of violating the principles laid down by Vladimir Lenin, Moscow stripped Rákosi of his prime ministership, Then to his dismay, Moscow hand-selected a man Rákosi despised to replace him as prime minister: Imre Nagy.[41]

---

[40] In 1948, there would be a second wave of land reform legislation, in which 170,000 hold of leased land was transferred from relatively large farmers to farm workers, smallholders, and cooperative farms for low rent payments.

[41] Moscow allowed Rákosi to remain as Party Secretary-General.

From Rákosi's perspective, Nagy lacked the requisite vigor and appetite for political intrigue. Nagy had been appointed Minister of the Interior in early 1946, but he lacked the stomach to be the ruthless leader the Party wanted to run the State Protection Authority. That was why Rákosi had him replaced by László Rajk. He saw Nagy as personally weak, too docile and ill-fitted to assume leadership of the Party. He planned to unseat Nagy, but knew he would have to wait until the political winds changed in Moscow.

Nagy, on the other hand, seized the moment and eagerly implemented sweeping reforms he called the "New Course." In widely popular speeches, he spoke idealistically of Communism with a human face, a resurgence of national pride, ending the purges, and closing notorious labor camps. He promised to raise the standard of living, and to consider the workers' interests. He permitted deportees to return. He allowed peasants to leave collective farms, cancelled compulsory agricultural production quotas, granted subsidies to private producers, and increased investments in the production of consumer goods. He quickly won the support of Party membership and intelligentsia for his courage to take on bureaucracy and excessive industrialization. He even released unjustly imprisoned loyal communists. One of those whom he released was János Kádár.[42]

An envious Rákosi was still pulling the strings behind the curtain and secretly undermining Nagy's initiatives. As a result, most of Nagy's reforms failed to come to fruition or alter the structure of the economy. However, it was at one meeting in Moscow that Nagy, himself, made the mistake that most displeased Soviet leadership. The Land Divider made it clear that he did not support the Stalin model of forced agricultural collectives.

---

[42] Kádár was appointed to head a district party office in Budapest.

Though I saved every cent I earned, after working at the Collective for a year, I was only able to afford bedding (sheets, pillows, pillow cases, comforters–two of each), two easy chairs, a small table, and a new blouse.

I actually received two marriage proposals in 1953. The first one came from a young man belonging to one of Tata's well-established families. He didn't even personally come to the house. Rather, he sent a dozen red long-stemmed roses with a card. I was rather offended by this impersonal gesture. I didn't know him. Did he think I could be so easily bought off? He was considerably older than I was. I told Nagyi that I refused to even write a thank you note. But she insisted that etiquette required a response. So she wrote a thoughtful note on my behalf. I don't even know what she said, but it put an end to the first marriage offer.

Ricsi's marriage proposal, which occurred during a Christmas visit, was joyously humorous event. The weather had abated and Father was working outside in the garden. Ricsi followed him around all day long but was too shy to broach the subject. Father, sensing Ricsi's intentions, kept him busy assisting with chores. Finally, late in the afternoon, Ricsi took a deep breath, professed his love, and requested permission to marry me. "You have my and Emi's blessing, as long as my daughter agrees," Father assured him. I happily consented. By this time, I had removed the protective wall around my heart. I was 100% in love!

Emi Mama in our Baj Vineyard

34

Zalaegerszeg, 1954

After graduating medical school in March of 1954, Ricsi was assigned to work as a general practitioner in Szolnok, a small city along the Tisza River in southeastern Hungary. He never wanted to be a general practitioner. His interest was in pediatrics. But per Party directives, the medical school assigned locations based on need, not on a doctor's personal desires. In Szolnok, unmarried medical staff were housed in a dormitory. Anticipating that I would soon join him, Ricsi wanted to insure that he would be assigned an apartment. Even though we were not yet married, he told the housing officials that we were. We rectified that problem a few weeks later. Ricsi hopped a train down to Tata. We went to the Tata town hall and obtained our marriage license. Immediately after our courthouse ceremony and a quick lunch, Ricsi jumped back onto a train and returned to Szolnok in time to start his shift at the hospital.

We were now married in the eyes of the state, but we didn't even have the time to consummate our marriage. I would remain a virgin until our real church wedding held in Tata on August 21, 1954. It was a modest wedding with twenty-two attendees consisting of only the immediate family. We even had to leave Ricsi's sisters off the invite list because we could not afford ten more people. Though his sisters were disappointed about not getting invited, we got along reasonably well with them once they understood our predicament.

A wonderful seamstress refashioned the same white eyelet dress I had worn to the graduation ball into my wedding dress. Emi-mama assembled a beautiful flower bouquet for me to carry. She and her sister Kata cooked up a fantastic meal. After the plates were cleared, Ricsi's father, István, stood to make an eloquent toast. Having learned to speak in theology school, he was a confident orator and only stopped after his wife, Rozsika-mama, started tugging on his jacket sleeve.

That same evening, Ricsi and I boarded the train to start our new life together in Szolnok. On the train, I pensively pressed my face against the window pane and said to Ricsi, "There is something that I must share with you. But I am finding it difficult to talk about."

Ricsi stared at me and imagined the worst. Was I not really a virgin? Was there another man? Had I been raped during the war? "Whatever it is," he responded reassuringly, "we will work through it."

So, I just blurted it out. "My period just started."

"Oh, is that all?" He laughed.

Both Ricsi and I came from households in which sex was considered a dirty, taboo subject. He joked that the only sex education he received at home was when his father noticed him as

Our wedding August 21, 1954

young child sitting in a bathtub with an erection. His father immediately fetched a glass of cold water and splashed it onto Ricsi's privates saying, "That's how we deal with that sort of thing."

I had been sitting in the bathtub on the eve of my wedding, when Emi-mama came in.

"What do you know about sex and men's bodies?" She asked.

"Nothing," I replied honestly.

"Do you know that a man's penis will grow and become hard?" She pressed. I was twenty-one and even that was news to me.

Before our wedding day, Ricsi had tried to shield me from his brother Pista's dirty jokes. The first few months after our wedding, Ricsi told and explained to me every dirty joke he could remember. That was my sex education.

Maybe that would have also been a good time to have confessed to Ricsi that I also did not know how to cook. The first time I cooked rice, I filled the pot halfway with rice, added a little water, and kept adding water as the rice continued to expand and overflow.

One patient gifted Ricsi with three small baby chicks. The darling little fur balls immediately latched on to us as surrogate parents. They trilled contently as they napped in our laps and peeped at us when we approached. The plan had been to eat them. But we became too attached and, instead, gave them away when they got big enough.

In January 1955, Hungary's leadership was summoned to Moscow for a dressing down. Rákosi's subterfuge had worked well. Based on a large dossier prepared by Russia's new envoy to Hungary, Yuri Andropov, Nagy's New Course was proving to be a miserable failure. Nagy was accused of economic incompetence, naivety, and bourgeois nationalism. Nagy was not fired outright, but Rákosi sensed that the political winds in Moscow had shifted back in his favor. He was about to oust Nagy from office, when Nagy beat him to the punch by suffering a heart attack. Months later as Nagy walked out the hospital, Rákosi charged him with the typical Stalinist-style purge list of transgressions against the Communist Party.

Nagy despairingly tried to convince the Hungarian Politburo of the falsity of Rákosi's charges. However, he was no match against the wily in-fighter Rákosi, who was determined to destroy his opponent. Though spared a prison sentence, Nagy was dismissed from his premiership and expelled from all party committees and functions. He was also prohibited from returning to teaching or any sort of wage-earning job. Rákosi was not satisfied with the end result. He wanted to see Nagy suffer public embarrassment. He demanded that Nagy publicly recant his heretical views, confess to the failure of the New Course, and submit to the ritual of self-criticism. Nagy refused, saying that "the New Course remains the only way to save Communism in Hungary."

Hungarian intellectuals began to complain about Rákosi's redeployment of harsh, heavy-industry-focused policies. Young communist journalists, who believed in Nagy's vision of increased liberalization, bravely spoke out. They exposed the hypocrisy of slogans devoid of meaning, the medieval cruelty, and the Party's insult to national pride. One journal released an extremely dangerous expose comparing the poverty of the masses to the luxurious Party leader mansions on Buda's Rózsadomb Hill. It described the special schools for their children, well-stocked shops for their wives, and even special bathing beaches at Lake Balaton shut off from the common people by barbed wire. It was an indictment, not of Communism, but of Rákosi Stalinism.

Rákosi dismissed journalists from the *Szabad Nép* newspaper and intimidated members of the Writers' Union. But in expelling leading journalists, Rákosi unwittingly gave birth to a group of "outcasts" who were willing to speak out for freedom and people's livelihood. As they had done during the revolution of 1848, the young intellectuals gave voice to the conscience of the nation. Intellectuals, writers and journalists united against Rákosi's neo-Stalinist resurgence. They cried out against the abuses of the totalitarian regime. They demanded a return to the ideals of socialism. The revolution began as a "revolution of the mind." Word of Nagy standing his ground against the tyrant Rákosi caused his popularity to soar. Writers began to call for Nagy's reinstatement.

Nine months and three days after our wedding, on May 24, 1955, Andris was born. I was working at the Szolnok library at the time of Andris' birth. At eight that morning I informed Ricsi that I was beginning to feel pain. "This is your first child," he said with the arrogant confidence of a young doctor. "You will not have the baby for quite a while. You walk to the library and tell them you won't be in. I will ride my bicycle to work and arrange for another doctor to cover my shift. Then I will come meet you at the library. From there we will take a cab to the hospital."

It took me an hour and a half to make what was typically a fifteen minute walk to the library. As soon as the library staff saw the condition I was in, they hailed me a cab.

The obstetrician-gynecologist stood smoking a cigarette out in front of the hospital when Ricsi finally arrived. "Congratulations." He said, "you have a son."

Around the time of Andris' birth, Ricsi received a letter from his former professor László Oroszlan, who had recently become the Director of the Children's Ward at the Zalaegerszeg Hospital. Dr. Oroszlan knew that Ricsi wanted to be a pediatrician. The letter was an invitation for Ricsi to join him as an *Alorvos* which translates to "under doctor" and equates to both a working doctor and resident.

Ricsi and Dr. Oroszlan came to terms and made final arrangements via mail. Even though this new position would enable Risci to transfer into pediatrics, the decision to leave Szolnok was not an easy one. After living for months in a storeroom within the village medical clinic, we had finally secured an apartment. As soon as the Szolnok Hospital would learn that he accepted a new position, we would be forced to give up that apartment. We would have to face the housing challenge all over again in our new location. Since we had no accommodations, Ricsi initially traveled alone to Zalaegerszeg. Andris and I went back home to Tata until Ricsi could secure us a residence.

After three months, Ricsi sent for us. Father sold his typewriter to buy us a couch that folded into a bed. Father also rented a truck. He and llonka drove us with our sparse furnishings to our new home. Besides the bedding and few items I bought as my dowry, we also brought a crib, one small table, two chairs, and one large armoire.

Ricsi was granted permission to convert one room in the Children's ward into our family residence. The entire living area of our new home was one sickroom large enough to hold six children's beds. To reach the toilet, I had to walk through the waiting room and the multi-desked doctors' office. So as to not disturb them during working hours, I usually used a chamber pot and emptied it down the little sink in our room.

We were the only family living in the children's ward, however, in the adjacent obstetrics-gynecology ward, a rawboned, pale, blond-haired gynecologist named Dr. Feri Husvét shared similar living arrangements with his slightly older German wife and their adorable three-year-old daughter, Kuki. They also had been told not expect an apartment of their own for at least three more years. Sharing such similar living arrangements, we became very close friends.

Since the doctors were typically on 12-hour shifts, the hospital fed them. Unofficially, there was always plenty of extra food for me as well. That covered our main meals. There was a pediatric ward milk kitchen located directly across from our room used to prepare a daily dish of creamed potatoes, carrots, and spinach blended in milk. This is what we fed Andris. After 6 p.m., I was permitted use of this milk kitchen, where I prepared eggs, tea, palacsinta (crepes), or sandwiches. The hospital forbade me to use onions or garlic because of the lingering smell. Once a patient gave us a dozen eggs. I scrambled up the entire dozen at once and invited all the working doctors for a snack. Still being such a novice cook, I badly over-salted the eggs. But since eggs were considered an infrequent luxury at this time, the staff politely ate them up.

Living within the medical ward, Andris was exposed to all of the sick children with their diseases. He was skinny and frequently sick himself. With a young, sick baby, and Ricsi always being on call, I rarely left the hospital. Fortunately, my feeling of isolation was offset by the strong brotherhood among the young doctors at Zalaegerszeg hospital. Our social life centered around these doctors and their families. We gathered many an evening for a cocktail, a coffee, a discussion, a game, or even a dance.

Zalaegerszeg hospital served the town and the surrounding county. Doctors teamed up to visit distant villages. They established a cycle of visiting each village approximately once every three months. Ricsi typically went in a group consisting of him (the pediatrician), a gynecologist, an internist, and a chauffeur who drove the government car. The specialized medical care they brought to these smaller communities (normally only supported by a general practitioner) was in high demand. Ricsi and his team of doctors were greeted with grateful open arms. After a full day of examinations and procedures, the villagers typically thanked the doctors by preparing a large meal. The wine and *Pálinka* liquor flowed freely. I became annoyed that Ricsi usually came home inebriated. And maybe a bit envious that he was out having a good time, while I was stuck back in our single room at the clinic. I wondered what was so good about being in this drunken state? Why do people drink to excess? I decided to find out.

We had a bottle of chocolate liquor that no one seemed to like. I found the taste more palatable than the other options. I drank the entire bottle. Soon I was vomiting in the sink. Ricsi held my head and laughed affectionately at my painful experimentation. This was the last time in my life that I ever drank to the point of getting sick.

Thus I lived simply and contentedly in our safe hospital compound, naively isolated from the discontent fomenting in the streets.

35

The Revolution, 1956

I mre Nagy did not want to be the leader of the revolution. In fact, he knew that Moscow was setting him up to be its fall guy. But if he didn't step up to lead in that moment of crisis, who else would?

A speech given by Nikita Khrushchev to the February 1956, Soviet Union Communist Party's Twentieth Congress had huge repercussions in Hungary.[43] Sensing the rising frustration in all of the Soviet satellite countries, he formally renounced Joseph Stalin. He said that Stalin had trampled on the Leninist principle of collective party leadership. That Stalin had rounded up thousands of people and sent them to Gulag work camps. That, three years prior, 98 of the 139 legitimately elected Congress members had

---

[43] Intended to be secret and internal, the speech was leaked via spy networks to the West and eventually published verbatim in the New York Times.

been arrested and shot. He declared that Stalin's "Cult of Personality" had run its course.

The speech triggered a de-Stalinization crusade that became a nightmare for Mátyás Rákosi. He was vilified for his own failure to de-Stalinize the Party in the manner Khrushchev had prescribed. The execution of László Rajk haunted him most of all. He was exposed for using fabricated evidence and forced to admit his role in staged trials that condemned faithful communists and Spanish Civil War veterans. Just as he had tried to make Imre Nagy publicly criticize himself back in 1955, Rákosi was now forced to officially rehabilitate László Rajk's legacy.

Young intellectuals found clever ways to navigate the risks of openly criticizing the Party and get their message out. The Petőfi Circle was a sanctioned communist youth debate club. Its meetings drew large crowds promoting cleverly named debate topics that exposed and destabilized the Party. A debate on socialist legality attacked the police state. A debate on socialist science exposed Russia's exploitation of Hungarian uranium.

In July, recently released ÁVH prisoner, Géza Losonczy, spoke at the most notable debate. More than 6,000 people attended this debate on the topic of free speech. Overwhelming the venue, people queued in the street to listen over loudspeakers to await his final speech of the event. He provided a detailed recounting of how Rákosi sacked and attempted to discredit Imre Nagy. He explained how Nagy was never granted a fair opportunity to defend himself. The crowd began to chant "Imre, Imre!" and "Down with the bald fathead!"

A few days after this debate, First Deputy Chairman Anastas Mikoyan flew to Budapest. Rákosi and Prime Minister András Hegedüs chauffeured the Soviet leader from Ferihegyi Airport back to Party headquarters in the heart of Budapest.

"Party Chairman Rákosi, how are you feeling?" Mikoyan asked. "I am well," Rákosi replied.

Mikoyan turned to him and said quietly "No, the Soviet leadership has decided that you are ill."

At that afternoon's Party meeting, Rákosi made a last-ditch effort to reclaim control. Holding out a piece of paper, he loudly announced, "I have here a list of 400 communists, including Imre Nagy, who shall be arrested for anti-Party conspiracy."

The room stared at him in stunned silence until Mikoyan softly asked, "Tell me Comrade Rákosi, what do you think of the Petőfi Circle?"

"They are a movement organized by enemies of the Party," Rákosi promptly responded.

"That's interesting," Mikoyan mused. "In Moscow, we hear that Petőfi Circle meetings repeatedly exult the Party. Wouldn't that make them a remarkable bunch of enemies?"

Seizing the moment, the Party's vulpine second in command, Ernő Gerő, turned against his leader. "Might I suggest, beloved and wise father of the people, that mass arrests are no longer reconcilable with our new brand of social legality?"

Looking back at that moment, Mikoyan might have salvaged the Party if he had at that point rehabilitated Imre Nagy. Nagy was popular with the masses. However, supporting Nagy would have required back-tracking on Moscow's claims of his unsuitability for office. It also meant giving a green light to liberalism and nationalist tendencies. That would have set bad examples for other satellite countries.

Instead, Mikoyan appointed Gerő, the man who outraged liberals, dissatisfied moderates, and perpetuated the growing schism in Party leadership.

Gerő's words bled with hypocrisy. He was as hard-driving of an intransigent reactionary as the worst of them. He had been involved in all of Rákosi's salami tactics and had little sympathy for Hungarian nationalist aspirations. Rákosi left Hungary for life-long "treatment" in the Soviet Union. But illness still festered back in Budapest. Soon, it would spread like the Spanish Flu.

On a miserably cold, wet October 6, over 100,000 spectators gathered at the national cemetery to witness the reinterment of László Rajk's remains. The solemnity of the event was even more symbolically profound because this burial ceremony took place on the anniversary of the execution of the 13 Hungarian generals killed after the Russian military crushed the 1848 Hungarian revolution.

Rajk's widow Julia, wrapped in a plastic raincoat, clutched the small hand of her seven-year-old son. The two had been reunited after her five year stint in prison. Julia had become an instant celebrity back in June when she made a surprise appearance at a packed Officers' Club meeting. Evoking tears among her listeners, she had described how, at the time of her arrest, the ÁVH had given her infant son a new name and sent him away to an orphanage. Her speech ended with a standing ovation, as she called for the punishment of her husband's murderers who had trampled underfoot all honesty and sentiment in this country. She had successfully portrayed her husband as a patriotic martyr, despite the fact that he had been one of the most villainous Party members when living.

A somber Imre Nagy stood next to Julia. Though stripped of all position and standing within the Party, his popularity had skyrocketed. Much of it based on the now widely spread rumor that he had stood up to Rákosi.

Heavy rains soaked and eventually dispersed the grim cemetery crowd. But after the rains subsided, a group of college students marched in what would be the first political demonstration to occur since the Party seized power nearly a decade earlier. The youthful, spirited crowd chanted "never again" and demanded the rehabilitation of Imre Nagy.

With First Secretary of the Hungarian Working People's Party, Ernő Gerő, away vacationing in Crimea, this bold gathering caught authorities off guard and, surprisingly, the government failed to react. Upon his return, Gerő admitted that he had not anticipated the profound affect this burial had upon the population. However, the significance of this event was not lost on Soviet Ambassador, Yuri Andropov, who sent warnings back to Khrushchev in Moscow about the growing unrest and the disappointing performance of the complacent Gerő.

Late in the afternoon of October 23, a much larger group of university students gathered and paraded along the Buda embankment. Large crowds gathered in open windows to cheer on the students as they marched past. One observer handed down a Hungarian flag with the "Rákosi" hammer and sickle coat-of-arms crudely cut out from its center. Students at the front of the procession held up this defaced flag as they entered Bem Square, which was named after the famous Polish military General Jozef Bem who fought valiantly for Hungary during the 1848 Revolution.

This march was ostensively to express solidarity with Poland's pro-reform movement. Poland was pushing back against its own Soviet installed government.[44] This situation was eerily similar to how, in 1848, uprisings in other countries stirred Hungarians to launch their own revolution. The hint of possibility became the spark that relit the flames of Hungarian nationalism.

The march leaders positioned themselves in front of General Bem's statue with its outstretched arm and its pointed index finger rallying his platoon to charge. Cheers erupted upon the arrival of the 700 cadets from the elite Petőfi Military School, attended by sons of the most loyal communists.

Earlier that day, with help from the Hungarian Writers' Union, the students had drafted a 16-point resolution. To make copies of the resolution, they interlaced carbon paper with regular paper and repeatedly typed out the set of demands. These included withdrawal of the Soviet troops from Hungary, free elections, liberty of speech and press, abolishment of surrendering of goods, the right to sell Hungarian uranium deposits on the free market, the removal of the Stalin statues, and the reappointment of Imre Nagy as prime minister. Cautious, but curious, people approached to read these resolution copies, which had been posted in squares and at trolley stops.

---

[44] In June, Soviet troops had violently squashed Poland's Poznan workers' strike. Poland's new Party Secretary, Władysław Gomułka, like Nagy in Hungary, was an increasingly popular leader who had been imprisoned in 1951 for "right-wing nationalist deviations." By October, the reinstated Gomulka had demanded concessions of autonomy and was staring down a threatened Russian invasion. Poland's brave defiance inspired these Hungarian students.

As the peaceful marchers left Bem Square and crossed the Danube River, workers who were just starting their commute home, joined the parade. The ballooning crowd headed toward the much larger Parliament Square. In symbolic parallels with the 1848 revolution, youthful students, writers, and intellectuals led the way. Their demands were eerily similar to those made a century earlier.

Impatient for action, a large contingent of protestors moved on to the Hungarian Radio station on Brody Sandor street to demand that the 16-point resolution be broadcast across Hungary. Valéria Benke, Director of Budapest Radio and a loyal Party member, foolishly tried to deceive the protestors. She had a microphone brought out and allowed the students to read their 16-point resolution. But the crowd quickly realized that something was amiss. People in the nearby flats heard music instead of the students' voices. The crowd became even more enraged when Ernő Gerő came on air to announce that he flatly refused to even consider the resolution. He condemned the Writer's Union and the students as enemies of the state.

Infuriated by Gerő's uncompromising statements and the station director's deceit, the mushrooming crowd swarmed the radio station building. ÁVH officers posted to defend it threw tear gas and opened fire on the unarmed crowd. This marked the first killing of the revolution.

An ambulance, bearing the universal large red cross symbol, arrived at the scene. Dragging their wounded toward the ambulance, the protestors were caught off-guard when the vehicle doors burst open and out popped additional armed ÁVH officers.

Another crowd had assembled in Heroes' Square below the towering forty foot tall statue of Stalin standing on its solid marble plinth. Protestors tied a steel cable noose around Stalin's neck and tried in vain to move the statue. Even with the cables attached to several trucks, the statue stood firm. Fearing that snapping cables might injure bystanders in the thickening crowd, the protestors shouted for people to stand clear.

A speeding truck arrived at the scene. Out jumped Technical School students carrying oxygen cylinders and blowtorches. The torches quickly cut through Stalin's steel ankles. The large statue toppled. Screaming in jubilant triumph, protestors climbed onto the prostrate giant and hugged one another. In tearing down the large statue, they had carried out one of their sixteen demands. It felt as if they toppled all of Communism. One of them planted a Hungarian flag into the empty giant shoes still attached to the marble plinth.

In front of the Parliament, the crowd began calling out for Imre Nagy to speak but he remained in his apartment dismissing the urgings of his acolytes to seize the moment. He opposed these demonstrations. In his heart, he was still a Party man. A devout communist. Holding a copy of the student's 16-points in his hand he complained, "Moscow will never evacuate Soviet troops. And free elections? Never."

His acolytes urged him on. "There is an undeniable patriotic fervor in this crowd. Today is different. You must heed their call."

"This protest will soon be stopped. And probably violently," Nagy mused. "Gerő wants me out there. This will give him an excuse to implicate me once and for all as a traitor."

Imre Nagy finally relented and appeared before the spirited but still peaceful people assembled in Parliament Square. By this point, the crowd had swelled to more than 200,000.

"Comrades," he began. But the crowd immediately booed him.

"We are citizens, not comrades," they shouted back.

"I come only to ask you to peacefully disperse. Please, go home...."

If the masses could hear him, they paid no heed to his uninspiring and unremarkable words. They began chanting "freedom of speech," "freedom of worship," and "we will never be slaves!" Into the night, the momentum of the protest continued to build. As word spread of the killings, the peaceful protest turned into a riot.

Around midnight, Moscow telephoned Imre Nagy to inform him that he had just been appointed prime minister. This put Nagy in an impossible situation. Moscow wanted to leverage his popularity and quell the protests before the Red Army needed to step in. But the rioters now demanded much more than what Nagy was willing or able to give them. The way they ignored his pleas earlier that evening in Parliament Square was clear evidence of how little influence he would really have over them.

Almost immediately after he reluctantly accepted the position, Ernő Gerő arrived to ask Nagy to sign a formal invitation for the Soviet government to send military troops in to quell the unrest. Nagy refused. He might have to be the Soviet's fall guy, but he would not take the blame for a brutal military intervention.

Nagy's refusal to sign the request did not alter the course of events. The following morning of October 24th, acting on orders based on a still unsigned request from the Hungarian government, six thousand Soviet troops and tanks entered Budapest. Because their objective was simply to quell a "small student-led uprising." The Soviets only sent in a small portion of their in-country military strength. Why bring an elephant to attack a flea?

However, that first influx of Soviet troops found themselves unprepared for the violent response they confronted. To slow Red Army progress, weaponless children built barricades in the streets. Lacking arms, the rebels countered with ingenuity. They covered slanted road sections with silk bedsheets and then poured soapy water over the silk. This caused the Soviet T34 tanks to slip and slide and crash into one another. They placed dinner plates on streets to simulate landmines. They built barricades using collected portraits of Lenin, Stalin, Rákosi, and other Soviet leaders so that the Russian tanks would have to choose between destroying those venerable icons or getting out of their tanks to remove them. Children threw stones at the infantry and scattered from the responding gunfire. They tossed Molotov cocktails at tanks and then quickly disappeared into narrow passageways and secret underground networks between buildings. And then, late that afternoon, Hungarian troops joined the resistance. The surprised Russians retreated. Overnight, the riot had evolved into a rebellion.

Rebels seized control of the Hungarian Radio building. However, by this time, the government had relocated the source of broadcasts to the Parliament Building. Every half hour, the Party-controlled radio station repeatedly broadcast the statement that "Fascist and reactionary elements have launched an armed attack against our public buildings and against the forces of law and order. In the interest of re-establishing law and order, all assemblies, meetings, and demonstrations are forbidden." This warning went unheeded. Rebels set police cars on fire and vandalized communist symbols. Fueled by a cathartic release of pent-up rage, this spontaneous rebellion surged onward without cohesive, clear objectives.

On October 25, Moscow blamed Ernő Gerő for his ill-advised commitment of Soviet troops. They replaced him as Party Chairman with János Kádár, a man free of the taint of Stalinism. Moscow had already begun to "develop" Kádár as a more moderate Party leader, who stood in the middle of the road between the liberal Nagy adherents and the doctrinaire Rákosi supporters. Despite having been imprisoned and tortured by the Party, he remained loyal and manageable. But Kádár would demonstrate no loyalty to Nagy who had him released from prison.

Word of Gerő's sacking failed to reach the protestors gathered out in Parliament Square. As they shouted out for Gerő's resignation, Soviet troops positioned on the roofs of the Parliament and the Ethnographic Museum across the square fired down on the crowd in a precarious crossfire. Within minutes, one hundred civilians were killed.

Word of this massacre spread quickly. More workers walked off their jobs to join the rebellion. A new revolutionary newspaper, entitled *Igazság* (The Truth) appeared on the streets demanding that the Soviet troops leave. This became the one unified demand in an otherwise chaotic and uncoordinated rebellion: the Russians had to leave.

On October 26th, Imre Nagy announced on public radio that he was forming a new government comprised of representatives from non-communist parties. Though he opposed the quixotic notion that Hungary could expel the Russians, he promised to negotiate a troop withdrawal with Moscow. However, he added, the first order of business must be to restore order and quell the fighting. Whether he agreed or not with the rebel cause, Nagy knew Moscow's retaliation would be merciless. He had witnessed firsthand cruel and heartless Russian purges back when he lived in Moscow. And he was afraid for the Hungarians. He tried to delay the inevitable by making Moscow believe that the population would soon fall in line.

But his modest proposal had no effect on the still growing rebellion. A fervor spread throughout the country. Rebels now controlled Debrecen, Pecs, Miskolc, and Csepel. Inspired by their unanticipated early successes, they showed no interest in stopping.

In his next radio speech on October 28, Nagy more firmly reiterated his promise to withdraw Soviet troops. He also said he would disband the ÁVH and restore the traditional Hungarian flag. He announced the swearing-in of the new government, and implored the disparate rebel factions to stop making inconsistent demands. He warned that if Hungary pushed too far, Moscow would withdraw all concessions. Any positive outcome could only occur with Moscow's blessing.

The country was stuck in an awkward standoff. The Soviets refused to leave until the rebels laid down their arms. The rebels refused to lay down arms until the Russians left. But on the evening of October 29, Nagy successfully negotiated his one true concession with Moscow. He convinced Khrushchev to give him

one more chance to restore order. Russia cancelled a pending
assault and agreed to a cease fire.

On the morning of October 30, Hungarians awoke to an
unexpected Red Army withdrawal from Budapest. Children lining
the streets booed and jeered at the retreating Soviet columns. The
euphoric, surprised rebels found themselves in command of the
city. Still unsure about the veracity of the ceasefire, people
cautiously filled the streets to inspect the damage. Those old
enough saw scenes reminiscent of the Siege of Budapest: streets
choked with rubble from buildings smashed by Soviet tank fire;
blown out shop windows; men in white coats sprinkling snow-
white lime powder on faces of statuesque corpses; small boys
collecting bullets.

The Russian retreat puzzled the rebels. It appeared voluntary,
organized, and indifferent to the state of the conflict. Had we
really fended off the Soviet army? Could the revolution actually
have succeeded? We may have injured them, but in no way had
we crushed them. Everyone knew the rebels lacked the means to
defeat the Soviet Army, but all logic went out the window on this
glorious day. We basked in defiant optimism. We cheered our
fearless young leaders. Our collective liberty-loving, tragically-
romantic spirit rose to heights not felt in a long time.

Rebels stormed Party headquarters on Köztársaság Square and
summarily executed 23 ÁVH officers. News reached Budapest
from the town of Mosonmagyarórvár where ÁVH officers had fired

on a crowd of unarmed protestors killing eighty-five men, women, and children. Seeking revenge for this massacre, a crowd in Pest lynched seven more ÁVH officers.

In the town of Rétság, directly to the north of Budapest, Hungarian army officers convinced the ÁVH guards to peacefully release Josef Cardinal Mindszenty, Archbishop of Esztergom from his life-sentence house arrest. Church bells pealed in joy when this venerated representative of the Catholic Church, a man who stood up to both the Nazi's and the Communists, returned to Budapest.

Rebels set up road blocks and checked the identification of passing cars and bicycles. On the peak of Gellért Hill, a crowd pulled down that statue of the Russian soldier that stood at the foot of the Freedom Statue towering over the city—the one of the woman holding up a laurel branch.

On Rózsadomb Hill, a group of rebels gained access to Rákosi's ostentatious villa. The villa had an American-style kitchen with brand new appliances, a brand new radio-phonograph, boxes of Dutch cigars and a bar filled with wine, champagne, and expensive imported liquors. On Rákosi's office desk they found his Party membership card and noted that his monthly dues were the same paid by ordinary workers.

Despite the evident destruction and death, people were jocular. They waived to one another with gestures of victory. They even reopened some of those havens of bourgeois decadence closed by the Communists—the coffee houses. But while Hungarians celebrated, Soviet tanks hovered around the outskirts of Budapest like sharks circling a school of fish.

Zalaegerszeg was within the rebel controlled sections of southwest Hungary. However, with Ricsi constantly on call and Andris sick we remained isolated in our little room on the hospital grounds. We were even disconnected from the action occurring nearby in the town center. Our little electric radio was our primary source of information about the revolution. I listened to that 12-inch box radio day and night. Its volume was so low that, to hear, I held my head close to the speaker. Ricsi and other hospital staff came in during their breaks so that I could summarize the quickly unfolding events.

Political debate and foreign diplomacy were taking place over the air waves. On the national radio station, Imre Nagy announced the end of the one-party system and pleaded for a peaceful transition of government. But, he was not the only voice on air. Radio Free Europe, backed by the U.S. CIA, encouraged the population to rise up against Soviet Communism and implied that Western support would imminently follow. An alternative Hungarian radio broadcast came on air, *Szabad* (Free) Kossuth Radio.[45] Its feverish call to action spread nearly as fast as the radio waves shared the news. It sent out desperate pleas to the Western world. The rebels had opened the window of opportunity. Now was the time for the West to support our struggle and intervene with United Nations forces to drive the Soviets out.

Tragically, Hungary once again found itself to be a disposable pawn in the chess match being played by greater super powers. President Eisenhower was weeks away from re-election. He had no desire to stir up an international incident that might give his opponent political leverage. He saw no payback in initiating conflict with the Soviet Union over Hungary.

---

[45] By the first of November, five other "free" radio stations were broadcasting.

Besides, American intelligence did not believe Imre Nagy would lead Hungary away from Communism. They had heard his pro-Party speeches, including Nagy's recent eulogy in remembrance of Stalin. Radio Free Europe urged the rebels to forge ahead and suggested Hungarians instead rally behind the freed Cardinal Mindszenty.

Ricsi felt the urge to somehow show his support for this anti-Stalinist revolution. But stuck on the Zalaegerszeg Hospital compound, what could he do? He reopened the chapel within this formerly-Catholic hospital. The communists had prohibited any religious activity on the government hospital grounds and had converted the little hospital chapel into a storage room. Ricsi pulled out the dusty furniture and supplies placed there, cleaned the room, reinstalled the pews, tore down the red star, and put up the old cross. He never could have imagined that such a simple act would totally turn our lives around.

On October 31, just as the last Russian troops were pulling out of Budapest, Anglo-French forces began bombing Egyptian targets. The world's fickle attention shifted away from Hungary to the Suez Canal crises. Western aggression in Egypt led Moscow to reconsider the Hungarian situation. How could Russia allow a satellite country to defect while British, French, and Israeli forces were concurrently crushing Egyptian leader Nasser's Suez Canal rebellion? A lack of response would to be seen as a sign of weakness.

Soviet interest in allowing Nagy time to establish a new government vanished. The arguments in favor of crushing the rebellion were too compelling to ignore. Rebel demands directly threatened communist rule. Anti-communist rhetoric in Hungary might spread and threaten neighboring satellite leaders' rule. And finally, Khrushchev needed to maintain authority within his own country. He could not risk giving party members any reason to question his lack of a forceful response in Hungary.

Yury V. Andropov, Moscow's chief representative in Budapest, was a slick deceitful rascal. During the lull in fighting, his first order of business was to get an actual signature on that Hungarian request for Soviet troops to suppress the rebellion. Nagy once again refused. Andropov settled for Rákosi's minion Hegedüs to sign the letter and back date it five days to October 24th.

On November 1, free radio stations were abuzz with chatter about Russian reinforcements coming across the borders from Romania, Czechoslovakia, and Ukraine. Andropov was back in the Parliament building meeting with Nagy.

"Trust me. What you are hearing about are nothing more than routine troop movements," the Ambassador cooed.

"Don't lie to me," Nagy demanded. "You are preparing for an overwhelming invasion."

"I assure you, Prime Minister, that Moscow intends to honor the cease fire and enter into discussions regarding troop withdrawals. You must agree that some Russian presence is needed to ensure the safety of the evacuating troops," Andropov calmly lied. "Let us schedule the meetings in which to work out the transfer of power and the schedule for evacuation of troops."

Meanwhile, Russian units quietly seized control of all of the major train junctions leading into Budapest. They took control of airports, including the Ferihegy Airport on the outskirts of Budapest. They also sent a force to the Austrian border to defend against a potential Western intervention. Top Soviet military leaders flew into Szolnok to personally command the operation.

In the evening of November 2, Nagy again went on the radio. Up until this point, he had carefully crafted his messages to stay within parameters of concessions palatable to Moscow. This time, he was speaking for the Western world to take notice. He knew that this speech would seal his fate with the Russians, but the window of opportunity was rapidly closing. He declared Hungary's withdrawal from the Warsaw Pact and Hungary's neutrality. He pleaded for United Nations intervention.

But distracted by the ongoing war in Egypt, none of the Western Alliance responded. The only reaction came from the Soviet Union, who viewed Nagy's appeal to the United Nations as a threat to the Soviet Union and a breach in the Soviet defensive buffer zone of satellite nations. While Nagy gave his radio address, János Kádár and two other top Party officials quietly slipped out of Budapest to the Russian military base Tököl on Csepel Island where they boarded a plane bound for Moscow.

Andropov's promised Russian-Hungarian talks began as scheduled at the Parliament building on the morning of November 3. Hungary's newly appointed minister of defense, Pál Meléter, led the delegation. The discussions were encouraging. Hungarians promised to return our armies to the barracks and to collect rebel arms. The Russians laid out detailed plans for troop evacuations, including a full scale military parade.

The first round of negotiations ended at 14:00 with plans to meet at 20:00 that evening at Russia's Tököl base. Sensing that this second meeting was a trap, a betrayal, Nagy asked Meléter to call him every half hour to confirm the safety of the delegates.

That evening, Meléter called twice to report that the resumed talks continued to be friendly and progress was being made. But before he could call a third time, Soviet policemen stormed into the room and arrested Meléter and the other Hungarian delegates. Meanwhile throughout the city, Soviet agents discreetly rounded up other Hungarian military leaders.

At midnight, Russian units moved into the city and positioned themselves at key intersections. Upon hearing the news, rebel leaders begged Imre Nagy to announce the attack and to direct Hungarian troops to defend the city.

"No," Nagy replied, "we dare not go to war against the Soviet Union. Arousing the population now will only lead to more deaths."

At 04:00 on November 4, the Russian commander gave the code word "Thunder." The sky lit up and the ground shook in a relentless barrage. This time the Soviet Army would not be embarrassed. They sent in 150,000 troops, 2,500 of their newest tanks, and plenty of air cover. Army leadership intended to over-perform on their promise to Khrushchev that they would "restore order" in the city within three days. MiG fighter jets strafed the city streets. Suspected rebel holdouts were completely leveled. Infantry units went from house to house, shooting, looting, and setting fires in their wake. Soviet troops failed to distinguish between civilian citizens and freedom fighters. They fired indiscriminately at anyone they encountered.

Hungarians sent out teletype messages to the West describing the attack and begging for help. Nagy made his final broadcast to the world at 05:15 in the morning. He appealed for international help. By noon, a deposed Nagy fled and took refuge in the Yugoslavian Embassy. Radio Hungary went silent. Cardinal Mindszenty took asylum within the American embassy, where he would live for the next fifteen years.

The Soviets threatened to relentlessly bomb Budapest if the rebels did not immediately surrender. Some rebels rejected the option of surrender. What was the point? Better to die on their own terms. They quoted Petőfi's poem written for another revolution a century earlier, "A miserable wretch is he who fears to die, my land, for thee." This small group of fierce but uncoordinated rebels resisted but were brutally crushed. In that brief futile defense, over 2,000 civilians died and another 13,000 were injured, most of them under 30 years old.

I kept listening to the radio for news, but by November 7 Rebel Radio, the last free radio station, was off air. The United Nations finally issued a request for the Soviets to withdraw, but no Western country took action to help the rebels. Returning from Moscow, János Kádár took to the radio waves and proclaimed himself head of a new "Hungarian Revolutionary Worker-Peasant Government." He declared that Imperialistic western powers financed this counter-revolution. He thanked the Soviets for helping to restore order after Nagy's disastrous and "illegal" government.

He also asked the nation to welcome the soldiers of the Russian army who helped Hungary overcome the counterrevolution of the reactionaries, those same Russian soldiers who were looting shops and hanging rebels from the bridges over the Danube River. In recognition of the Cold War, the Russians stuffed money into the mouths and slung signs around the necks of the corpses that read "These men fought for capitalists."

Though the official end of the revolution was declared on November 11, 1956, workers continued to passively protest by refusing to return to work. A general workers' strike gripped the country. By November 19, only 25% of the strikers had returned to work. Kádár threatened to withhold food from Budapest if the strike continued. Still, few paid him heed. Citizens called him a Soviet string-puppet, with Ivan Serov, the Soviet Union's head of security police, pulling the strings.

Having been lured out of the Yugoslavian embassy with a promise of safe passage, Imre Nagy was immediately arrested and taken to Romania. On November 25, the Kádár regime informed the Budapest Workers Council that, if the workers' strike stopped immediately, Nagy could return to government and Russian troops would withdraw from the country. But by now, no one trusted the new regime. Nagy, Meléter, and other leaders were later charged with treason and executed.

To break the workers' strike, the government began deporting able-bodied workers to slave labor camps. Tens of thousands were jailed or deported to the Soviet Union. The Russian-controlled Hungarian government tightened their nationwide dragnet in search of anyone who had in any way been engaged in the fight for freedom. Young revolutionaries were jailed until their 18th birthday, when they were hauled out and executed. All of these events triggered a massive wave of emigration. Fearing retribution, a ragged, desperate stream of refugees crossed the border into Austria.

Ricsi and I heard that Russians were shooting escapees as they tried to cross. But we also heard of times when the Soviets simply allowed people to cross. It all seemed so capricious and unpredictable. We felt tremendous pity for the over 80,000 refugees who had crossed into Austria by the end of November. We could do nothing more than return to our everyday routines at the hospital.

36

Graz, Austria 1956 - 1957

Our guide pointed to a sign, upon which "Austria" was written. "This is as far as I go. Walk up to any farmhouse you come across. They expect refugees these days. They will help you."

We exchanged hugs and handed him all the Hungarian Forint we had brought with us. It represented our entire savings, money we were accumulating with dreams of one day buying an automobile. However, at that time, Hungarian currency was worthless outside of the country. Besides, we felt good about giving what we had to this heroic man who had repeatedly taken personal risk to lead us and many others to freedom. We entered Austria with no money. From that point forward, we were totally dependent upon the charity of others.

After walking thirty minutes, we knocked on the door of a simple, small farmhouse. It was 2:30 in the morning when the sleepy couple opened the door. Seeing our large contingent, the farm couple curtly apologized that they could only accommodate the two couples with small children. We and the Husvéts entered the warm kitchen as the others continued their journey.

The farmer's wife noticed that Andris was shivering and blue with cold. She removed her own sleeping son from his crib and placed Andris in it. She served us hot tea.

Early the next morning, the farmer led us to the main road where buses rounded up sixty refugees and dropped us off at a school converted into a refugee processing center.

We were acutely aware that these people of Jennesdorf, a small village of 1,300 inhabitants, had already helped thousands of refugees who crossed before us. Though we were among the last waves passing through their communities, they continued to be kind and patient. We Hungarian refugees gave them nothing in return. In fact, that first day we were withdrawn and only partially "present." We puttered around like dazed zombies as we received food and drink and rummaged through a well-picked-over pile of donated used clothes.

Still feeling the sedative, Andris slept through the day while we just sat against a wall. When he finally woke that evening, he couldn't even sit up. He hungrily gulped down a half liter of hot chocolate and immediately fell back to sleep. I eventually fell asleep along that processing center wall. The next morning, Andris woke with a high fever and babbled like a little drunken soldier.

The villagers organized a Christmas Eve reception for the refugees. But, because of Andris' fever, I could not attend. Ricsi went to get us some food. Left alone that Christmas Eve, the stress of the last four days and the realization that I might never see my family again flooded my thoughts. The dam burst and I quietly sobbed.

I did, however, attend a Christmas morning meal offered by another local family. Unburdened by the stress of escaping, we enjoyed the pleasant two mile walk from the town center to the farm. This was the first time I ever tasted turkey. I found it odd that our host family served only several types of salad with the turkey. No starch, no potatoes, noodles, or rice. Though these were simple farmers, they had a notably higher standard of living than similar farmers just across the border. Their shelves were well stocked. In this village of 1,300, there were 300 private automobiles! Such ratios were unheard of back home.

Back at the Jennesdorf camp, we found a vacant spot along the wall and passed the day listening to funny banter among the refugees. A little girl in our group vomited all night. After she was taken to the hospital in the morning, we learned that she had both meningitis and scarlet fever. Since the latter is extremely contagious, it was a miracle that no one else caught either disease.

On Friday, December 28, Red Cross officials escorted us to the station where we boarded a train bound for Graz. By the time the train arrived at the Graz train station, the number of refugees arriving that day had grown to 1,500. A long line of buses drove us to an "industrial hall, " where we unexpectedly ran into three good friends from Zalaegerszeg. After warm embraces, we shared escape stories. They had snuck away a week before we did. Neither of us would have suspected that other was going to escape.

Maybe it was because these were the holiday days between Christmas and New Years, but nothing seemed to be happening at this dismal industrial hall. After just three days, Ricsi struggled to contain his impatience. He grimaced with frustration. But on New Year's Eve, just as I began to worry that he might make a scene, we were magically called out of the crowd and driven in a jeep to spend the evening at the Hotel Elefant, located in the center of Graz on Murplatz, only a block away from the Mura River.

We were assigned a small, warm room located in the back of the ground floor of the quaint and subtly elegant three-story hotel. There was only one bathing room on the middle floor and the windows of our room looked out on a large brick wall that blocked out sunlight to the extent that we relied on electrical lighting during the day. Nevertheless, I was happy to be somewhat isolated from the other guests so that our rambunctious son did not disturb them. Overall, we were overwhelmed by this unexpected gift of a clean bed with white sheets and soft pillows, and very accommodating hotel staff. What an unexpected wonderful way to ring in the new year! What anonymously-given generosity!

We eventually learned that the American-funded Austrian *Arztekammer* (Medical Society) was sponsoring us, Dr. Husvét, two other doctors-–who happened to be from Debrecen–and five other doctors and their families in the hotel. How unexpected and fortunate we were to have been called out of that crowd of 1,500 refugees stuck back in that dismal Graz industrial hall. We befriended these families and passed time watching movies or playing the card game "66."

The *Arztekammer* also paid for all of our meals. It took a while for Andris to learn to behave like a proper little gentleman suitable to the hotel environment. Each meal was a tussle. His misbehavior started at breakfast, worsened at lunch, and was intolerably embarrassing at dinner. We were so exhausted by the time we got back to our room that we often joined Andris for his afternoon nap. We solved the meal challenge by requesting room service for breakfast – consisting of coffee, milk, butter, jam and a soft boiled egg. After breakfast, Ricsi read the newspapers to practice his German. I took care of the room and kept Andris entertained. Between 1:00 and 2:00, we took Andris for long walks before entering the restaurant building for an a la carte lunch. While I finished my meal, Andris climbed into Ricsi's lap and spooned spongecake with whipped cream into his mouth.

Andris fully recovered on this steady diet of milk, eggs, meat, butter, and jam. He was fully potty-trained day and night. He happily played by himself. He could keep himself entertained for two hours with just a matchbox, a little train, and a rag doll. His vocabulary grew rapidly. As new parents, we embraced those first few expressions of independent thought. He found a cottontail and called it *habos pipi* which was his own combination of words "frothy" and "baby chick."

Paperwork consumed our first few days at the Hotel Elefant. We registered with the police; got finger printed; received identification papers. We also registered for asylum in the United States. One can understand the Austrians wanting to be overly careful because lawbreakers were mixed in among the refugees.

We lived the lives of penniless millionaires. We still wore the same clothes we arrived with. I washed Ricsi's two shirts every other day. My mostly knitted clothes were shrinking but still usable. I wondered when we might be able to get some new clothes. I even tried to wash Andris's blanket. But using the small sink in our room, it turned out to be a task better attempted only once.

As the days passed, we spent more time outside the four walls of our hotel room. Situated in the Mura River Valley and surrounded by snow-capped mountains, Graz was a friendly, busy, prospering city. The factories were tucked away on the outskirts, leaving a meticulously clean and litter-free city center full of narrow streets, vibrant shops, and well-dressed "free" people carelessly browsing lovely merchandise. As we perused the daily market stalls lining

317

the main square, we sometimes encountered groups of Hungarians on the street. By their old worn-out clothes and boisterous un-Austrian behavior, they were easy to spot. But we also noticed how happy they were. How different we all felt to be free of the dread of living under a repressive regime.

This being our very first journey out of Hungary, we made new discoveries around every corner. The surrounding beauty and prosperity reminded us of what a ruined, poverty-stricken country Hungary was. Ricsi often made it a point to walk by the Western Train Station, where he would pause and muse about journeying in that direction.

As wonderful as we found Graz and the Hotel Elefant, Ricsi was fixated on getting us to America. One of the many stunning churches in town was located right next to our hotel. We entered this Franciscan seminary in an attempt to locate Father Batori, one of my former Tata high school instructors who had been driven out by the communists while I was a student. The seminary sent us to the Jesuits who were politely accommodating and told us to return the next day when a Hungarian priest would be there. When we returned the next day, this so-called Hungarian priest, though born in the Bacskai region, could not speak a word of Hungarian. He was a sweet old man, but unable to be of assistance. Ricsi did not give up. Eventually he succeeded in locating Father Batori in Boston. In addition to Father Batori and Catholic organizations, we wrote letters to the Vietorisz family in Pittsburgh.

Ellie Petentail, an old family friend from Vienna whom we had never met, sent us a gift of 500 shillings (about $20). We still had no concept of Austrian currency, but managed to buy me much needed warm boots to replace my worn-out walking shoes and cigarettes for Ricsi. With the balance, we were not able to even buy Andris an apple.

Three weeks passed without a response to our letters of inquiry. Ricsi was getting antsy. When the much-anticipated letters from America finally arrived, both Erzsébet-*néni* and Father Batori sent affidavits stating their willingness to sponsor us. With nothing but time on his hand, Ricsi read and re-read these letters. As he dissected them, he complained that these carefully worded letters implied help but gave him no confidence of our ability to emigrate. This, and rumors that America's quota for doctors had been filled, left him crestfallen.

We also received letters from Hungary encouraging us to return home. My father let us know that he was able to retrieve our furniture and possessions from Zalaegerszeg. He was holding them for us in Tata. Everyone was worried about us and assured us that we would be welcomed back with open arms.

Ricsi's brother Pista tried to convince us that we would have better opportunities back in Hungary. The alpha-male he was, Pista had easily slipped into the role of family patriarch when my father-in-law died. His protective oversight of Ricsi and their sisters was over-shadowed by his unyielding and controlling delivery. Our escape took him completely by surprise. His letters subtly chastised his baby brother and this depressed Ricsi. Despite my own misgivings about the way ahead and indecision regarding those appeals to return home, I tried to elevate Ricsi's spirits by expressing a positive outlook and cheering him on.

Ever the idea guy with a mind that never rested, Ricsi was always coming up with new angles to pursue. At the *Arztekammer* office, he befriended the wonderfully kind, elderly secretary who helped him telephone contacts in Salzburg, Vienna, and New York.

Ricsi visited the local hospital, which he found to be cleaner and much more modern than the Zalaegerszeg Hospital. However, he noted that their standard procedures were no better than those of Hungarian doctors. Resourcing, not education, led to the differences.

Ricsi learned that the Vienna *Arztekammer* office was giving out 500 shillings to refugees who were Hungarian doctors. Lacking money for local transportation, he and Dr. Husvét began walking at the crack of dawn to catch the first train to Vienna. They were happy to discover that the train ticket to Vienna was less expensive than anticipated. The blue, two-car express pulled out of the station just as the morning sun lit up the foothills of the Alps. The vista became unutterably beautiful. The incline steepened and the train slowed and then entered a series of long tunnels. Each time the train emerged from a tunnel, a new picturesque scene was revealed. Glistening castle ruins, deep, snow-filled valleys dotted with toy-model homes. An ancient aqueduct bisected the hillside. Curtains of steam rose from the sun-baked, snow-capped Semmering Pass. Behind the train, the narrowing tracks wrapped along steep crags.

At Vienna's still war-ruined Southern Train Terminal, Ricsi rode his first shiny, steel, double escalator up to catch the number 7 bus to Stephan Platz. A friendly policeman left his post to walk the two doctors past the gothic spired Stephan Church to the Vienna Arztekammer office, where they quickly procured their 500-shilling gifts. Back on the bustling streets of Vienna, they celebrated their successful adventure at a modest cafe with an outrageously expensive cup of coffee.

I had superstitiously come to believe that Friday was our lucky day. We crossed the border on a Friday. We left Jennersdorf on a Friday. And now the kindly Ärztekammer secretary told us that if everything went according to plan we would depart Graz for Salzburg on Friday, January 25th. Salzburg was a dream come true! Rumor was that, in Salzburg, refugees with affidavits were quickly processed. We had two affidavits!

But that evening, another doctor pessimistically opined that we probably would not leave after all. No dark rumor would break my spirit. I refused to give up hope that our Friday luck would continue and excitedly prepared for the trip. I imagined us saying our goodbyes to Graz, the Mur river, the Slossberg, and the Elefant Hotel staff.

On Friday, a bellhop knocked on our door to inform us that we were to assemble at the sports hall at six that evening. At noon, we ate our last lunch at the Schiff restaurant. Just as I had pictured it, we exchanged tearful goodbyes with the waitresses and the wife of the owner. We were so touched by their kindness and respectful service, even when they knew that we didn't even have a penny to leave as a tip. The wonderful Arztekammer secretary escorted us to the sports hall. She was one of those people who was intrinsically motivated to help others and who derived such cheerful joy in giving without expectation of reward. God revealed himself to us in the form of these kind people whom we met along the way.

We spent that night with a large crowd of refugees, not in the sports hall itself, but in the dirty, cramped, depressing sports hall locker room. We could tell that it had been used as a holding area for refugees before. The dirt, litter, and smell of human sweat was a stark reminder that we were a month behind the majority of Hungarians who passed through Austria. Also at this time, Andris was recovering from conjunctivitis. In this dusty space, his eyes again swelled up to the point that he could barely open them. This stage of the refugee process seemed more unorganized than it should have been. There were too few Hungarian speakers working the crowd. But any inconvenience or confusion was overshadowed by our anticipation of reaching Salzburg.

The following morning, our convoy of eleven large buses rose above meadows shrouded in deep fog into sunny bright mountain roads above the clouds. Sunshine melted away the tops of the clouds to reveal the Bachstein glacier, waterfalls fed by melting snow, and those same spectacular mountains Ricsi had first seen during his trip to Vienna. The buses stopped in a small town where we received a snack and a few glasses of beer and where Andris could do his "business." Along narrow roads approaching the Salzach valley, the buses slowed to a crawl in heavy fog. We finally arrived in Salzburg, the town made famous by the composer Mozart.

The quaint cityscape transfigured into ugly gray military buildings as we entered Camp Roeder. Refugees were divided into groups of 100 and assigned to bunkbed-filled barracks. Ricsi took an upper bunk and Andris and I shared the lower bed. But the depressing environs did not diminish our buoyant expectations. We saw this camp as only a brief stepping stone on our way to America.

In the following morning's sparkling fog-free clarity, we saw that beyond our immediate perimeter of industrial grey camp barracks, we were surrounded by the spectacular Berchtesgaden Alps. Apparently, much of the camp staff had slipped off for a holiday break and those who remained struggled to support our large influx. For the first few meals, we had to wait in line for two to three hours. But we paid it no mind because we believed we would imminently be departing this camp.

Waiting in a food line, I spotted my childhood cousin and friend Klára with Margít-Néni's daughter Éva, Éva's husband Zoltán, and baby Bori. They had already been at this camp for 3 weeks. It was a bit disheartening to learn that even though they were registered in Vienna rather than Graz–which put them much further ahead in the queue–they were no further along in the processing than we were.

There were still 60,000 Hungarian refugees waiting in Austria. America issued only 6,160 "escapee" visas. Those were quickly exhausted. After that, refugees had to compete for work visas granted under the "parolee" provisions of the Immigration and Nationality Act. At first those also moved quickly. But now, America had dramatically slowed its immigration approval processing.

Nothing happened. We whiled away day after day at Camp Roeder. One uneventful day was indistinguishable from the next. We sat around, chatted, and waited. On warmer days, we basked for hours in the mountain sunshine. On Groundhog Day, it was so sunny that men and women removed their tops to sun themselves. We doubted that the groundhog would ever go back into his burrow.

After experiencing our private hotel room at Hotel Elefánt, we grew impatiently intolerant of evenings in the crowded barracks. Curtain walls delineated our private family space, which consisted of a chair and a bunk bed. At 10 p.m. the lights went off. The prattle of children quieted down. Then began a nightly cabaret of adults telling funny stories.

There were also disturbances. One night, a camp staff member came looking for a doctor because a child had fallen from a bunk bed. Ricsi sent the boy to the hospital for stitches on a head wound. An hour and a half later the boy's younger brother also fell from the same bed and cut his chin. Another night, Dr. Husvét attended to a woman who had a panic attack. Once the refugees learned Ricsi was a doctor, there was never a quiet moment. Our passionate countrymen often knifed one another. We jokingly thanked them for shortening the queue.

Refugees were allowed to leave Camp Roeder to wander about in Salzburg. Klára and Éva gave us our first opportunity to leave Andris with a babysitter. Ricsi and I spent our "date" wandering for hours through the hilly town. We crossed every vehicular and narrow pedestrian bridge over the Salzach river. I was surprised to see that, even though I was chilled to the bone, the snow-white swans happily swam in the icy river. We were reluctant to enter a restaurant because of the cost. But, in the end, hunger and the cold compelled us to enter. We remembered longingly how, at the Hotel Elefant we could order whatever we desired without a thought about price. Now we carefully studied the menu to pick the most affordable meal. After lunch we visited Mozart's birthplace. After buying a pound of chocolate, we returned to the camp with all of our money spent.

A month passed in this camp and the only thing that changed was that people complained more. Tempers flared more quickly. More fights ensued. People kept saying that no one cared any longer about us refugees. That the world's attention had wained.

On March 7th, Éva, Zoltán, their daughter Bori, and Klára all received visas and airplane tickets to America. But in a surprising turn of events, just one half hour before they were scheduled to board the plane, the Consulate called Klára in for questioning.

They asked her if she used to walk with Zoltán. She confirmed that they occasionally walked together to get the mail. That was all the evidence they needed to accuse Klára of being Zoltán's lover. In front of her, they tore up her visa and airline ticket, and sent her out of the camp. We later found out that three people had testified that they had witnessed their infidelities. This was a completely fabricated accusation. Zoltán and Éva had basically adopted Klára into their family because she was there all alone. We suspected that someone was desperate to move ahead in the queue and hoped to take Klára's place. We were shocked that the Consulate would blindly and inhumanely act this way without even trying to find out the truth. Éva and family left for America. Klára left for Vienna.

The despair among refugees became more palpable as each day passed. Since our arrival, there had been 40 suicide attempts. I call them "attempts" because the camp never revealed the final disposition of those who tried. There were rumors that camp officials planned to lock down the gates and not let anyone into or out of the camp. Camp officials started opining that we, who came across in December, were opportunists rather than freedom fighters. That we should be treated as immigrants instead of refugees. Hearing that the quota for America had been filled, we registered to go to Canada. Some refugees were being sent to other camps, but we did not want to leave this camp. We feared that those other camps would be more remote and more difficult from which to gain passage to America.

On March 12th, Ricsi and Dr. Husvét traveled to Vienna to pick up another gift of 200 shillings each. However, the cost of transportation there and back was 130 shillings. They received a net gain of 70 shillings and a pleasant, scenic trip out of the camp.

We also received a $10 check in the mail from Erzsébet-*néni* in Pittsburg. Good timing because we were again out of money.

A refugee friend from Tata shared the name of a distant cousin who lived on the outskirts of Salzburg and would set us up with some new clothes. At exactly the prearranged two p.m. meeting time on March 16th, we and the Husvéts arrived at an elegant mansion. A servant led us into a library to wait while the family finished their lunch. A short while later, Count Grove entered and escorted us into another room for coffee. In perfect Hungarian, he asked about our situation. After coffee, his wife drove us in her BMW to a Red Cross center, where we were able to pick through a large room full of donated clothes. Ricsi found a good pair of shoes and a necktie. I found two sweaters, a short fur jacket, and clothes for Andris.

Never one to sit idle, Ricsi found a new way to fill his days. He described it in our March 18 diary entry:

An acquaintance who works at the NCWC Hospital informed me that the hospital was looking to hire a new doctor. At the hospital office, an unpleasant staff officer told me Dr. Vale is on vacation and that no decisions could be made without him. He added that the position would only last for three years. Undaunted, I stayed the morning and observed how this remarkably small hospital operates. One X-ray machine, and only 4 of its 12 beds occupied. Apparently, these doctors only make money by bringing in their own private patients.

Determined to make inroads, I returned the following morning to the NCWC Hospital. Fortunately, this time a much friendlier office secretary tipped me off about a possible position at the larger Landes Krankenhous Hospital, which even has a pediatric ward.

Finding my way to the bigger hospital, I met the wonderful Mrs. Meyer, who spoke good Hungarian. What a relief to be able to explain my quest in my own language rather than struggling with my broken German. What a wonderful coincidence, Mrs. Meyer spent three years in Debrecen. We hit it off instantly. She immediately called up Dr. Zederbauer, Director of the Pediatric Ward. He was out of the office, so she penned me a letter of introduction to take to him.

Returning to camp that evening, I related my good fortune to Feri Husvét, who begged that I bring him along. He and I were making plans for the following day when a large skirmish broke out among two groups of refugees. Police officers came in and the camp was put into lockdown. The gates were secured and nobody was allowed to enter or leave the camp.

I would not be denied the chance to meet with Dr. Zederbauer. Feri and I woke before the crack of dawn, climbed the fence, and escaped from the locked camp. Having left so early we reached the hospital long before the doctor's anticipated arrival. We waited for hours. The doctor never showed up. Exasperated, we went back to the main hospital office to visit with Mrs. Meyer. She made some calls and learned that Dr. Zederbauer's car had broken down. However, the day was not completely for naught. Mrs. Meyer arranged for both of us to receive honorary appointments. We would not receive salaries, but we could take free meals and were given our own mail boxes. Camp Roeder's gates were reopened by the time we returned. We reentered without issue.

The next morning at the hospital, Dr. Zederbauer barely even glanced at my letter of introduction. He said he knew of us and invited us to accompany him on his two-hour morning rounds. Dr. Zederbauer didn't examine the children directly. Rather, he consulted with the individual doctors responsible for each patient. He shared unique ideas about medicine. For example, he gave Terramycin (an antibiotic) to every child as a prophylactic against diarrhea. He got this idea from a veterinary journal and decided to implement it on children. It seemed to work. For otitis, he didn't perforate the ear; he let it either naturally perforate or heal by itself. He also listened to the lungs through the mouth, which I had never tried. For keloid treatment, he used radioactive cobalt. And for some reason, Salzburg had far fewer mastoiditis cases than we dealt with in Hungary.

From this day forward, I established a leisurely daily routine in which I followed doctors making their morning rounds. Afterwards, I studied English. By 11 a.m., if doctors didn't have any more patients to attend to, they just went home. As a result, I had lots of free time to study. After lunch, I checked the mail box which Mrs. Meyer set up for me. In the afternoon, Feri and I took indirect walks back to camp both for the exercise and to postpone our return.

Klára returned to the camp from Vienna bringing terrible news that for several weeks no new refugees will be allowed to enter into the USA. As this news spread throughout the camp, panic ensued. I, at least, got out each day to visit the hospital. The less fortunate, less educated people, do nothing but sit and wait.

On April 3, 1957, Ricsi_wrote in our diary:

Last night, on the eve of my name day, we shared cocktails with friends. But as the alcohol began to take effect, our celebratory mood deteriorated into overshadowing talk that we all arrived to this camp

328

too late. That we missed the window of global interest in refugees. That the camp staff saw us as neither the first wave of fleeing communists, nor the patriotic rebels fleeing retaliation by the Russians. We left too late.

Today, I penned 8 letters to people abroad, which I hope will yield good news and maybe some money. I hope that by my birthday [May 30], we will no longer be in this camp.

The number of suicide attempts in the camp continues to climb. I counted 47. Though we will never act this stupidly, I, too, am very depressed.

Today, we said our tearful goodbyes to a couple bound for New Zealand. He is a young former priest who reminded me of my father. Both Maria and I became very attached to this couple and it was difficult to see them go.

No one gives us any sign of hope. It appears that everyone has given up on helping us. We receive no new information. I wouldn't mind staying here in Austria, but the Austrians clearly do not want us here. In America, the competition for doctor positions will likely be as challenging as it is here. My once clear vision of our future is now uncertain. Maybe I will change careers from medicine to chemistry. Both Maria and I could apply for scholarships at Austrian universities. With scholarships, we might be able to save enough money to live, assuming we qualify for free Kindercare.

The waiting game continues. We wait for letters, but none come. I keep going to the hospital but even that has become less satisfying. I observe a lot of chatter and loitering but not much work.

If I wasn't so obsessed about our uncertain future, there really would be much to enjoy in Salzburg. My afternoon walks are resplendent. I have visited every church and even found fascinating Roman ruin excavations. Some evenings they show movies in the camp. We saw "The Hunchback of Notre Dame," staring Anthony

*Quinn, "Carmen Jones," with Harry Belafonte, and "Rock & Roll,"
starring Elvis Presley. We were not impressed with this last movie. It
was crude and noisy. We hope this movie is not a reflection of typical
American life.*

On the afternoon of April 13, two venerable elderly friends
stopped by the camp for a visit. Karcsi and Lupa both left Hungary
in 1945 and had been living in Austria since. We could only offer
our guests larded bread with fresh onion slices. They graciously
and appreciatively accepted our offering, and stayed until 10 p.m.
as we drank, told stories, and even sang.

Imagine! Karcsi, who had been trying since 1945 to legally get his
wife out of Hungary, finally made progress with help from an
American professor, Dr. Williams, in Vienna associated with the
American Academy of Sciences. Kindly old Karcsi told us that he
also had already spoken to this doctor about us. The doctor had
given Karcsi a questionnaire to pass along to us. We promptly
filled it out and returned it to Karcsi.

Ricsi's stress level rose as each day passed. He obsessed about
not getting responses to his many letters of inquiry. He smoked
way too much. He began suggesting that we should just return to
Hungary. That even a short imprisonment might be worth it. He
questioned his career choice. He predicted that his path in life

would be determined, not by his talents or his interests, but rather by which job offer got us out of this camp.

On the afternoon of Ash Wednesday, I waited at the Post Office until they sorted through every last letter. But, once again, we received no mail. Ricsi reported that he also had received no mail in his hospital mailbox. His hopes to get to America or Canada were plummeting. Desperate to find a way out of the camp, he penned a letter to the Hungarian Consulate in Vietnam:

17 April 1957, Salzburg, Austria
To the Hungarian Ambassador to Vietnam,

I understand that South Vietnam is looking for doctors. I would like to learn more about these opportunities. My wife, our eighteen-month-old son, and I are currently at the military Camp Roeder near Salzburg.

As a student in the Medical University of Debrecen, I worked in the microbiology institute. After graduating in 1954, I worked in Szolnok as a medical practitioner. In 1955, I moved to Zalaegerszeg where I worked at the Children's Clinic. There, while completing my residency, I had two interns working under me.

I am currently reading medical journals in both German and English, but am not yet able to speak either language. May I inquire about the potential job openings and what salary they might offer? Pending agreement of terms, please take this inquiry as my willingness to work in Vietnam.

Sincerely,

Dr. Richard Répásy

However, he never sent this letter. He was so lethargic that his nose wiped the floor. There was nothing I could do to better our situation.

Out of other ideas to cheer him up, I eventually suggested that we go up to Vienna to find this "Dr. Williams" since we had received no response to our completed questionnaire. Klára showed us how she caught free rides on the buses returning to Vienna after dropping new camp refugees. Ricsi was not very enthusiastic about the idea of begging a ride but agreed to go if I went along. I packed a little food and arranged a babysitter for Andris. Ricsi approached the drivers with such self-defeated, negative energy that none of them would even talk to him. But then Klára, with her youthful charm, beauty, and better language skills, persuaded one driver to take us along with three other *potyautas* (free riders). The bus arrived at the outskirts of Vienna thirty minutes after midnight. The driver dropped us off on a quiet street and pointed in the direction of a train station, which he said was only a five minute walk away. The city was shut down until dawn. The houses were dark. The streets deserted. It started to rain. We were glad we brought our winter coats with us.

Unfortunately, the station to which this driver had directed us was only the turnaround point for the electric trolley. It didn't even provide any type of shelter from the increasing rain. Uncertain if we were even correctly heading toward central Vienna, we followed the tracks along desolate streets. We finally chanced upon a person who pointed us in the direction of the Westbanhof train station. The rain intensified. We reached the station at two-thirty in the morning. The station doors were closed and locked. By this point, we were completely soaked through and Ricsi's mood could not have gotten any worse.

"What a silly idea it was to come to Vienna," he said, and then added as soon as I tried to respond, "don't even say a word to me."

We finally came across and entered a small run down pub that stayed open until 4 a.m. Digging into into our 55 shillings, we ordered a couple of drinks and proceeded to people watch in this surprisingly active, seedy little bar. Seemingly oblivious to the early morning hour, a group of men played an animated game of cards. They slapped money down on the table and argued, I assumed, about cheating. In another corner, a man of about twenty was engaged in intimate conversation with a woman who looked to be about sixty. Their quiet chat erupted into loud argument. She knocked the drink out of the young man's hand and sauntered off with a tirade of profanities and an exaggerated backside wiggle.

When the bar closed, we made our way back to the now open Westbahnhof Station. Cleaning crews were hard at work with large noisy vacuum cleaners. The heat wouldn't come on until 6 a.m. and we shivered in the cold hall. Luckily, the restrooms had hot showers that thawed out our frozen bodies. The cafe opened and we shared a cup of warm coffee. This left us with only 15 shillings.

The sun crested the horizon as we walked out of the station. An hour and a half later, pounding rain drove us to take shelter in Saint Stephen's Cathedral. This was the Thursday before Easter. The Cardinal was conducting mass. Acting as if we had arrived for that service, we sat and admired the statues and art of this opulent church. I quietly prayed that this trip to Vienna would be worth all the discomfort we had endured so far. In his ever-contemplative mind, Ricsi had already itemized our objectives for the day: pick up our monthly allotment of 200 Shillings from Arztekammer, locate Dr. Williams, secure an interview with the Academy of

Sciences, and pay a courtesy call to Ellie Petentail, the old family friend who, without actually ever meeting us, had sent us money.

Step one went off without a hitch. Once we had the 200 Shillings in our possession, Ricsi's mood improved. Our luck continued at the university. Dr. Williams was in his office. Ricsi continued to brighten. Dr. Williams was an elderly, pleasant, and unpretentious man despite his influential position. There was something about him that made me feel very optimistic that he would help us. He apologized that he had to run off to a meeting but scheduled to see us later that afternoon.

We exited his office to find that the rain had stopped—another promising sign. With several hours to kill we took care of our other tasks. We telephoned Ellie and arranged to visit after completing our business in Vienna. We made our way to Vienna's refugee office where we were able to obtain free train tickets back to Salzburg. On the way, we were overwhelmed by the kindness of the Viennese. When we asked for directions, a trolley conductor jumped off the trolley with us and walked nearly half a block with us before the driver honked for him to return. Waiting for another trolley, we asked a lady for directions. When we boarded the trolley, we asked the conductor to tell us when to get off. The conductor replied that the lady had already made arrangements for him to take care of us. We stopped for lunch. It costs us an unaffordable 60 shillings, but we badly needed a meal.

In the afternoon, Dr. Williams drove us to Schmidt Plaz #1, where Dr. Csapo interviewed Ricsi with the disinterested perfunctory motions of a bureaucrat who would not have wasted his time were he not doing a favor for Dr. Williams. But at the end of the interview, Dr. Csapo told Risci that he would recommend him favorably to the consulate.

We spent a pleasant evening with Ellie. She served us dinner and then gave us a short car tour before dropping us off at the train station. We were very touched by her kindness and exchanged warm goodbyes. The express train arrived back in Salzburg at 3 a.m. on Good Friday. As we walked from the station back to Camp Roeder, it started to rain again. But, this time, the rain did not diminish our buoyant mood. It was another lucky Friday.

The morning of April 29th started out the same as many mornings had before. Ricsi went off to the hospital and I took Andris out for some sun. At 11:00, as I walked back to our barracks, I heard the names "Répásy" and "Husvét" over the camp loudspeaker. We were to report to the processing center. I rushed to an office to telephone Ricsi at the hospital. As soon as he arrived, we were sent for passport photographs and medical checkups.

On May 2nd, learning that we passed the medical checkups, we were then fingerprinted and scheduled for consulate interviews. I was extremely apprehensive when I learned that my interviewer would be a man with a very bad reputation at the camp. He was a fierce anti-communist, and would reject anyone for the most insignificant shreds of evidence that they were communist. For three hours he grilled me about Ricsi's work, every nuance about his daily routine as a pediatrician in Hungary.

Because my interview lasted until past 5 p.m., Ricsi's interview was postponed until the next afternoon. His lasted just as long as mine, but he emerged feeling very good about how it went. Our responses were consistent. That same evening, the camp staff informed us that we were approved and would leave for Munich in three days. The days flew by as I busily prepared for our journey. I washed and ironed our clothes and said goodbye to those we left behind. It was especially difficult to say goodbye to Klára, to see her left behind, alone with no family connections.

We left Camp Roeder by bus on a rainy May 7 morning. The rain quickly turned to snow. It felt as if the old country was making its last ditch effort to prevent our departure. Arriving at a U.S. military airbase in Munich, a military jeep escorted our caravan directly to the tarmac. By 1:00 p.m. we sat aboard a four-propellor military transport plane. The low clouds were heavy with rain, but the weather held. Within minutes, the plane soared above the stratus and we saw no more of the European continent. At 5:00 p.m., the plane refueled in Scotland. In the warm terminal they served us soup and coffee. This was the first public restroom I encountered that provided soap and towels. Leaving Scotland, the clouds temporarily cleared, granting us our first glimpse of the vast Atlantic Ocean. On the plane, we were served a meal that included a fruit we had never before tasted: pineapple! At 2:00 a.m., the plane refueled again in Nova Scotia. At 7:00 a.m., we landed at McGuire Air Force Base, in New Jersey. We were in America!

37

Epilogue - America

On the tarmac as we boarded buses, our escorts asked if anyone in our group spoke English. No one stepped forward. So they appointed Ricsi to serve as translator for the group. He and I had a good laugh at this. On the ride from New Jersey to Brooklyn as the morning sun silhouetted the growing skyline, the entire bus was contemplatively silent. Our quiet reverie was soon disrupted by noisy traffic from the crowded streets as we approached the Hotel George.

Of the 32,000 refugees who preceded us, 5,000 arrived by boat. Like us, the rest flew over on military air transports that landed at McGuire Air Base. Nearly all of them had been taken to Camp Kilmer, in Piscataway, New Jersey, for processing. However, by the time our plane landed, the White House had declared the refugee program successfully completed. Camp Kilmer no longer accepted refugees. With media fanfare, the last refugees walked out of Camp Kilmer and the entire Hungarian refugee processing operation was officially terminated. That same week, the refugees we had left behind in Camp Roeder staged a hunger strike to protest America's termination of granting immigration visas.

Our timing could not have been luckier. Had we not taken that trip to Vienna to meet with Dr. Williams, we would still be among those protesting in Austrian refugee camps. Had we come only a week earlier, we would have ended up in the noisy Camp Kilmer military barracks. Instead, we were situated in the heart of Brooklyn in a hotel room of our very own.

The Hotel George was a monumental 26-stories tall. Our large and sunny room even had its own bathroom! The Husvéts were only 2 doors down. Andris and Kuki happily played together in the large rooms. Back at the refugee camp, we had tended to sleep in and eat later meals to make the days feel shorter. But at this hotel, we adhered to strict schedules no matter how uncivilized American meal-times seemed: Breakfast 7-8:00, Lunch 11-12:00, and dinner 3:30-5:00. This stood as a reminder that it would take a while to adapt to American customs. The food was plentiful but bland. Andris openly expressed his disgust and survived on eggs, bread, and butter. Owning only clothes appropriate for snowy Austrian weather, we found the 85-degree New York weather stifling. The enormous fans twirling above did little to mitigate the heat.

The immigration processors were bent on moving us out as quickly as possible. We efficiently repeated the administrative processing and medical checkups we had taken those last days at Camp Roeder. When staff learned of the Vietorisz family living in Pittsburgh, they immediately contacted them. Érzsébet-*néni* called her daughters to find out if any of them could take us in until we got our feet under us. Éva's husband, John Condit, invited us to their apartment in Évanston. The staff advised Ricsi that Chicago would be a good place to make his way as a physician and then quickly arranged for our departure.

Érzsébet-*néni* suggested that we see as much of New York City as possible because we probably would not get back there for a very long time if at all. She lamented that they never had the opportunity to do so. Not speaking English, and not knowing the layout of the city, we timidly explored the littered streets in the vicinity of the hotel. We much preferred the expansive views of the city from the top of the hotel. The 26th floor! From above, we didn't notice the filth. We admired the skyscrapers, ships in the harbor, and the glowing nighttime sky with its neon advertisements and street lights. Besides, the entire family found the elevator as thrilling as a carnival ride.

This was the first time I had ever directly observed a person of color. Walking in front of us towards a wedding in the ballroom were voluptuous bridesmaids in beautiful dresses and with large stylish hairdos of various colors: blond, brunette, red, and even pink. As we neared, they turned around. I was surprised to see elderly black faces under those wigs. We also observed that the black hotel staff spoke a different dialect. I wanted to borrow an iron for Ricsi's suit. He carefully wrote out the request in English, and then stood in front of the mirror practicing pronunciation of the simple phrase. As we went in search of a bellhop, I told Ricsi how proud I was of him for being able to speak English. When Ricsi carefully read his prepared request, the bellhop stared at him, dumbfounded. After an awkward silence, he responded "I am sorry man, I don't speak Hungarian." It reminded me of my failed attempt to speak Russian to the soldiers in the Gellért Hotel after the siege.

Only three days after landing in America, two gentlemen from the refugee organization escorted us by taxi and ferry across the

Hudson River to the Grand Central train terminal. They bought us tickets for an 8 p.m. train and hung signs around our necks on which our names were written and the stop we were to meet our contacts. Wearing our winter clothes, including my furry winter jacket, we waited for four hours in miserable heat. As we boarded the train, the conductor advised us that we would arrive at 4:30 p.m. Despite the heat, the train was comfortable. We had room to stretch our legs. At 4:30 a.m., we gathered our belongings and prepared to disembark. But to our surprise the train did not stop at any time close to this hour. We now understood what "p.m." meant.

The following afternoon, we detrained in Chicago and were immediately approached by a man who introduced himself as John Condit. With him was my cousin and childhood friend, Éva's sister, Zsuzsa. How did he recognize us so quickly? Oh yes! We were the only ones wearing winter clothes and had signs hanging from our necks.

Zsuzsa and John drove us to Evanston via the biggest, busiest 4-lane highway we had ever seen. Éva greeted us with a delicious meal of lentil soup supplemented with sliced hotdogs. She was very sweet. They put us into one of the three bedrooms in their small apartment.

Unfortunately, Andris and Michaela did not get along. Michaela was reticent. Andris was rambunctious and used to playing with older children. Liz was only one year old, and Éva was pregnant with her third child. Éva and I tried our best, but we were both distressed by the children's failure to get along better.

John taught us English using the Robert Frost poem *Whose Woods These Are*. He sent me down to the grocery store with a small shopping list. With one exception, I got everything right. He wanted McCormicks seasoned salt into which he dipped carrot sticks. Instead, I bought McCormicks garlic salt. Éva taught me how to shave my legs and underarms–American style. John lent Ricsi $100 to buy a suit for his job search.

In the first two weeks, Ricsi went all by himself to visit eight hospitals and laboratories. He soon landed a job at Mt. Sinai Hospital in the Immune-Hematology lab. He had hoped to quickly learn English from his fellow lab workers, but to his dismay, they were all also foreigners: Chinese, Poles, Japanese, and Indians. The only English speakers he encountered were the black workers in the animal labs. He spent his lunch hours with them and picked up idiomatic phrases that greatly amused John Condit. At Mt Sinai, Ricsi met a German doctor, Dr.Davidson, who later helped Ricsi get his residency at Cook County Hospital in Chicago.

We quickly realized that hosting us was a challenging burden for Éva and John. They were not wealthy. They had only been married for three years. Despite their graciousness, we felt the tension. Their quarters were obviously too tight for all of us. We spent sleepless nights discussing how we might get out of their hair as fast as possible.

I started to look for a job as well. On my behalf, Éva put an ad in the local newspaper. The ad stated that I was a refugee looking for a housekeeping job. In the coming weeks we received several responses to our job searches. After six weeks, we had moved out of Éva & John's apartment.

I began to work as a live-in maid for the Fishers, a Polish-Jewish couple with two daughters aged six and eight. After living in Éva and John's simple apartment, our accommodation expectations were very modest. We were completely blown away to be offered a two-bedroom, one bath apartment within their elegant twelve-bedroom brick mansion. Including the basement, this house had 4 stories! The large interconnected rooms had many windows and were bright and cheery. The dining area ceiling was recessed in an elegantly articulated circular dome with a magnificent chandelier in the center.

In a city, it would have consumed an entire block, but this mansion was centered in a large oak tree sheltered lawn, located at 1111 Sheridan Road in Wilmette, Illinois. From the top floor I could see up and down the coast and out over the expansive blue of Lake Michigan. Across Sheridan Road, a path led down to a secluded beach.

But there was only one catch. Andris wasn't allowed to live with us. This rule was reasonable. I would not have been able to do my job if I was watching Andris all day long. I needed to be attentive to the needs of the Fisher family. John Condit solved our dilemma. He arranged for Andris to stay with his sister Betty, and her husband, Bucky Ball. They had two sons, Pier and Hunt, of similar age. Though I was filled with anxiety over our separation, Andris thrived there. An advantage of being separated from me was that Andris learned English much more quickly. Betty took care of the kids for 5 days a week. On my two days off, I went over to her house and took care of the kids. The arrangement suited Betty because it gave her a chance to get away on weekends. We became very good friends.

I started work each morning at 6:30 a.m. just as Ricsi left for the lab. Twelve hours later, we reunited. Because of his travel, Ricsi was usually more exhausted than I. However, we made the most of our evenings alone together, something rarely experienced for the past two years. Most nights, I was able to set aside a share of the Fisher meal for me and Ricsi. There was a little TV in our room. This was our first time to ever have such a luxury. Even though we didn't understand the conversation, we watched all the evening programs.

Ricsi's first job paid only $50/week–so little that he could not even afford cigarettes or an occasional beer. With my base salary of $25/week, I actually made more than him when I did additional babysitting for the Fishers at ten dollars a day.

The days passed quickly as we fell into our routines. I prepared breakfast, helped the girls get ready for school, made the beds, cleaned the five bathrooms, helped Mrs. Fisher in the kitchen, tended to the girls after school, and cleaned up the kitchen after dinner. Other help came weekly to do the vacuuming, laundry, and heavy cleaning. Mrs. Fisher and I spent hours in her large well-stocked kitchen. My inability to keep up my end of the conversation did not diminish her love to talk. Slowly, I learned English from this delightful Jewish mother hen. Mr. Fisher had made a fortune selling fabrics. He was probably 20 years older than his comely wife. Both of them were very kind and unpretentious despite their wealth.

Zsuzsa gifted us with tickets to seven operas; Monday nights at 8 p.m. We were very proud to note that among the most famous opera singers of the time, Mario Demonaco, Gussi Bjoerling, Anna Moffo, Aldo Protti, Julietta Simionto, Renata Tebaldi, and Tito Gobbi, there were also Hungarian artists Leslie Csabai and George Solti.

Ricsi was flummoxed when Mr. Fisher asked him why he allowed his wife to do such menial work. Mr. Fisher offered to loan us money but Ricsi hated the idea of borrowing money. Instead, he established our three-year life plan. Until he finished his residency, I needed to be self-sufficient. I would get a job to support the family, pay our rent, and cover Andris' daycare. Being a housemaid may have been menial work, but it gave us free room and board and we were able to bank my salary.

That September, Ricsi was the first of us to get a driver's license. Up to that point, his commute required walking to the Linden station, taking the elevated train downtown, and then walking or bussing over to Mt. Sinai Hospital. It took over two hours each way, and cold weather was coming. For never having driven before, he looked naturally confident and handsome behind the steering wheel. He wore dark sunglasses and a cigarette perpetually dangled from his lips. He bought a very old blue Ford. The insurance cost almost as much as the car!

I experienced my first Halloween. It struck me as unusual because in Hungary and throughout Europe we only celebrated All Saints Day on the following day. Rather than visiting cemeteries full of flowers and candles, I made costumes for the Fisher girls. One wanted to dress as a Chinese woman. I sewed cotton balls on a blouse to make her a fluffy fringed robe. The other girl wanted to be a princess. I rarely sewed in Hungary, but I enjoyed the challenge and loved working with the girls. I escorted them around the neighborhood. The entire experience was fascinating.

Driving home late on the evening of November 2, Ricsi had his first car accident. The accident occurred close to the Fisher home and Mrs. Fisher went to pick him up. Fortunately, nobody was hurt. But our old Ford was totaled. With the insurance money, Ricsi bought our second old car. This one had a manual transmission.

On November 7, the Fishers left to winter in Florida. They would stay away until spring when warm weather returned to Chicago. In their absence, my only job requirement was to housesit. I still received my weekly salary and Fraser, the milkman, continued to deliver the weekly milk, cheese, and eggs. And Andris was now permitted to come and live with us! The Fishers were so accommodating because they desperately wanted someone to stay in the house. In prior years while they were away, the house had been burglarized. So it turned out to be a mutually beneficial arrangement even though I was a bit scared to spend all day alone in this large mansion.

What a blessing it was for Ricsi to have met Dr. Davidson at Mt Sinai! With the doctor's recommendation, Cook County Hospital granted Ricsi an internship. They said that the county-trained doctors were the best in the city. They performed surgeries from sunrise to sunset. Ricsi's work hours increased but he was thrilled to actually be involved in medicine again.

Ricsi met two Hungarian refugee doctors working at Cook County Hospital. The three doctors became fast friends and made the most of their many hours at the hospital. Being on call for 24 hours, they created their own diversions. Joe Bogdan, who had started 5 months earlier, boastfully demonstrated how to engage with a patient. Grabbing a tongue depressor, he yelled "Tikki Tonga!" Ricsi quickly realized that Joe spoke no better English than he. One day, they had a bet to see whose patient had the largest penis. Using medical instruments, they went around taking measurements of each of their patients.

The sixth of December is *Mikulás Télapó* (St Nicholas Day) in Hungary. It is the day that a Santa Claus-like Mikulás puts gifts into the good children's boots left on the windowsills, while his frightening helper, Krampusz, takes the bad children away. For

345

Hungarians, it represents the beginning of the Christmas holiday season. It was strange to pass this day without this celebration. It was a reminder that I was not in Hungary any more. I missed my family back home.

I also obtained my drivers license! Ricsi took me out driving to teach me to drive, but he was an impatient instructor. He actually made me more nervous than I already was. And I wouldn't let him forget that he had just totaled our first car. Struggling to work the stick shift, I stalled the car in the middle of a busy intersection. He began yelling and I got out of the car and walked home. The next day, I hired a driving instructor for four half-hour lessons. The instructor gave me three sheets of likely test questions. I still couldn't speak English but memorized the patterns of the questions. Somehow I passed the test. But I honestly did not know how to drive and I didn't understand the rules. I persistently worried that I was doing something wrong. Whenever I saw a policeman, I broke into a cold sweat. Andris, on the other hand, loved policemen. I cringed in terror as he shouted out in joy whenever he spotted a police car.

Ricsi invited colleagues and our few friends over for a holiday party at the Fisher mansion. We were like teenagers having a party when our parents away. It started to snow heavily and the men started drinking. By the time guests were ready to leave, the cars were buried. Our new old car was stuck in the snow. Ricsi got behind the wheel of the car. A friend started to push our car with his car. Their communication broke down. Ricsi tried to move in one direction while the car was being pushed in the other. Suddenly, our transmission gave out. In less than three months, Ricsi had totaled two cars.

Ricsi spent Christmas evening on call at Cook County Hospital. Andy—as we now called him—and I celebrated alone in the big empty Fisher mansion. Andy learned English much faster than I. Over and over, I read him the story of the three little pigs. Each time, he corrected my pronunciation. After Andy fell asleep, I thought back on our Christmas the year before. I had been alone then as well. We had just crossed the border. Because of Andy's high fever I could not join the holiday dinner. Alone to my thoughts I could not help feeling overwhelmed about leaving home and family, and not knowing what lay ahead of us. I spent my second Christmas in a row crying.

We bought our third car from a very seedy Western Avenue dealership. We paid $100 for a black Ford. The rear trunk needed to be tied down with wire to stay closed. The dealer promised, but never provided, us with the title to the vehicle. Because he almost lived at the hospital during this period, Ricsi rarely used the car. I was the one who drove it. For nearly a year, I drove without a valid registration or plates. This added to my panic whenever a police car neared.

Finally, I decided enough was enough. In a rage, I drove back down to the dealership and parked the car facing the dealership's large picture window. Inside, three salesmen scrutinized me with disdainful amusement. I marched in and laid out three alternative scenarios, "Today, I will leave with a title to the vehicle, or you will give me back my $100, otherwise I will drive this car through your front picture window."

Trembling, I took the bus home with $100 in my pocket.

In the first three months of Ricsi's internship at Cook County, he delivered 320 babies. At other hospitals, a doctor might deliver, maybe, 40 in that same period. He also assisted with emergency surgeries. The near-west side of the Loop, where the hospital was situated, was the most dangerous part of Chicago. Most shootings and stabbings went to Cook County.

Throughout his internship, Ricsi intensively studied for his "Educational Commission for Foreign Medical Graduates (ECFMG)" certification test. He needed to pass this feared, grueling test in order to practice medicine in America. The odds of passing this test the first time were very low, especially for someone lacking English language skills. In late 1959, Ricsi would pass it on his first try. I was so proud of my smart husband.

Though the Fishers were very kind to me, I needed to show that I was capable of doing much more than housekeeping. In January of 1959, I began working as a lab-assistant in Dr. László Lorand's bio-chemistry laboratory at Northwestern University. By May, I had put down a deposit on an apartment located on Central Street in Evanston, adjacent to the Metra train station. Soon after the Fishers returned, we announced that we were moving on. I felt guilty for abandoning the Fishers. But they were completely supportive. They even gave us a mattress that became the only piece of furniture in our new cockroach-infested apartment.

My one year of university chemical engineering studies came back to me and I enjoyed helping with the research. I now earned $250/month working in Dr. Lorand's lab. From that salary, I paid rent and $80/month for Andy's Roycemore Nursery School. After one year, we moved again to a nicer apartment on Maine Street. I worked at this laboratory until April 20, 1961, three days before the birth of our second child, Ricky, at Evanston Hospital.

In 1962, we rented a house in Northbrook. And by April of 1965, only months before Matt's birth, we moved into our Thornwood Lane home in Northfield.

After settling in America, we rarely saw the Husvéts–the family with whom we escaped and shared those stressful months in the refugee camps. Sadly, we grew apart as we pursued different paths in this new world. Only once did we find the time and money to visit them in New Haven, Connecticut, where Dr. Husvét was a successful gynecologist until he began to lose his eyesight and could no longer perform surgeries. They moved to Denver where he helped their son establish a woodworking business. Though our relationship died off, I still think about them when I look at the two large healthy maple trees growing in our yard that they gave us as eighteen-inch saplings the first time we visited them in New Haven. The trees are a reminder of friends who stuck by our side when we needed them most.

We lived our American dream. We started out with nothing and ended up comfortable. True to our natures, Ricsi laid out our life plans and I executed them. We were able to set aside a portion of our earnings to send back to Hungary. Though we worked hard and endured difficulties along the way, I recognize that our good fortune was due to the kindness and selfless generosity of others– those who carried our son, who guided us through forests and city streets, who gifted us with cash and clothes or funded our accommodations at the Hotel Elefant, who shared their own homes, and who gave us jobs, references, tips, and recommendations. Dr. Williams facilitated our visa. Dr. Davidson introduced Ricsi to Cook County hospital management. The Vietorisz family gave us a way out of the refugee processing facility. Dr. Lorand–we found out years later–had sponsored our visa through the National Academy of Science. I am eternally indebted to those who helped us achieve our dreams. I don't know if I have given back to this world as much as it has given to me, but I do know that I look back on my life without regrets. My first twenty-three years in Hungary needed to unfold exactly as they did to bring me to where I am today. I am blessed and thankful. I pray that this story inspires future generations to live thankful, rewarding, and generous lives.

Made in the USA
Monee, IL
20 October 2023

44891745R00197